The Company of A CHORUS LINE has collectively appeared:

On Broadway in: *A Joyful Noise, Applause, Beg Borrow and Steal, Bajour, Bye Bye Birdie, Bravo Giovanni, Breakfast At Tiffany's, Cafe Crown, Coco, Company, Conquering Hero, Don't Bother Me I Can't Cope, Follies, Folies Bergeres, Flower Drum Song, Funny Girl, Georgy, Golden Boy, Golden Rainbow, Hair, Hallelujah Baby!, Heathen!, Henry Sweet Henry, High Spirits, Her First Roman, Here's Love, How To Succeed in Business Without Really Trying, Irene, Jennie, Jesus Christ Superstar, La Grosse Valise, Little Me, Lolita My Love, Lost in the Stars, Lysistrata, Mack and Mabel, Minnie's Boys, Milk and Honey, Molly, Music! Music!, Noel Coward's Sweet Potatoe, Nowhere To Go But Up, Of Mice and Men, On the Town, Pajama Game, Pippin, Purlie, Rachel Lily Rosenbloom (And Don't You Ever Forget It!), Promises Promises, Seesaw, Sgt. Pepper's Lonely Heart's Club Band, Showboat, Skyscraper, Smith, Stop the World I Want To Get Off, Subways Are For Sleeping, Sugar, Sweet Charity, The Boyfriend, The Education of Hyman Kaplan, The Gay Life, The Happy Time, The King and I, The Rothschilds, The Selling of the President, Ulysses in Nighttown, Via Galactica, West Side Story, Walking Happy, Wild and Wonderful, Words and Music* and *Zenda.*

In National Companies in: *A Funny Thing Happened on the Way to the Forum, Applause, Cabaret, Carnival, Company, Disney on Parade, Follies, Hallelujah Baby!, Hello Dolly!, How To Succeed in Business Without Really Trying, Irene, Purlie, Seesaw, The Boyfriend, The Me Nobody Knows, The Music Man* and *Your Own Thing.*

In Bus and Truck Tours in: *Applause, Call Me Madam, Can Can, Hello Dolly!, Hello Sucker!, On A Clear Day You Can See Forever, Promises Promises, Your Own Thing* and *West Side Story.*

They have appeared in eighty-eight different shows in which they have given a total of 37,095 performances. Collectively they have had 612 years of dance training with 748 teachers — counting duplications. They spend approximately $894 a month on dance lessons. While appearing in the shows mentioned they have sustained 30 back, 26 knee and 36 ankle injuries.

The characters portrayed in A CHORUS LINE are, for the most part, based upon the lives and experiences of Broadway dancers. This show is dedicated to anyone who has ever danced in a chorus or marched in step . . . anywhere.

CAST
(in alphabetical order)

Roy	SCOTT ALLEN
Kristine	RENEE BAUGHMAN
Sheila	CAROLE BISHOP
Val	PAMELA BLAIR
Mike	WAYNE CILENTO
Butch	CHUCK CISSEL
Larry	CLIVE CLERK
Maggie	KAY COLE
Richie	RONALD DENNIS
Tricia	DONNA DRAKE
Tom	BRANDT EDWARDS
Judy	PATRICIA GARLAND
Lois	CAROLYN KIRSCH
Don	RON KUHLMAN
Bebe	NANCY LANE
Connie	BAAYORK LEE
Diana	PRISCILLA LOPEZ
Zach	ROBERT LuPONE
Mark	CAMERON MASON
Cassie	DONNA McKECHNIE
Al	DON PERCASSI
Frank	MICHAEL SERRECCHIA
Greg	MICHEL STUART
Bobby	THOMAS J. WALSH
Paul	SAMMY WILLIAMS
Vicki	CRISSY WILZAK

MUSICAL NUMBERS

I Hope I Get It	Company
I Can Do That	Mike
"And . . ."	Bobby, Richie, Val, Judy
At the Ballet	Sheila, Bebe, Maggie
Sing!	Kristine, Al
Hello Twelve, Hello Thirteen, Hello Love	Company
Nothing	Diana
Dance: Ten; Looks: Three	Val
The Music and the Mirror	Cassie
One	Company
The Tap Combination	Company
What I Did For Love	Diana and Company
One: Reprise	Company

AN AUDITION   Time: Now   Place: Here

A CHORUS LINE *IS PERFORMED WITHOUT AN INTERMISSION*

UNDERSTUDIES never substitute for listed players unless a specific announcement for the appearance is made at the time of the performance.

Al, Mike—John Mineo; Paul, Richie—Chuck Cissel; Kristine, Connie, Maggie—Donna Drake; Don, Mark—Brandt Edwards; Cassie, Sheila—Carolyn Kirsch; Diana, Bebe—Carole Schweid; Larry, Greg, Bobby—Michael Serrecchia; Val, Judy—Crissy Wilzak; Zach—Clive Clerk.

THE ORCHESTRA

Personnel Manager—Herbert Harris; *Associate Conductor*—Jerry Goldberg; *Keyboards*—Fran Liebergall; *Guitars*—George Davis; *Bass Guitar*—Roland Wilson; *Uprite Bass*—Jaime Austria; *Harp*—Bernice Horowitz; *Drums*—Allen Herman; *Percussion*—Benjamin Herman; *Reeds*—Joseph Maggio, Buzz Brauner, Norman Wells, Marvin Roth; *Trumpets*—Bob Millikan, James Morreale, Al Mattaliano; *Trombones*—Vincent Forchetti, Gordon Early Anderson; *Bass Trombone*—Blaise Turi.

What They Did for Love

·······································

The Untold Story Behind the Making of

A CHORUS LINE

Denny Martin Flinn

Photographs by Martha Swope

A BANTAM TRADE PAPERBACK

BANTAM BOOKS
NEW YORK • TORONTO • LONDON • SYDNEY • AUCKLAND

WHAT THEY DID FOR LOVE
A Bantam Book / July 1989

Grateful acknowledgment is made for permission to reprint lyrics from "Move On" by Stephen Sondheim, copyright © 1984 Revelation Music Publishing Corp. and Rilting Music Inc. A Tommy Valando Publication.

BOOK DESIGN BY ANN GOLD

Library of Congress Cataloging-in-Publication Data

Flinn, Denny Martin.
   What they did for love : the untold story behind the making of A chorus line / Denny Martin Flinn ; photographs by Martha Swope.
      p.   cm.
   ISBN 0-553-34593-1
   1. Hamlisch, Marvin.   Chorus line.   2. Bennett, Michael, 1943 Apr.
   8–   I. Swope, Martha.   II. Title.
   ML410.H1745F6   1989
   792—dc19   88-47842
                                                              CIP
                                                              MN

Published simultaneously in the United States and Canada

Bantam Books are published by Bantam Books, a division of Bantam Doubleday Dell Publishing Group, Inc. Its trademark, consisting of the words "Bantam Books" and the portrayal of a rooster, is Registered in U.S. Patent and Trademark Office and in other countries. Marca Registrada. Bantam Books, 666 Fifth Avenue, New York, New York 10103.

PRINTED IN THE UNITED STATES OF AMERICA

0 9 8 7 6 5 4 3 2 1

ACKNOWLEDGMENTS

. . . .

My wife, Barbara, participated in all the interviews. Without her this book would never have been completed.

Thanks also to Barry Kleinbort and Edward Strauss, who brought to bear on the manuscript—and my life—their extraordinary knowledge of the American musical theater; and to Deborah Schneider, agent, and May Wuthrich, editor, for their continuing faith.

The dancers quoted herein, and many others who did their time in *A Chorus Line*, spoke about the show and their lives in a markedly open and trusting manner. For that trust, I can only say that I hope this story satisfies their desire for a fair and interesting account. Whatever enjoyment the reader finds is due in large measure to them.

DMF

One
for the road

CONTENTS

· · · · · · · · · · · · · · · · · · ·

PROLOGUE

· · · · · · · · · · · · · · · · · ·

The Shubert Theatre. August 10, 1987.

Probably no one in the celebrity-studded audience was seeing *A Chorus Line* for the first time. It had opened in this theater almost twelve years earlier. Tonight's performance would be number 5,001. The musical about dancers' lives, which created a sensation when it opened in 1975, would be the first show ever to run that long on Broadway.

In the cast tonight would be nineteen winners of an unusual lottery. In the two years since the stock and amateur rights had been released, thousands of young dancers around the United States had appeared in more than 350 productions at high schools and colleges, in summer stock, dinner theaters, and community theaters. In a "Chance to Dance" contest, these dancers were invited to apply to the New York Shakespeare Festival for an opportunity to appear in one performance on Broadway. Their letters, sorted by role, were placed in a top hat, from which producer Joseph Papp picked one dancer for each part. The winners and their guests were flown to New York—where the original version of the musical was still running—and were taught the show's finale by the dance captain.

The group included a mother of five from Salt Lake City, a real estate agent from Maryland, an account executive from Atlanta. That night they would join their Broadway counterparts onstage for "What I Did for Love," and again for the show's finale. They would be onstage when the show crossed the five-thousand-performance mark and became the only Broadway musical in history to reach that plateau.*

*Just to put that achievement in perspective, the book *Broadway's Greatest Musicals* uses as its criterion any musical that has played five *hundred* performances.

· 1

And yet the success was marked with sadness. Michael Bennett, who had conceived, directed, choreographed, and masterminded *A Chorus Line* as the penultimate achievement of a luminous theater career, would not be present. A month earlier, he had passed away.

Tonight, when the audience applauded the musical **before** it began, when the producer cut the five-foot cake baked in the shape of the show's famous top hat, when the nineteen nervous young dancers made their first appearance on a Broadway stage in the legendary musical they had grown up adoring, even when the post-performance celebration was marred by a near fistfight between the producer and one of the authors, the ghost of Michael Bennett would hover in the air as sharply as his dancers circumscribed the stage.

Michael would most have loved the idea of celebrating this milestone with anonymous young dancers from across the country. He worshipped dancers, and though he choreographed some of the musical theater's greatest solos, he was happiest working with the chorus. And his chorus numbers—either for the chorus behind the star or, better yet, the chorus alone—were his greatest achievements. For two decades his dances had sparkled along Broadway in hit shows. They opened, closed, and stopped more than a dozen musicals.

During Michael's career the musicals he was involved with became permeated with his sensibility, and dance became more and more integral to them, until the shows themselves danced, virtually **flew**, from beginning to end. And then he stripped away the show itself and settled on a project that was **about** dance. He called it *A Chorus Line*, a title that reflected its guise of simplicity, and it succeeded beyond even his own wildest dreams.

After Michael died, a memorial service was held at the theater. Many of his professional associates spoke about him, and Stephen Sondheim sang Michael's favorite song, "Move On" from *Sunday in the Park with George.*

> *Stop worrying where you're going,*
> *Move on.*
> *If you can know where you're going*
> *You're gone.*
> *Just keep moving on.*

Then the current cast performed *A Chorus Line*'s famous finale. But this time, when the set revolved to reveal the sunburst drop that backed the number, it had been replaced by an enormous picture of Michael, arms outstretched toward the audience, the sign DREAMS lit up behind him. Because Michael had been one of Broadway's great makers of dreams come true, for himself and for many of those in the audience, and because those dreams had affected so many, it was a highly emotional moment, all the more stunning for its theatricality—which Michael would certainly have approved of.

But tonight, because the audience had come to celebrate the show's five thousand performances, there was a joyfulness in the air that was in marked contrast both to the memorial and to the first public performance years before, when the original cast had trembled in anticipation of what the audience might think of them in this odd new musical.

Still, the young dancers who were going to dance on Broadway for the first time tonight did plenty of trembling. *To dance on Broadway.* For many of them the dream had begun when they first saw *A Chorus Line* in their hometowns, to which a company had trouped as the musical's fame spread out from Broadway. Tonight, when their turn came, they danced smiling onto the stage, one after the other in their glittering costumes and top hats, and fulfilled that dream.

None of them had known the choreographer, and none of them had any idea of the process by which *A Chorus Line* had come into being.

This is the story of the original dancers in that show. It was their desire, their greatest joy, to dance on Broadway. And they all did, in various combinations, in more than a hundred musicals. Their odyssey, which began for some as far away as Trinidad and for others as close as Brooklyn, reached an extraordinary climax when they became the original cast of *A Chorus Line.*

Behind the slick singing and dancing, behind the award-winning performances of the original cast, behind the historic, record-breaking run, is the unique story of the dancers who were *A Chorus Line.* Behind the dazzle of light reflected off sequins lies the pain and joy of an arduous and emotional adventure in the dramatic world of the Broadway musical theater.

The full story begins years earlier at a neighboring Broadway theater. . . .

CHAPTER I

·················

Coming Together

I n the winter of 1973, a Broadway musical disappeared into the inglorious Valhalla of notorious flops. The musical was called *Rachel Lily Rosenbloom (And Don't You Ever Forget It!)*. An unfortunate title by any account, now referred to—when it is at all—as *Rachel Lily Rosenbomb and Maybe We Better Forget It.*

Rachel (all musicals are quickly abbreviated by the dancers to their shortest possible title) was a rock musical with book, music, and lyrics by Paul Jabara. Starring Paul Jabara.

The producer who brought this particular stiff to life was Robert Stigwood, the entertainment mogul responsible for the musicals *Jesus Christ Superstar* and *Evita*, as well as the films *Saturday Night Fever* and *Grease.*

Stigwood was thought to have produced the show as something of a favor to Jabara. Ron Link was hired to direct. He had never before directed a Broadway musical. Some of the cast came to believe he had never before **seen** a Broadway musical.

Stigwood left others to oversee the preparations and disappeared to his haven in the Caribbean. When he returned, the musical was a mess. He fired Link, postponed previews, and brought in Tom Eyen, an off-off-Broadway director best known for *The Dirtiest Show in Town.* Tom Eyen had never directed a Broadway musical either.

Eyen's contribution included cutting a good many of the dances that choreographer Tony Stevens, his assistant Michon Peacock, and a dozen of Broadway's best dancers, had sweated over for weeks.* *Rachel* was Tony's first Broadway musical as a choreogra-

---

*In *Rachel's* chorus: Richard Cooper Bayne, Carole (Kelly) Bishop, Judy Gibson, Michon Peacock, Jozella Reed, Jane Robertson, Thomas Walsh, Anthony White, Rhoda Farber, Wayne Cilento.

pher, and things had not been going well. During previews he sat in the last row at the back of the Broadhurst Theatre and cringed, praying that the building would burn down before the show could be seen by the public.

Traditionally, when a musical goes bad, the choreographer is the first to be fired. That is because he is the least to blame. So Tony got the blame and then the old heave-ho. Grover Dale, whose most recent credit was the musical *Seesaw*, from which he himself had been replaced, was brought in. Dale's contributions to *Rachel* included a first-act finale, choreographed for his wife, in which she was bludgeoned to death by the two singing "Dykettes," and a chorus number in which all the boys wore vine-leaf G-strings and salaamed upstage, in tempo, naked posteriors pointing toward the audience. If not the dirtiest show in town, it was certainly the most tasteless.

Rachel was withdrawn before the critics could get at it, and it sank without a trace. To his credit, Robert Stigwood returned the entire loss to his investors out of his own pocket.

All right, it happened. It's over. Forget it. File it with *Ari, Wild and Wonderful, Her First Roman, Mata Hari, A Mother's Kisses, Prettybelle,* and *Lolita My Love,* just to name a few.

But one extraordinary circumstance followed. Out of the frustration of this really terrible show, out of a growing impatience on the part of dancers with the ineptitude of so many producers, writers, and directors, came the first tangible impetus toward another musical that within two years would be called, by many in the New York theater community, the greatest musical ever.

"Out of that show," Tony Stevens says, "it became clear that most of us—the dancers in the show, the chorus people—knew more about how to put a show together than many of the producers we had worked for. That we approached the work with much more discipline, and with a sense of movement and freedom that other people didn't have."

Tony Stevens had grown up in the Midwest with a single dream: "To go to New York, dance on Broadway, and be the Gene Kelly of my generation." During his first three years in New York he danced in *The Fig Leaves Are Falling*, which lasted four nights; *Billy*, which lasted one night; and *Jimmy*, which managed a couple of months. But Tony left *Jimmy* after one month to do *Georgy*. Four nights. He did *The Boy Friend*, which ran nearly a summer, and then he danced in two more flops, the off-Broadway *Ballad of Johnny Pot* and the Broadway revival of *On the Town*. He did eight shows in three years and received what he would come to call an "amazing education."

But the dream with which he had come to New York, to get into a hit Broadway musical, had never materialized. So Tony turned to choreography. His assignments included *Ringelevio*, a new musical that never got past its Buffalo tryout, and *Spotlight*, a clunky pre-Broadway show that was scuttled in Washington.

His assistant on *Rachel*, Michon Peacock, came to the city from St. Paul, Minnesota, with the same dreams. She danced in a number of shows and faced many similar situations. She felt bad about another aspect of the whole thing. "Tom Eyen was very degrading to dancers," she felt, "and Ron Link was not much better." In the hurly-burly chaos of a big musical, dancers were pushed around, abused, blamed, and not listened to. She went through the *Rachel* experience close to Tony. Together they fell to wondering why the hell a thing like this happened so often.

After *Rachel* closed, Michon went home for Christmas. She was unhappy after a series of similar, frustrating shows and spent a lot of time pondering what she could do about it.

This trip home proved not so much a vacation as a retreat, and she relied heavily on her religion. As a follower of Nichiren Daishonin, who introduced the practice of chanting *Nam Myoho Renge Kyo* in thirteenth-century Japan, she set up a small shrine in her bedroom, and chanted to get to the bottom of her unhappy situation.

The philosophy of Nichiren Shoshu Buddhism teaches that life and the environment are inseparable, and that as much as the individual is influenced by his environment, so does he have the power to exert influence over it. More specifically, he can effect change through self-reformation.

Michon began to develop a new view of her situation. She realized that if things were going to change, it was the dancers themselves who would have to change them.

"We created that environment in which we are seen as individuals who don't know anything, who can't express ourselves, who are not capable of contributing anything other than 'five, six, seven, eight, go.' So when I got back to the city, I called Tony."

Tony Stevens and Michon Peacock got together to talk about all this. They discussed the problem for hours, between themselves and with other dancers. Was there actually anything they could do about this situation?

They conceived of a company, *composed completely of dancers*, who would write, produce, direct, design, and choreograph their own shows. This dancers' repertory company seemed like a viable way to avoid the ridiculous ineptitude under which they so often suffered.

Lacking the pull to get all the people and the funding they required, Tony and Michon realized they would need a more powerful and established personality to help them get the project off the ground. They decided to approach Michael Bennett. Bennett had begun his career as a dancer and was now one of Broadway's best director-choreographers. Since Michon knew Michael better than Tony, she was elected to contact him.

"I chanted for a couple of hours and then called him," Michon recalls. "And sure enough, he wanted to see us the next day."

The three assembled to discuss it. Michael was immediately intrigued. "We decided," recalls Michon, "we would hold a talk session to find out where dancers have come from and gone to, and to create something, either a book, a magazine article, a play, something. We were all gypsies and we had a mutual interest in making gypsies more functional and more appreciated in the profession."

A gypsy is a musical-comedy dancer. There is no known derivation of the nickname, though Betty Comden and Adolph Green claim it's because "dancers go camping from show to show." A special exuberance separates the gypsy from the ordinary concert dancer. They are singers and actors as well as dancers, and play characters more closely related to real life than the princes and princesses of ballet or the abstract images of modern dance.

A gypsy travels a great deal, for the Broadway musical is in demand everywhere. Yet their community is a close one, and even in the heyday of American musicals, when dozens of hit shows danced across the country, most dancers knew one another, whether casually, intimately, or by reputation.

They stand next to one another in class at the barre, in lineups before leering producers, and behind the stars. They sweat together, party together, laugh and cry together, love and hate one another. They blend their voices in song and their bodies in dance. They are an insular group, with their own language and customs. As a subculture, they are virtually unknown to audiences who, when cheering a musical, rarely see the chorus boys and girls as individuals.

Michon got the use of a studio—a Nickolaus Exercise Center on the Lower East Side donated by Bill Thompson, a Buddhist former dancer and co-founder of the Nickolaus Exercise Centers—and she, Tony, and Michael began telephoning dancers. They approached dancers who had larger ambitions, who wanted to sing, act, design, write, choreograph, and/or direct as well. Since one of their objectives was to get a sense of the life of the gypsy, they also chose dancers who, they felt, spanned the spectrum of that experience.

A number of people turned them down. Some were afraid they might be called on to assert themselves verbally, when their art and confidence lay in nonverbal communication. Some thought it was just Tony, the "would-be choreographer," attempting to establish himself. For others, the prospect of all those egos in one room was threatening and overwhelming. But some were attracted by Michael Bennett's status in the theatrical community. And for many who had experienced shows like *Rachel*, a dancers' repertory company held promise. Slowly a group was assembled.

Tony Stevens and Michon Peacock. Michael Bennett and Donna McKechnie. Trish and Jacki Garland, sisters. Steve Boockvor and Denise Pence Boockvor, married only a year. Sammy Williams and Thommie Walsh and Wayne Cilento. Kelly Bishop and Andy Bew. Chris Chadman and Candy Brown. Nick Dante. Priscilla Lopez. Renee Baughman. Steve Anthony.

On Saturday, January 18, 1974, at midnight, they would meet

to dance, talk, and discover—if they could—who they were and what their lives meant.

Though no one knew it at the time, that meeting would be the beginning of the most remarkable chorus line in Broadway history.

CHAPTER II
· · · · · · · · · · · · · · · · · · · ·

The Meeting

It was long past dark when the two dozen dancers headed for the Lower East Side. Some had just completed matinee and evening performances of Broadway shows and set out from their stage doors. Neon signs flashed and crowds of people pushed against one another on Broadway streets. In groups of twos and threes the dancers made their way downtown through the city traffic. The winter air was cold and crisp, the temperature dropping rapidly.

For those with the courage to attend—and many refused—there was the inducement that one of Broadway's best choreographers would be present. If Michael Bennett had not yet established to the public the full extent of his talent, these dancers knew just how brilliant he could be. For nearly a decade insiders had known that Michael was by far the best musical-comedy mind of his generation. Always ambitiously seeking to do innovative work, he was also the most connected to, and respectful of, dancers as artists.

If one thing set these dancers apart from those who did not attend, it was perhaps the nature of their commitment to their work. Their dedication to and love for theater dance transcended whatever trepidations accompanied them downtown.

But perhaps one other trait set them apart as well. Michael, Tony, and Michon had worked hard to assemble the right list. They were looking for more than skilled dancers. In his work Michael had always attempted to personalize the chorus. With each successive show he had gone a step further in creating a set of characters within the ensemble, and to do this he needed unique individuals. The assortment of dancers who arrived that night were more than the classic musical comedy chorus boys and girls. They were the most special of a special breed.

The excitement began to mount as the dancers climbed the stairway and milled around, gossiping, in the dressing rooms. There was the buzz of friendship as gypsy acquaintances were renewed, and the chill of competition, too. As the dancers changed their clothes and prepared to test themselves and one another once again, a palpable tension filled the air.

There are hundreds of applicants for every dance job. Everyone there had competed for the same shows, and for the attention of one or another choreographer, including Michael Bennett. This is the constant reality of a dancer's life, and it carries over to class, rehearsals, and friendships. The dancer getting dressed feels a curious combination of emotions, for in tights and leotard he is at once most exposed and most comfortable.

They gathered in the studio, and the room filled with music. The evening was going to begin with a jazz class. Tony led the dancers through stretching and strengthening exercises, then moved on to more technically oriented jumps and turns. Finally he taught a routine that each picked up quickly and fit to his or her own body. Dancing in smaller groups, they corrected themselves in the mirror, all of them surreptitiously comparing themselves to the others. The room became humid and close.

The unusual nature of what would follow drew the ordinary air of excitement to fever pitch. For some, the uncertainty of the evening was overcome here, the tension broken, by the workout. For others, there was a feeling of impatience. They had already performed two shows that day and had not gone downtown at midnight to take a class or learn Tony Stevens's choreography.

Then Michael arrived, late, during the dancing, with his favorite dancer, Donna McKechnie, on his arm.

Michael Bennett, born Michael DiFiglia in Buffalo, New York, to a Sicilian auto-plant machinist father and an East European Jewish mother, had pursued his dream of becoming a Broadway choreographer since childhood. Dance lessons at the age of three, performances at local hospitals and orphanages with "Mrs. Dunn's Little Stars of Tomorrow" by the age of nine, and a consuming interest in the theater and the films of Gene Kelly and Fred

Astaire, led to Michael's dropping out of high school to dance in a European tour of *West Side Story* for Jerome Robbins, the preeminent musical comedy director-choreographer of the preceding generation. In short order Michael had moved into choreography, then direction; he had employed, and could employ again, any of the dancers in the room.

His most recent musical had been *Seesaw*.

When *Seesaw* opened on Broadway on March 18, 1973, it barely resembled the musical that had left town to try out in Detroit several weeks earlier. This new musical was based on William Gibson's successful play *Two for the Seesaw*. The play had only two characters, played by Henry Fonda and Anne Bancroft, but the musical had a big chorus. It was originally choreographed by Grover Dale and directed by Edwin Sherrin, who had never before directed a Broadway musical. Out of town, the show was a disaster.

In an attempt to save it from quick obscurity, the producers hired Michael Bennett, Broadway's reigning musical-comedy doctor. Michael brought in his own entourage, including his close assistant, Bob Avian, and his dance captain, Baayork Lee. He replaced Lainie Kazan in the lead with Michele Lee, and a supporting actor with the world's tallest tap dancer, Tommy Tune. Then, to make room for his own dancers, he looked around at the existing chorus members. He choreographed a jazz combination in rehearsal, and the dancers found themselves auditioning for him two by two.

That evening during the performance, thirteen or fourteen people were fired, and Michael delegated Grover Dale, now working for him, to bear the news. The dancers remember Dale's haunting the wings during a performance, tapping people on the shoulder and saying: "Don't bother coming back tomorrow. You're fired."

While Michael's near frantic efforts to fix the musical were rehearsed during the day, the old version was still being performed at night. Among the dancers who had been given their notice, there was a lack of enthusiasm for the work. As dance captain, Michon made every effort to keep the company from falling apart, but their anger over how they were being treated made the backstage atmosphere tense.

One night before the show Michon gathered them together and quietly drew on their pride of profession. She warned them that every job, every performance, affected their careers, and asked them how they wanted to think of themselves and be thought of by others. They banded together and determined to do their last few shows to the best of their ability.

Michon had been with the show from the beginning, and though she was not among those let go, she hated the way Michael fired so many dancers. She attempted to get out of her contract. But Michael recognized her leadership capabilities and asked her to stay. They developed a guarded truce, which slowly blossomed into a satisfying working relationship.

"He tried to explain things to me," Michon says, "and he made tremendous efforts. He would ask me to help with certain things because I knew the people and could work with them."

Michael oversaw the staging and rewriting of *Seesaw*, and drew on some of the dancers to help with the choreography: Wayne Cilento, Steve Anthony, and Mitzi Hamilton invented steps for one of the numbers; Grover Dale worked on one number and Thommie Walsh on another, and Bob Avian and Baayork Lee on several. The show came to Broadway and succeeded. When the book writer, Michael Stewart, refused to have his name bruited about, Michael took his billing, and "Written, Directed, and Choreographed by Michael Bennett" appeared on Broadway for the first time.

But to Michael, *Seesaw* was never a work of art. He had merely created a flashy entertainment and in the process had proven his ability to oversee the reconstruction of a flop musical quickly.

Inevitably the show's Broadway run began to stumble financially, and once again Michael turned to Michon. Michael called her into the stage manager's office one night and said, "There's only one thing we haven't tried yet."

"What?" Michon asked.

"Chanting," he replied.

Michon felt an intense excitement about his suggestion of how they might attack the problem of a drop in box office activity. Michael had dabbled in Buddhism several years before, but she, a deep believer, felt confident that if the entire chorus were to join forces they could turn the situation around. One night thirteen people, including Tommy Tune and other dancers from the show, came to Michon's apartment. For an hour they chanted *Nam Myoho Renge Kyo* for the success of their show.

The very next day, in a major publicity coup, New York's Mayor John V. Lindsay agreed to make a special appearance onstage in place of his near look-alike, leading man Ken Howard. He allowed himself to be mugged to music and picked up by a dancing prostitute in the opening sequence. Photos of Michon and the girls doing the "hooker" number with Mayor Lindsay ran on the front page of the *Daily News* and the *Post*. Sales went up. The show was saved.

Seesaw was only the most recent in a string of Michael's exceptional shows.

When Michael Bennett, short, dark, intense, with close-cropped black hair and a neat Amish beard, and Donna McKechnie, tall, with the athletic grace of a great dancer, walked into the room, everyone's eyes turned to them. The dancing tightened up and a palpable energy emanated from the group. Michael's late entrance only heightened the excitement, as he had known it would. Shortly after their arrival, the dancing concluded.

Delicatessen sandwiches Michael had ordered were devoured; then everyone gathered in another room. The group consisted of three different circles of dancers: Michael's own inner circle; Bob Fosse dancers, loyal to another of the reigning director-choreographers on Broadway; and a group of select dancers who perform yearly in the Milliken industrial show, a lavish musical comedy staged for the fabric convention. There were people who really didn't like each other, and people who didn't trust each other. Cliques within cliques.

Michael, Tony, and Michon had written out one hundred questions for each performer to answer: real name, stage name, age, astrological sign, where you came from, what your childhood was like, life as a dancer, and on to your experiences coming to New York and in the professional theater. Everyone sat on the floor in a circle and Michael laid down the ground rules. Going around the circle, each dancer would answer the fundamental biographical questions, structured in sections: childhood, adolescence, pre-New York dancing career, and New York to the present.

Each dancer would speak about the same subject; then they would move on to the next and go around again. Anyone in the circle could ask additional questions. The rules established, they were ready to begin. Michael turned on the tape recorder.

Tony Stevens's family, the Italian side, were all exceptional ballroom dancers. **I had an aunt who was a nun that we used to call Sister Rubberlegs. She used to love to jitterbug.** When his mom and dad got up to dance, everyone would stop and watch. Then it would be the baby's turn and he would jitterbug with his father, getting thrown into the air in all the jitterbug lifts. They took him to dancing school when he was three. **I took a year of dance and I quit 'cause they made me a poodle in the recital.**

After that he tried the piano for two years but he couldn't sit still long enough. By eight he was back at the dance studio. **The thing that was strange was that it was so easy for me. I'd just go and do it. I guess it's like some guys play ball or do something really naturally.**

There was nothing very challenging for a long time, until I started taking class in St. Louis. **Then I started meeting all these little Jewish girls who knew what ballet was about, taking it very seriously. I started thinking: "There's a lot more to this than just squatting and jumping around." So by the time I got into high school I was taking four or five classes a week. I thought I better apply myself to see if I'm going to do this or not.**

Theater in St. Louis is the Municipal Opera. Two giant oak trees form the proscenium of this twelve-thousand-seat outdoor arena, which presents ten or twelve shows in the same number of weeks and hires dancers from May to September. **So many places, dancing is not a reality, but here it was a real, tangible thing. You could work and you made eighty dollars a week and that was big money. I mean you could have a summer job dancing. So you really planned. When you got old enough you worked all winter for the audition, which came in March.**

When Tony didn't get the job, it was a big disappointment. He went to rehearsals anyway, to watch his friends. **Then the very same guy that got it instead of me broke his ankle, right in front of me. Fell down and broke his ankle. "Who can take him to the hospital?" And there I am, and the choreographer remem-**

bered me from the audition and I took that guy to the hospital and got his job. I had just turned eighteen.

During that season of stock he met New York professionals for the first time. In September he piled into the car with his new friends and drove to the city.

In my senior year I had just gobbled up everything I could about New York. I studied maps, I did everything just to absorb it, and it really felt like home. All I really wanted to do when I was a teenager was to go to New York and be the best dancer anybody had ever seen. I just wanted to be a dancer on Broadway and be the best.

Michon Peacock was a tomboy. **Also very slouched, stoop-shouldered, bowlegged, swaybacked, and had other physical impairments.** She was accident prone and by the time she was eleven had broken her leg playing football. The doctor recommended dance class.

Even that small expense was a hardship for her parents, who were terribly poor. Her father drank and her mother worked constantly to support four children. After the first year they could not afford to send her to dance school, but the teacher, a Jewish cantor and musical-comedy fan who performed as a song-and-dance man in New Jersey stock, had spotted talent and taken to the girl. **He was wonderful. He trained me. He really took great pains with me. I started to practically live there. It was an excuse to get out of the house.**

By the time she was fourteen she had started working as a dancer and got her union card for performing with St. Paul's Civic Opera Company. She did dozens of musicals and operas in her teens, and met and worked with the stars and New York choreographers who came to St. Paul. She graduated from high school and, like many young dancers faced with the same decision, opted for a total commitment to dance instead of college. It was 1964. She had not yet turned eighteen when she headed for New York.

I messed myself up like crazy. Alcoholic at seventeen and a half. O.D.'d on New York. I lasted in New York till the end of the World's Fair, went home with mononucleosis, and tried to get myself settled down a little bit.

Back home, Michon worked as a legal secretary, played a

couple of leading roles in community theater, accumulated a little money, and determined to try the city again.

She got a job in a provincial area outside of Montreal which she thought would help her get back to New York. There was this big building in the middle of the highway. You lived where you worked. The room that I stayed in was disgusting. Turned out to be a strip joint. I got up there and the person I was supposed to replace was a woman stripping other women on stage. After I saw the show I went up and locked myself in my room and just started crying and crying. How am I gonna get out of this? I had fifty dollars on me. So I cried my way out of it and they let me go. It cost me forty-five dollars by cab from Newark Airport to my girlfriend's place, so I had five dollars when I arrived in New York.

When Sammy Williams was just a little boy, his sister was taking dance lessons, and his mother brought him along to watch. He sat on the floor with his back to the mirror, mesmerized by the music, the dancing, the sound of the taps, and, most of all, the costumes. Little by little he began to practice the steps secretly at home.

One day the Trenton, New Jersey, dance teacher coaxed Sammy onto his feet. He never sat down again.

To tap-dancing, Sammy added jazz, which was just beginning to become popular in the 1950's. After school he hurried to the studio for classes and rehearsals, for recitals, and performances for local organizations, psychiatric wards, benefits, Elks clubs. Between the ages of eight and fourteen, dancing was Sammy's entire life. When his teacher suffered a heart attack and had to retire, Sammy began doing plays and musicals.

His family had very little money, and by the time he was a senior in high school, Sammy still had not seen a show on Broadway. He was dancing in a production of *The King and I* under the direction of a Broadway actor who was simultaneously serving as standby for Anthony Newley in *The Roar of the Greasepaint, the Smell of the Crowd.* For his convenience, the director asked the cast to rehearse in the city on matinee days. Then, unexpectedly, Sammy's director had to go on. Instead of their rehearsal, the director arranged for them to see the Broadway musical.

It was at the Shubert Theatre. The high school senior sat way up in the balcony, looking down at the stage, and was overwhelmed. It was then that Sammy understood what he wanted in life. To have his own moment under the lights, alone on stage.

He was attending night school at a local community college when they put on a production of *Carousel* under the direction of Tommy Tune, a Broadway dancer who encouraged Sammy to read the trade papers and attend New York auditions. He auditioned for Michael Bennett for *Henry, Sweet Henry,* but didn't get the job. He did, however, get cast in a summer stock tour, his first professional show. Performing for a living, doing eight shows a week in the tents of New England, Sammy was in heaven.

While touring for the summer, Sammy and his roommate spotted an audition notice for a new Broadway musical called *The Happy Time,* to be directed and choreographed by Gower Champion. They were looking for teenagers, and Sammy's roommate pointed out that Sammy—young, short, and slight—was perfect. Having just got his first professional job, Sammy was content and not anxious to go, but his roommate continued to press him until he agreed. Following their performance one night, he took a plane into the city, stayed at the YMCA, and auditioned the next morning for Champion. He left the theater with his first Broadway contract.

The show was to try out in Los Angeles, and at the airport Sammy received a big disappointment. They informed him he would be the swing boy. He had to ask what that was. It meant that he would understudy all the rest of the boys. Realizing he would not be onstage regularly, he was crestfallen. But he worked for months to absorb all of Gower Champion's varied choreography, learning all the parts, and eventually went on many times.

Back in the city, Sammy lived in a hotel. During the entire run of *Happy Time* he was like a kid in a candy store. Living on his own in the city, with a good paycheck, he bought clothes and knickknacks, went to movies and other shows, and partied all night. After nine months the musical closed, and Sammy was on his own.

But he had friends in the business now, and they taught him its realities. He moved out of the hotel and into a small apartment on the Upper West Side. He signed up for unemployment and he began the dancer's round of auditions. It had all started when he sat on the floor of a dance studio in Trenton, New Jersey, with his back to the mirror, watching his older sister dance. Where he thought to himself: **I can do that.**

At fifteen, Andy Bew tried out for the first national touring company of *Hello, Dolly!* when it played his hometown of San Francisco. He was hired to dance in the show and his mom was hired to travel with him as chaperone for the kids. One summer weekend when the show was in Chicago, he and his mother and a girl he was going with were boating on a lake in Waukegan. There was an accident and Andy's mother drowned. **The boat went over the top of her and that was it.**

The *Dolly* company coalesced around him, holding him together after that. **We went back out on the road and toured around the entire United States for another nine months. Now I'm completely on my own at sixteen years old. Overnight, grow up. Welcome to the world.** In Houston he and a friend graduated from high school through correspondence courses. That night Carol Channing took her curtain call in cap and gown, and announced to the audience: "I want to let my two friends here take the bow. I have something special to give them." And she presented their diplomas.

The tour ended and Andy returned to his father's house in California and tried to reconnect with some of his high school friends. **I was so far removed at this point. I guess I was a man of the world. I had a Corvette. I had money. I couldn't associate with any of them.** He got a call from David Merrick's office. Gower Champion, *Dolly*'s director, was forming the original company of the new musical *The Happy Time* and had asked for Andy.

He was eighteen when the show brought him to New York.

Steve Boockvor is from the Bronx; his father, an immigrant. **I was about two years old. I bounced around on the street corner by the radio store that had a loudspeaker outside. People were throwing change and carrying on. I guess I did that for some time.** His mother sent him to tap dance school for one hour a week, and he stayed until he was twelve.

The real joy came from the trips downtown. **That was the big** time, going out to see a Broadway show. *Where's Charley? South Pacific.* You'd wait sometimes four months to see a Broadway show. We weren't rich people, came from a mixed neighborhood, mostly Italians and Jews. To go to the theater was something else. We ate in Horn and Hardart, the Automat, and popped the nickels in for my sandwich. I loved it. My father and I, we had a ball. Broadway was fabulous then.

One of the kids from the neighborhood was attending the High School of Performing Arts, the school immortalized by the film and televison show *Fame.* He was kind of daring me. "You can't go to that school!" he'd say. That's all I had to hear. I mean, kids dared me to jump off roofs. This was a zip. At the age of twelve and a half, Steve took a record and his tap shoes and, spurning his mother's offer to accompany him, went downtown to audition for the only high school in the country that trains teenagers for the stage. When the dance department invited him to enroll, he didn't know what to do. He hadn't come to get in, only to prove that he could. He was popular in his own high school, vice-president of his freshman class, good at baseball. Just a kid. To this day he isn't sure why he said yes. But he's glad he did. Performing Arts taught me about art, taught me about painting, taught me about books. I went to a school where they were teaching things that I never knew existed. I didn't know what a dancer was. They taught me a lot of things, and instead of winding up in the garment district or as a policeman or as a bum . . .

The Rehearsal Club no longer exists, but over the years it housed a thousand hopeful young girls who had come uninvited to a strange city to break into show business. A classic play (and subsequent film), *Stage Door,* is set there, and its alumnae include several stars. For a girl lugging a suitcase and clutching a single address on a piece of paper, the Rehearsal Club brownstone was no figment of Hollywood forties nostalgia, but a haven and a beginning.

Denise Pence wrote a cute little letter to the lady and said, "I'm a real nice girl, I don't even have a traffic ticket." Without the club, she might never have come to New York at all. I hated New York on first seeing it. It was so dirty and the building was old and decrepit. I remember calling my mother on the pay phone outside my room: "This is awful here!" Then I started meeting people in the Rehearsal Club and it was incredible. All of a sudden I started picking up on the energy. It was just so thrilling. They were talking about auditions. Two weeks later there was an audition for *The Rothschilds.*

It was an enormous cattle call. Hundreds of girls auditioned. They took four, and Denise got her first Broadway show. In rehearsals she was partnered with Steve Boockvor, by now an experienced Broadway gypsy.

He asked her out. She said no. Then I went back to the Rehearsal Club and I said, Denise, you're being ridiculous. You don't know anybody in this city. How the hell are you going to meet anybody if you keep saying no. So I said yes. Boy! The first Broadway show he took me to see was *Oh! Calcutta!*

Steve: I was looking to get laid. I got the tickets for nothing!

His real name is Kenneth Allen Brown. His Hebrew name is Yakov Avraham. His professional name is Christopher Chadman.

I always danced. Since I could breathe. It made me the block weirdo. I always knew I was different. That was very painful for a long time.

I'll tell ya, everything that was dancing, I saw. *West Side Story, Cabaret.* I wanted to be Joel Grey. TV. I'd sit home and watch *The Ed Sullivan Show, American Bandstand.*

The family spent summers at Shore Haven Beach Club in the Bronx. They gave cha-cha lessons after the show. There'd be all the alta-kockers and this little kid taking lessons. There was also this little girl, so the emcee put us together, choreographed a little routine, and put us in the show. We were an instant hit. I danced there for ten years, amateur, ballroom.

At thirteen he attended High School of the Performing Arts as a ballet student. They tried to throw me out because I wasn't doing very well. My facility was not very good; I didn't have good stretch; I have no turnout. They barely passed me for three years. They kept me out of performances because they said I wasn't ready. They told me to give it up, but I thought I'd rather be suffering with this than not doing it at all. I had no alternative. It was just a passion. That's all I knew. That's all I felt.

When he settled in the city, Chris went to all the auditions he could. I thought that's what you do. To go backstage, Broadway theaters, and audition. Wow! But I didn't really think I would get the job. I really thought I was a terrible dancer.

I remember [choreographer] Lee Theodore yelled out from the house: "Being nervous is not gonna get you this job, Chadman!" I mean, gimme a break. What do you want from my life! Then she hired me! I was out of my mind. It was incredible. I got my first show! I was eighteen years old and I was dancing on Broadway. *Darling of the Day*. Ran about a minute. Throughout rehearsals she made me very, very nervous. But she used me. So I just went from show to show to show after that.

Trish and Jacki Garland came from Lawrence, Kansas. Their mother was a farmer's daughter whose unrealized dream was to become a nurse. Determined to give her daughters the opportunity and support she'd never had, she took in laundry to pay for their dance lessons. Her neighbors never understood why she spent all that time taking her girls to dance schools and performances. Maybe she'd never get out of Kansas, but both her children would.

The sisters were very different. Jacki, older and shorter, was the acrobat. Trish, taller and younger, was the ballerina. They began their studies with the local teacher.

Trish: I had a terrible time there because she didn't seem to care for me as much as she did Jacki. One time she said I was ready to do a back flip—I knew I wasn't, and I landed on my head. We used to do contests in Kansas. All the county fairs and state fairs. Jacki would do her acrobatics and I would do ballet. We always won.

Jacki: Generally I took first. I think she took first once and I couldn't take this defeat! How dare she!

Trish: Ballet protected me. I was real good. I was also with my dance teacher, who I loved and who I wanted to be my mother because I thought my mother loved Jacki more than me. For a year I did not talk to my mother. I kissed my dancing teacher or I'd comb her hair, but I would not kiss my mother for a year. I was about ten. It must have devastated her, now that I think of it.

· 23

In their early teens both girls moved on, leaving Kansas behind. Jacki was accepted into the New York City Ballet School summer program; Trish got a scholarship to San Francisco Ballet.

Trish: **Mother was always encouraging me and that was very difficult for my father, to let me go at that age. It wasn't as hard for my mom because she knew there was something I had to do, but for my dad, I was the baby.** While she was in San Fransisco, their father was killed in an automobile accident. Even though she was alone, their mother still encouraged her children's ambitions, and refused to ask them to come home. **She said you have to do what you have to do.**

Wayne Cilento went to a Catholic grammar school in Westchester, New York. **I always liked Open House dancing. I always danced with the black people. Just regular social dancing.** He auditioned for the high school musical, choreographed by the female physical education teacher, who saw immediately that Wayne had a natural ability and started pushing him to start dance classes. **So I said, "Okay, fine, but I'm *not wearing tights.*"**

Wayne attended modern dance and jazz classes twice a week, wearing shorts and pretending to be an athlete. During the day he was a student at Westchester Community College. Then the teacher took him to see his first Broadway show. **I couldn't believe it. I said, "They're really doing that for a living?" She said, "That's it." I said, "Okay, fine, that's it."** Searching through *Dance* magazine, he found that Brockport University had a dance curriculum, and transferred there. **Okay, so here I am. I'm eighteen now and I knew I had a lot to catch up with. From a person who wasn't gonna wear tights and was never gonna take a ballet class in his whole life, I decided I was gonna be a dancer. So I went to Brockport and I do the same thing. I had an interview with the head of the department and I said, "No tights. You want me to dance? No tights." I think it was a week later, I had every get-up on my body that you could possibly think of. I had modern drag, ballet drag, jazz drag. I had outfits for days. I took two ballet classes a day, three modern classes, and a repertory class. I was dead. I just danced from morning to night.**

Candy Brown was glued to the television set any time dancers performed. **I just knew I was Jimmy Cagney. I saw him tap and** that was the end. I was Gene Kelly. I never was Cyd Charisse or Ginger Rogers. I was Fred Astaire. Nobody bothered to tell me I was black, you couldn't be Fred Astaire. She grew up in Queens, New York, attending Bernice Johnson's dancing school when she was two years old. Our warm-ups were walking splits across the floor! Everybody who came out of there had six o'clock kicks and lots of sell. The training was: If your shoe falls off, keep dancing!

Candy's family, after following her Air Force father around the country, finally settled in Brooklyn. She returned to her dance lessons, this time venturing into Manhattan. There she spotted the trade newspapers *Show Business* and *Backstage*. I was so dumb. I went, Oh, they have their own secret newspaper.

I thought from watching old musicals like *Forty-Second Street* on TV that people would say, "Okay, girls, do the routine," and everybody would know it. I thought there was a set thing that everybody just knew when you went to an audition. I said, Well, I'm gonna be so slick. I'm gonna go to an audition, I'm gonna learn the routine, and then I'm gonna come back and study for a year till I got this routine *down*, and then I'm gonna go get a job. So I went to this audition for the national tour of *Hello, Dolly!* with Pearl Bailey.

When I got there, the choreographer would show you a step and you would do the step. There was a lot of tap and waltz-cloggy kind of stuff. Very stylized. There was one girl—Wynette Turner; we're friends to this day. Well, Wynette did it like it was her own nightclub act, and I said, I like that. I'm gonna do it like that. Then we got to the ballet combination. I ended up backwards. I said, Well, I'll give 'em teeth. What can I tell ya. *I got the Gig!*

For Candy it was a growing experience. We did a month on Broadway. Can you imagine? Nineteen, twenty years old, coming from nothing to Broadway! Then we were off, on tour. I was still kinda starry-eyed. It was the first time I really saw a homosexual. First time I was alone on the road, living in hotels.

After six months the tour ended. I went, Oh shit! I got lucky and now what am I gonna do? I'm a big fraud. I had to go on unemployment. Oh! It was like going on welfare. My mother went down there with me and, oh, it was horrible. But all the kids had said, "We do it all the time. Don't worry about it."

Back in the city, Candy auditioned for the Milliken Breakfast Show.

At that time, it was common knowledge that black dancers need not audition. One black girl who was very fair-skinned had been doing the show, but Candy assumed that one was the limit. At Candy's audition the choreographer fought for her and she was admitted to the Milliken ranks. **Out of all those people [thirty-one girls, thirteen boys, and fourteen children] they only let one in, so for me to do the job, the girl that had been doing it, that was the end of her.**

When Bob Fosse returned to Broadway after a long absence to direct and choreograph a television special for Liza Minnelli, Candy auditioned, but they needed only five girls and at the audition they took one who was black. **I went, Oh, they'll never take two out of five. I got the call that night. I was trying to act so calm. Yes? Rehearsals? Okay. Fine. Thank you. I hung up the phone. Wahooo!!**

She had never heard of the special's renowned director-choreographer. **A couple of weeks into rehearsal I was watching an old movie on TV—*My Sister Eileen*—and I saw these two guys dance. I said, That's just what Mr. Fosse is talking about. They were so sharp, so clean. I didn't know it was Bob Fosse! I was really impressed. It wasn't until near the end that I saw a program with his biography. He had all these awards and had been married to Gwen Verdon. Oh!**

By this time Candy's family was impressed with their show-business relative. The televison taping was black-tie. **Everyone was getting two, four, six tickets. I must've gotten about sixty, and they said, "Now, Candy, this is formal. Are you sure?" Everybody showed up, tuxedo and gowns and all. When the show aired they bought a brand new color TV.**

That night after it was over I went to tell Mr. Fosse how much I enjoyed working with him. He was sitting in the theater and I said, "Excuse me, I just wanted to say thank you," and he said, "Oh, Candy, I want you to meet a friend of mine," and this lady turned around and it was *Gwen Verdon*. I had to sit down. My heart just stopped. She was my idol. Oh, I fell apart.

Kelly Bishop's mother had wanted to be a dancer but dropped out in favor of a marriage that was, ultimately, a failure. **She** wanted something better for her kids, so she got me into ballet very early. Every ballet company that came to Denver, my mother shlepped me down there. By seven, Kelly began her training, with every plan to be a ballet dancer.

After her high school graduation she came straight to New York.

I wanted to get there. I wanted to study there. I wanted to get into a ballet company. I was lonesome at first and of course intimidated on the subway, but I never was frightened of New York. Mother came a few years later and said to me: "If I'd known what I was sending you off to, I never would've done that."

Her first New York audition was for American Ballet Theatre. She had taken classes with the company while they were on tour and the teachers had been encouraging. But Lucia Chase did not want her.

It was my first shock that you don't get the job that everybody says you're going to get.

Though it was not a preferred job among ballet dancers, Kelly became a member of the Radio City Music Hall corps de ballet. The schedule of four or five shows a day with rehearsals interspersed was the only vaudeville-style format left in the country.

Putting those pointe shoes on five times a day, your feet are raw enough as it is. I had never really liked pointe work all that much anyway. It was very painful for me. Finally I thought, I just don't want to do this. I don't want to have to sleep every night with my feet up on the wall to keep the throbbing out of my toes.

The 1964 World's Fair was employing a lot of dancers, and Kelly found work in a show called *Wonderworld* for choreographer Michael Kidd. It was an enormous show. It had thirty-two dancers and thirty-two singers and thirty-two swimmers and motorcycles. I loved it. I loved those gypsy dancers. This is a world of people who are kind of funky and fun, an easygoing bunch of people. I liked the dancing, too. I found myself getting into jazz very easily.

Kelly's jazz education was launched on a vacation when she landed a job in Lake Tahoe and Las Vegas with the Ron Lewis show *Viva Les Girls*.

God, to be a Ron Lewis dancer was a terrifying and wonderful thing. It was so innovative, but we're talking years ago. It was even more unusual. A whole group came from Jack Cole, who must have been the most evil genius around. Gwen Verdon and Chita Rivera and Matt Mattox and Ron Field and Ron Lewis. All of these really brilliant dancers, teachers, and choreographers came from Jack Cole, so he must've been something else.

As for her experience with Ron Lewis in Vegas: It was a killer show. It didn't stop from the beginning till the end. You'd never dance for him without working everything—your head, your eyebrows, your smile, your shoulders. It was the hardest and the best. When you weren't dancing you slept. There was nothing else you could do, because you were so tired.

I think there must be some masochism involved. Most of our ballet teachers, they were real interesting people, but the whole concept of that kind of training, with the stick and the yelling—there is a sadomasochistic relationship that goes on there. Ron Lewis would do the same thing. One of the worst things was the way he put people down, sent people running out of the room crying because they couldn't do the steps. He's a madman.

I remember when I was rehearsing my first show with him. I was doubling, which you do a lot in Vegas. Especially with Ron—he doesn't understand sleeping. I was dancing at the Tropicana at night and rehearsing my first *Viva Les Girls* during the day, and I got to a point one day where I was just so tired I sat down on the stage and started crying because I was so driven and I was so tired and I couldn't get the combination.

Then, someone involved with the show gave Kelly a pill. I took it and perked up and got the combination and went on with the rehearsal. They were amphetamines. We didn't know. People were not that aware then. Unfortunately, that tended to happen with most of the dancers.

The competition in his group was so intense and Ron Lewis is so intense. He will not expect a step out of you if he can't do it himself better. He'll do it over and over again. On that level he's admirable.

But you find yourself—at least in those days when it was also a kind of cult thing—taking amphetamines. This pill made me feel good and I didn't eat as much, and of course every dancer in the world wants to look like a toothpick. We also had no days off, two shows a night, seven days a week.

Early on I hurt myself doing a jump split and was in terrible pain and determined not to stop. My "show pill" made the pain go away. It was my own choice but I was kind of hooked at that point, because it was the only way I could keep the pain away.

After two and a half years, Kelly left the clubs. I had done the best show with the best choreographer. Now I either got topless or I got back to New York. You don't become a star dancer in Vegas if you have your top on. It wasn't the direction I wanted to go in. So I decided to go back and see what would happen.

As a young child, Donna McKechnie would dance around the house with her arms high in the air. She was desperately seeking a father figure and her arms held an imaginary Indian chief. Her mother assumed that Donna held her arms in the classic ballet position "high fifth," and so introduced her to the world of dance. As it turned out, Donna would find love, security, and her Indian chief at the ballet.

When I was born my father picked my mother up from the hospital and said, "I thought this was going to help but I guess not." My mother told me that when I was fifteen.

When my father was in the war I lived with my grandmother and my mother, and his picture was in my room. That was my father, an eight-by-ten glossy. Every night I would kiss him goodnight. When my mother got a telegram that he was back, she dressed me in a little white dress and said, "We're going to meet Daddy." So we went to the train station and there was a *person* and it scared me to death. They came together and hugged and I screamed bloody murder. I couldn't go near him for six months. I couldn't accept the fact that he was real. The early quest for a father figure was like a lifelong search in a way.

Later she came to see her parents' marriage as really troubled, with their inability to communicate what they really felt. I think they loved each other, but I think they had a hard time being with each other, and so a lot of feelings came out in indirect ways, and my sister and I got the brunt of it. That was very painful. It took her many years of psychoanalysis to face the fact that she would never be able to please them. All she could feel was a driving ambition to get out.

Dancing provided her that opportunity. She had started ballet lessons at the age of seven, holding on to the back of a folding chair until she was tall enough to reach the barre. Her intense love for those hours when music and dancing filled the emptiness in her adolescent life fit perfectly with an unmistakable natural ability. And a dancer was born.

There followed the usual round of increasing dedication to classes, participation in recitals and local companies—Donna was a founding member of the Detroit City Ballet—and the usual introduction to musical comedy through stock shows.

I always knew that I had to get to New York. I just knew that I had to get out of Detroit, and New York seemed to be the place to go because that's where the dancing was. I don't know where I heard it. I lived from the age of seven or eight just trying to get out. I didn't graduate high school. I came to New York at about fifteen. I had planned my escape, and so when I left I literally ran. They didn't know where I was. I came to the city that I'd dreamt about as I grew up.

I lived all over the place. At the Y.W.C.A. on East Thirty-eighth Street, the Y on Eighth Avenue. I was living hand-to-mouth. I lived at some of the most sleazy hotels. The Knicker-bocker Hotel—I lived there. I lived at a place they tore down on Sixty-ninth Street that was really a cathouse. I was so dumb.

Her first job out of New York was a concert tour of one-night stands of the South with five older professional dancers. They traveled with their own U-Haul truck, carrying sets and costumes, making $75 a week. **I thought it was the most glorious thing in life.**

Donna auditioned for Lucia Chase's American Ballet Theatre. During a week of classes, applicants were weeded out until five remained. Lucia pulled Donna aside and explained that she was still too young, the company was going to Russia that year, and would she mind studying at the school for a year and joining them the next. Donna took that as a rejection and left the school. She went immediately to Radio City Music Hall and auditioned for the ballet corps. She was accepted, but lasted only ten days. **I couldn't stand it. It was holding plastic tulips and putting them down on** the beat. I just walked out on dress rehearsal. I didn't know that you were supposed to give notice. I just left. They were frantic— they thought I got hit by a truck or something. They called the Y finally to track me down.

It was then that Donna McKechnie discovered the world of the American musical theater. She got a job in a company of *West Side Story* that Lenny Dale was doing. Remember Lenny Dale? Lenny was one of the greatest dancers in New York at that time. He was a real weirdo. He was an incredible dancer and he was teaching jazz in New York. In this period I'm starting to take jazz from Jay Norman, Jaime Rogers. Timmy Everett was teaching up at June Taylor's.

After *West Side*, Donna went to the 46th Street Theatre and auditioned for Cy Feuer and Bob Fosse, who hired her for a new musical they were preparing, *How to Succeed in Business Without Really Trying*.

I remember being in rehearsals for *How to Succeed* when I finally got down off my little pedestal about the ballet world. We were rehearsing onstage and a light bulb went off in my head and I thought, I really like this stuff. My first line was, "Oh, that Mr. Toynbee, he thinks I'm a yo-yo." I said that one line and I thought that was fantastic.

So Donna left ballet for good.

I was very shy and inhibited, and dancing satisfied a way of communicating and feeling closer to people and to myself. It had a lot to do with the way the show worked, the way Fosse used us, that we were all part of it. Because we were actors. And I *loved* his way of staging humor.

And watching Bobby Morse—there was something, an effervescence about him, a spontaneity. There was stardust. He was very magical and everybody sensed that it was a winner show from the first reading.

It was the mid-1970s, the era Tom Wolfe labeled the "Me decade." Encounter groups and sensitivity sessions and having a shrink were at the height of popularity. Whether they were influenced by the times or the late hour or the shared and similar confidences, the dancers slowly opened up and talked about their lives.

Little by little, as they went around the room, the dancers told their stories. Hour by hour, going deeper and deeper into their personal and professional lives. Around and around again, until the layers began to peel away and their deepest truths were exposed.

Chris Chadman remembers thinking, " 'Oh, God, I gotta sit and listen to all these people tell their story.' Sometimes it would get interesting, sometimes I was bored, and the whole time I kept thinking, 'What am I gonna say?' I wanted mine to be the best story. But the process had a momentum all its own. By the time they came to me, it didn't come out at all like I planned."

Tony Stevens saw that as they started to go around the circle, "Somebody would share something a little personal and then someone else would share something a little more personal and that would make you think, 'Oh, I know exactly what they're talking about.' It started adopting a group encounter sort of form to it. All of a sudden you wanted it to get around to you because you desperately wanted to tell something."

Michon Peacock found it interesting to watch people when somebody next to them was talking. People were genuinely shocked by what they were hearing. "Some of the people in that room couldn't stand each other. They had no concept of the reality of another person's life. What had gone into it until that moment. I think they began to appreciate each other in a totally different way."

Dancers, it began to appear, had misunderstandings about one another. You thought you knew who someone was, and that turned out to be an act the person had constructed in order to cope.

Chris Chadman was the only gypsy living on the East Side. "I had this whole reputation that I was a big snob and that I was conceited and that I was aloof, and what they didn't know was that I was just insecure and scared like everyone else. I always got dressed to come to work. People would ask, 'Why are you so dressed up all the time?' It's because I like clothes. That's partly true, but there's more. I thought that if I acted successful, maybe I would become successful."

Some relationships that already existed were altered. Michael, who had worked with Donna McKechnie several times over the course of ten years, knew little about her personal life. That night he heard for the first time about her drive to leave home and enter the world of New York dance. The Garland sisters, who had seldom acknowledged, let alone discussed, their rivalry, sat side by side and spoke about the childhood they had shared. Jacki found it easier to speak than her younger sister. Trish always felt in the shadow of her sister: "I always thought I was adopted. I used to run away from home all the time. I didn't think that I was loved. I never had my own bike."

Steve Boockvor remembers: "We all let it hang out that night. There was a lot of baring of souls. I felt for the first time that Trish Garland was a human being. Nick Dante wiped me out with his story. I mean, your heart went out to these people. They were airing some very intimate details about themselves."

Nick Dante's story had a powerful impact on many of the dancers present. He had been asked to leave Cardinal Spellman High School in New York City because he was gay. He wanted to stay and cope but the authorities thought the other students would not be able to deal with it. So he dropped out and became a drag queen, dancing as a "pony"—a boy who dresses as a girl—in the famous drag show *The Jewel Box Revue*. For three years he wore a dress onstage, and later realized that his conditioning toward effeminacy by the stereotypical images of the straight world had pushed him toward making this choice in life-style. When he started to view his fellow performers as sad, he left that world and took up studying dance seriously for in order to enter the legitimate musical comedy field. Later he came to see the other ponies as having real dignity, and himself as being too insecure about his own homosexuality to realize it. Though Dante was unknown to many of the dancers present, no one there will ever forget the effect of his story.

Tony remembers: "You got very secure in that room with everyone. You got very, very secure."

With everyone relating a section of his or her life, and then moving on to the next dancer, each of them got and gave a little bit at a time. In that way trust was built. Andy Bew had never before spoken of the effect his mother's drowning had on him. "By the time I got to when the accident was, we had gone around the room twice and it was getting pretty late in the evening. So everybody was a little bit looser. It was difficult for me to talk about it. I had chosen to close it off. But I opened up and let it come out. It was a breakthrough. I was finally able to unload all this junk I'd been carrying around for years."

Many of the dancers had never talked about their lives or even looked into and dealt with their own problems. Sammy Williams, the slight young dancer, at first refused even to attend the meeting. He did not want to talk about his life. But Michael Bennett would be there and Sammy suspected the event could be important to his career. After a lot of coaxing by his friend Thommie Walsh, Sammy agreed to go.

Their experiences as dancers had been punctuated by a fierce sense of rivalry and competition. But for a short time, in the shelter of that room, they poured out the most intimate details of their lives. Their disappointments, their fears, their joy in dance.

A group of people who had shared a sense of professional camaraderie suddenly found they shared an even stronger sense of community. They were shocked to learn that so many of them had come from alcoholic homes. They spoke about their upbringing, their families, their sexuality, their peers, their early unformed and unfamiliar desires. Of being on the outside but wanting to be on the inside.

Michon Peacock: "The realizations that went on were phenomenal. People cried most of the time. I don't think Renee Baughman ever stopped crying. It was very, very, very moving."

Tony Stevens: "There was a lot of pain in the room, a lot, and there was a lot of guilt for not having somebody else's pain. A lot of 'I've been your rival all this time; we competed for the same parts.' Yet everybody realized they were in the room because they were dancers. We all understood that joy that nobody else could ever experience, just dancing together. An incredible bond was created."

Joy was shared as well as pain. Kelly Bishop, just about to turn thirty, was really looking forward to it. "I just loved the concept of being that adult."

Candy Brown wondered at first what the hell was going on. "As usual, it was annoying, such a big group and I was the only black person there. But at the same time, it was a nice group. I think we were all just so young and so willing to try things. It was beautiful that everybody just opened up so much. I mean the stories—oh, my God, I was stunned. In fact I felt like I was the disappointing one. I said, I know they think I'm from some ghetto and I got all these troubles, and I didn't. I had probably the most all-American, wonderful, happy life anybody could ever want. I was a cheerleader. I was in the choir. And all these broken homes and drunken parents, and I'm just in tears through all these stories. People ran away from home to dance and all that. My parents were so happy that I was doing *something* that they didn't care."

Donna, sitting next to Michael, was the last to speak in each section. At first she felt alien, as if she had not been invited there to be part of it but to accompany Michael. Her career had already transcended the others'. But as the evening continued, she came to feel more and more a part of it. Since childhood she had wanted to belong to a group, but had always felt like a misfit. Donna's childhood was a traumatic one, and she spoke about it in detail in that room.

"That night it was wonderful to be in that group finally and hear everyone open up. To be in a group of peers, men and women of different sexual persuasions; people you go to class with and you don't really know; people that you'd known over the years in shows. When they started revealing a story, I went, 'Oh, it's like me.' It's like showing pain a certain respect."

Wayne Cilento: "Well, God, we just poured out our lives. I mean, we didn't hold back anything. We just told everything."

They had begun the meeting at midnight and talked into the cold January dawn. They did a brief dance warm-up to refresh themselves and continued on through the morning. By noon on Sunday they had all laid out the events leading up to their arrival in New York. They had talked for twelve hours. It was time to close.

By the end of the intense meeting the dancers were exhilarated. They closed their eyes and held hands, passing the "energy" from one to another, spinning it faster and faster around the circle. While the room seemed to buzz with energy, a peaceful quiet fell on the group. Outside, noon church bells began to chime. Finally they all opened their eyes. And then they began to cry.

The dancers all remember the event vividly. Their common bonds had created an unusual intimacy, which will forever be a part of their lives. Many had released years of pent-up feelings.

They went home silently, tracing the deserted Sunday morning streets, devastated by the evening yet exhilarated by the whole experience. It had snowed the night before, and there was a fresh white layer on the city. The day was sunny and bright, the air crisp and clear.

That night, those dancers shared something that will never be undone. Each will always feel close to the others and protective of the group. No matter what the future would bring, what happened that night could never be erased.

CHAPTER III

....

Evolution

A second talk session was scheduled for three weeks later. The dancers were both apprehensive and eager to continue the process. They had all had a very special experience. Would it happen again?

Michael had hoped to keep the original group intact, but inevitably that could not be. Dancers are an itinerant lot, with jobs taking them suddenly far away. A few of the original participants dropped out, and since word had gotten around the gypsy community about what had taken place—"Really? Well, how cosmic was it?"—there were new dancers ready to step into their places. Mitzi Hamilton had been invited to the first meeting, but was recovering from breast-enlargement surgery and was unable to attend. Because she was so eager to participate, and the second session coincided with the end of her period of recovery, Michael gave his consent and she joined the group.

All headed for the studio expecting a replay of the original meeting.

Once again the session began with dancing. This time Wayne Cilento taught the combination. "I was a nervous wreck. Michael was there and I taught this forever combination. I was proving to everyone that I could dance. Everyone was moaning and groaning. 'Oh, would you stop already. Why is it so long and hard?' "

When they began the talk session, Michael asked Mitzi to begin. "Okay, Mitzi," he said, "since you couldn't make it last time, you have to tell us all about yourself."

"I had to go first," Mitzi remembers. "It was real frightening. They were all sitting there staring at me. Luckily, people started passing around joints and I thought, 'Oh, great, we'll get stoned and relax.' "

Mitzi Hamilton grew up as Carol Patricie in a Chicago neighborhood. When she was a baby, her grandmother used to whisper in her ear: "You're going to be a ballerina." They watched dancers on TV and listened to Vaughn Monroe sing "Ballerina." By the time she was four or five, Mitzi started saying, **I wanna be a dancer. I want to go to dancing school.** Her mother thought it was a cute idea, and sent her to a neighborhood studio that offered everything from acrobatics to baton twirling.

There was a young man who lived upstairs. He played the trumpet. He was seventeen or eighteen, and when she was seven or eight he used to drive her to dance class on Saturday afternoon. **He used to take me the long way and a couple of times he parked and seduced me into going down on him, giving him a hand job, that sort of thing. I didn't dare tell anyone, because I was afraid. To this day I'm turned on by a trumpet.**

By the time Carol was sixteen she had been studying for ten years. She got her first professional job in a chorus line playing outdoor state fairs. But her father disowned her, and she had to pay her high school tuition and graduation expenses. **He didn't want to know about me being a dancer. We were a lower-middle-class Italian family and he expected me to be at home and help my mother in the kitchen and learn how to cook and eventually get married and have a family and live in the neighborhood. He couldn't believe I was going off on my own. My mother and he had big fights about it. He wouldn't speak to me unless he called me a name. My mother, God bless her soul, used to throw herself bodily between the two of us. It was pretty ugly for about three years till I was nineteen. Then I moved out of the house.**

Carol Patricie became Carol Petri. She performed in and around Chicago in revues, joined the national touring company of *How to Succeed in Business,* and moved to New York. Then she performed in *Minsky's Burlesque Follies.* **We weren't topless but we wore pretty scanty costumes. I didn't care—it was a job.** A girlfriend in the show encouraged her to take a new name. "You just can't be Carol Petri. Who's that?" Wanting to put her past behind her, she chose a more show-biz moniker and became Mitzi Hamilton.

I was on a plane traveling somewhere and I read an article about Marilyn Monroe having her chin done. I had a weak chin and I thought, "Well, if she could alter her looks to be what she wants, I could too." I decided I would have my nose done first, just to sort of get things going. I went to this doctor and he said that because of my facial structure it was best to have them both done at the same time. They take away from the nose and add to the chin. So that's what I did. I had it done twice, because I wasn't pleased with it the first time. I didn't feel he had made it strong enough.

Next she added to her breasts. I did it for myself. I always felt like a very sensual person. I felt that I have only one life to live and I thought, "How dare I not have gotten tits?" Really, I've got this one life, I wanna have tits.

Mitzi was proud of her brand-new breasts and showed them off in the small Italian T-shirt she wore to the meeting. Michael walked right over to her, put his hands on her tits, and said, "They're beautiful."

After Mitzi talked, the others picked up where they had left off. Inevitably the second session was anticlimactic. The dancers had come expecting to have another magical experience. Everyone walked away feeling a little let-down.

The first meeting was remarkable for its spontaneity. Unprepared, the dancers launched into their life stories with the courage of the naïve. There was drama and humor, laughter and tears, as emotional scars were exposed. From story to story no one knew what to expect, from themselves or those around them.

The second meeting was more predictable. Dancers arrived with their stories prepared, their jokes set. Perhaps the change in subject matter also had something to do with it. The pain of childhood memories gave way to the exhilaration of a new career in a new city.

At the end of the session, Michael posed his final question: "What do you do when you can't dance anymore?" It was a painful subject that no one in the room had seriously considered. Answers were tentatively explored. As the dancers confronted the subject

....

for the first time, the room erupted, with everyone talking at once. The discussion led back to the question that had lingered in the background all along. Why were they dancers?

After the second session Tony and Michon and Nick Dante met with Michael at his office. They knew they were at a threshold with the project and were eager to continue. They saw Michael as the natural leader. He sat behind his desk, looked at the three of them, and said, "Well, I don't know what it's going to be. . . . We got a lot of material here. . . . I think the best thing is a book." Michon would never forget the moment. "We're sitting across from him going, 'A book? A book! A *book!* That doesn't have anything to do with anything we've been trying to do.' I was so freaked out that after all of this information on their lives and their designs and their pasts and their dreams and all this stuff and he's just thinking about a book! It was really disturbing to me."

Michael had become involved in the talk sessions out of personal curiosity more than any need to participate in a dancers' repertory company. If he had connected the result of those sessions—the lives of dancers recorded on two dozen hours of tape—with the idea of a new musical, he did not mention it at this stage.

In discussing how to proceed, they had to consider Michael's immediate schedule. He had signed to direct Herb Gardner's Broadway comedy *Thieves*, starring Valerie Harper. He had to cast and rehearse the show, then go out of town for tryouts.

They all agreed that, in Michael's absence, Tony and Michon would carry on. The project evolved in two directions simultaneously.

Project A was principally Tony and Michon's original desire for a company, at first called the Broadway Creative Commune, then renamed the Ensemble Theatre. They continued meeting with dancers to discuss it, got a friendly accountant to explain the ramifications of a nonprofit corporation, and proposed a charter:

"The Ensemble Theatre, Inc. is a company of professional dancers formed to further develop their theatrical talents, such as: choreography, direction, design, writing, acting, singing, etc., by creating and performing new theatrical pieces originating from and composed by members of the company. The qualities particular to the company will in turn provide a source for original theatrical forms and entertainments to support and foster the growth of the American theater."

The formation of such a company proved slow going.

Not everyone who could provide concrete help was willing to do so. Andy Bew expressed it for several: "I guess what Tony was talking about is that we're going to get together and we're going to choreograph a piece for all of us and then you'll be involved in this number and I'll choreograph a piece and we'll help each other work out routines and do stuff, and I'm going, 'Hold the phone, Joe. I went to Juilliard for three years. You expect me to come down here and give you my knowledge overnight and not get paid for it?' I said, 'You'll work for me someday, but I'm not going to come in here and give my time up.' I put in a lot of hours learning what I wanted to learn and I wasn't about to get up and give it away."

Then there had to be someone in charge. It was going to take a lot of time and a lot of effort to get the group focused and keep things moving. Tony would have to give up choreography and Michon performing if either were to devote the amount of time necessary to organize and administer the company. So far no one had emerged to take control.

Meanwhile, additional meetings were sparsely attended. Chris Chadman: "After Michael disappeared I think people lost faith. I guess everyone felt Michael, because he was established, could pull it off. He had the money and the clout and the name. But who are Michon and Tony? Nothing personal, but they didn't have the power."

Michon Peacock watched it all fizzle out. "We all tried so hard and we couldn't get past that point. No one jumped up to say, 'I'll do it.'"

Project B was Michael's. In his absence and on his behalf, Nick Dante, interested in writing, continued to interview dancers individually. Then, while *Thieves* was still in out-of-town tryouts, "artistic differences" caused Michael and Valerie Harper to quit the production. They were replaced by Charles Grodin as director and Marlo Thomas as star. Michael returned to New York ready to resume work on his own version of the dancers' project.

One evening at dinner together, Michael, Donna McKechnie,

and Michael's close collaborator Bob Avian spoke about their past and their hopes for the future. Donna's devotion to musical theater had not paid off. Her success as a dancer had not translated into a major career. Michael's greatest dream was to create a show of his own. By 1974 he had choreographed for other directors (*A Joyful Noise, Henry, Sweet Henry, Promises, Promises, Coco, Company*), directed a play (*Twigs*), co-directed a musical (*Follies*), and doctored a musical out of town (*Seesaw*). But he had not yet created a musical all his own.

In the back of his mind, for a number of years now, was a show *for* dancers. He envisioned a musical that, like the Jerome Robbins ballet *Afternoon of a Faun*, would be set in a mirrored rehearsal room. He yearned for a project in which dance and drama would be completely integrated.

Finally Michael met again with Tony and Michon and Nick Dante.

"Listen," Michael said. "I don't know what it is, but it was too incredible and we all know that. If you give me the tapes I'll do something. I think I can get Joe Papp interested in doing a workshop. I don't know what it is, but I'll do something with it."

"So the three of us went away very low and concerned about the whole thing," Tony recalls. "I remember us sitting at the Triple Inn drinking very heavily and tyring to decide, because it was ours to decide what to do with. Anyway, we all decided that it was better that it had a life. He had the power and the resources, and we did not."

Each signed a short contract giving Michael control of all the dialogue that had been recorded in the marathon group meetings. Then, Michael gave each of the three of them a dollar.

"So we signed our little releases and wished him Godspeed. It was a very off-centered kind of feeling. We knew it was great, but we didn't know what was going to happen and we were so close to it. There was a fear that it would be misused. More than losing a million dollars or whatever, which never really entered our minds at that time, we were afraid that somebody was going to get used or hurt. More than anything else we didn't want that to happen.

"There are things that are destined to be. They take their own shape. Now I know what Michael had in his mind. The human drama was greater than anybody ever expected."

"I think now," Michon adds, "that Michael knew all along that it was going to be a musical."

Michael and Nick Dante continued the interviews, speaking again with certain dancers, talking with new dancers, gathering more and more material. Dante typed up the transcripts and assembled dossiers on each potential character.

Michael played the tapes of the meeting for Joe Papp, founder and producer of the off-Broadway New York Shakespeare Festival, who offered to sponsor a workshop. Nick Dante set out to write the book.

Dante had grown up in New York and, after leaving *The Jewel Box Revue*, had studied dance for nearly three years before he found the confidence to attend musical comedy auditions. He first found work at the St. Louis Muni, where he danced in the chorus for three summer seasons, then appeared on Broadway and on television. Following his first summer stock season he returned to the creative writing he had abandoned when he quit high school. He had been interested in the idea of a dancers' repertory company because of his own writing, and had, at the first meeting, told the dramatic story of his childhood and the indignity of his drag-show years. It was a story that had shocked and moved the other dancers, and left a profound impression on Michael for its intrinsic dramatic value.

"The major reason Michael asked me to write the show," Nick believes, "was that he needed my story and he knew that he wouldn't get it otherwise. He didn't know if I could write. If I couldn't write, who cared. He could write the show and stick my name on it." In fact, Michael invited him with the proviso that they would bring in other writers if they found it necessary. "For a while," Nick recalls, "I felt like the little fag dancer that tagged along."

By now the original impetus of a repertory company formed by dancers had completely dissolved. The biographical material recorded at the group meetings had become the property of Michael Bennett, to do with as he saw fit.

"Trust me," he said.

CHAPTER IV
······················
Preparation

Joseph Papp founded the New York Shakespeare Festival in 1954 in the Emmanuel Presbyterian Church on Manhattan's Lower East Side. By 1974 it was by far the largest non-profit theater company in the United States, with free summer performances of Shakespeare outdoors in Central Park and year-round activity at a complex of theaters, rehearsal rooms, offices, and workshops on Lafayette Street in the East Village, in the old Astor Library, which he had talked the city into leasing to him for one dollar a year.

Shakespeare had long since become only a small part of the company's total activity, which soon included all kinds of plays and performances. Most of the work produced by Papp was adventurous, avant-garde, and often received mixed reviews—the price one pays for consistently supporting original material.

At the same time, the greater the risk, the greater the reward. When his productions have succeeded, Papp has enjoyed a level of success unprecedented in the nonprofit theater community. The Shakespeare Festival hosted the world premiere of the rock musical *Hair*, Jason Miller's Pulitzer Prize drama *That Championship Season*, and *No Place to Be Somebody*, for which Charles Gordone received the first Pulitzer Prize ever awarded to a black playwright. The Festival claims a substantial list of playwrights, directors, and actors who were given their earliest opportunities there and went on to major careers. There was no place in town more receptive to unusual material.

Michael Bennett had no book, music, or lyrics. He had no star. He didn't even know if he had a show. All he had was a mountain of taped conversations recording the lives of dozens of

Broadway gypsies. He played a couple of the tapes for Joe Papp and outlined a sketchy idea for a musical. Papp gave his support. The Festival would pay each of the two dozen people who would participate in the workshop—dancers, writers, director, and his assistants—$100 a week.

Michael's decision to turn to Papp instead of a commercial Broadway producer was a reflection of his shrewd business acumen. In the first place, commercial investors expect results. Even if Michael wasn't sure himself, he would have had to bluff others into thinking something was there. And because he was known as a hit-maker, there would have been additional pressure on him to succeed.

In the commercial theater, failure and success is very clear. A director's reputation rests on his ability to be associated with shows that earn substantial profits. Downtown, the difference between success and failure is not defined by the accountants' ledger. The nonprofit theater company succeeds as long as it continues to raise philanthropic money in sufficient quantity, receive grants, provide serious theater to a community, and employ artists. Uptown, a failure could put his whole career in jeopardy. Downtown, Michael could have a failure, throw up his hands, and say it had all been a noble experiment. His reputation would remain intact. The Shakespeare Festival would be a cocoon to protect Michael from artistic compromise, for already a musical had begun to take shape in his mind, a musical without precedent in form and substance. The audience would have to suspend their understanding of the ordinary musical comedy formula, and perhaps it would be more willing to do so for the New York Shakespeare Festival than on Broadway.

Michael did have a feeling that the raw material could be molded into a musical, and his instincts were commercial. But at the same time the project was, for everyone involved and especially for Michael, intensely personal.

Michael was going through a period of disillusionment. *Seesaw* had been a frenzied exercise in show-doctoring, and *Thieves* had ended unhappily. He missed working with dancers, their strict sense of discipline and their shared creativity. Michael often said that the most idyllic time in his life was when he was a chorus boy. It was then he had first realized his youthful dreams and had forged some of his closest and most enduring friendships. In retrospect, the innocence and camaraderie of that period held nostalgic appeal for him.

But ambitious dancers do not remain in the chorus. They turn to choreography as a means of advancing their careers. And in that change of role, a schism is created. They are forever separated from the group that gave them their earliest sense of belonging. Part of Michael yearned to re-experience that feeling.

This show would fulfill his personal need to return to those carefree days. Even if Michael himself could never again be one of the gypsies, at least he could find a way to live among them again.

The show would also represent the chance Michael needed to step up to the top plateau of his profession. He would conceive, direct, and choreograph the show, and, most importantly, he would supervise every phase of the writing. The production would thus be symbolic in two ways: He would make an advance in his career while simultaneously taking a step back to the happiest time in his life.

His first task was to assemble a staff. Now that he had taken over the project, there was no longer any question of a company of dancers who would supervise themselves. From now on it would be his show. And he would choose the people he wanted to join him. Bob Avian would be his assistant. Avian, taller and a few years older than Michael, had been a dancer in the European tour of *West Side Story*, the show Michael had left high school to join. Since then they had worked together on nearly all of Michael's shows. The more responsiblity Michael took on, the more Avian did, becoming increasingly involved in the choreography, the direction, and the producing of his projects.

Avian was a man who paid attention to detail. He was particularly adept at fleshing out the minutiae of dance steps, staging, and acting. It was one of Michael's greatest talents to be able to see the big picture. His shows always benefited enormously from a powerful sense of structure, the inner rhythm that keeps a great musical moving forward quickly. But he worked closely with Avian as his co-choreographer, as well as with the dancers, in inventing the steps that would be needed to execute the patterns.

This method gave Michael a larger vocabulary than his own personal dance style, and enabled him to embrace a much wider variety of dance numbers.

Among Avian's talents were a gentle manner and a cool head. Often his treatment of the dancers gave them as much confidence as Bennett's treatment filled them with awe and fear.

For the score, Michael asked Marvin Hamlisch to do the music and Edward Kleban to do the lyrics. They would be writing together for the first time. Ed Kleban had been around Broadway musicals for years, working as a record producer of several original cast albums, and writing, as both composer and lyricist, special material for singers and scores for unproduced Broadway musicals. Michael's choice of Kleban to write the lyrics demonstrated a keen understanding of what was needed. The songs would have to grow organically out of the material, just as the whole show would. An ordinary pop lyricist would not be able to achieve that, having neither the understanding of how theater lyrics work like dialogue to further the plot, nor experience in the theater from which to draw ideas.

If the project lacked name credibility, that was changed dramatically when Michael enlisted Marvin Hamlisch to compose the score. Hamlisch had recently won three Oscars for *The Way We Were* and *The Sting.* He was Hollywood's hottest composer. What many people did not know was that he had gone to Hollywood following a theater apprenticeship that involved playing rehearsal piano for Broadway musicals, conducting, and writing dance arrangements. He and Michael had worked together as choreographer and dance arranger respectively on the 1967 musical *Henry, Sweet Henry.* Though he had yet to write a Broadway score, his heart was in the theater and his credentials were impeccable.

The creative team Michael had brought downtown was not accustomed to working for $100 a week, nor to taking the subway south. From the start the idea of the experimental project as a purely artistic endeavor had to be dispelled. Michael did not know yet just what he had, but whatever it turned out to be, it would be first class.

Next he had to assemble a cast. Michael was not committed to keeping the original group together. He thought legal releases authorizing him to use the material that had been recorded were necessary. So, out of the blue, each of the original dancers received from Michael a one-page release form which gave Michael permission to quote from their stories. They were asked to sign it for $1. They all did.

For the show, however, they would have to audition. Wayne Cilento: "Were we pissed? Oh, yeah!"

Michael set up shop at the Shakespeare Festival and began inviting dancers to audition. Each day the waiting room was crowded with dancers who had come downtown to dance, sing, and read for the writers, Michael, and Avian. Experienced gypsies clustered together, exchanging Broadway gossip, speculating about Michael's latest project, and scrutinizing unfamiliar faces. Those who had attended the talk sessions were shocked to find themselves auditioning for roles they had actually lived.

Michael handed Wayne Cilento a monologue describing Wayne's experience with *Seesaw* in his own words. "I talk awful—my Bronx accent. So I'm trying to read it but I couldn't, and I said, 'I can't read this.' "

Michael said, "Put the paper down and just talk to us."

Kelly Bishop was asked to read from her own life story. "He gave me this piece of paper to read, and here I'm reading verbatim what I had said on the tape, including the little spaces where I normally take a breath.

"I didn't know that he was going to do that, but it made me feel terrific. I thought, 'Gee, I'm so interesting that he's going to write this down about me.' I'm in this dark little theater, very severe light on me, and I'm walking around with this piece of paper reading this thing to these three or four people in the audience and I felt like a real actress. I had a great time.

"When I'm finished they have a little tête-à-tête up in the audience and then Michael comes down to me and says, 'Don't say anything to anyone but you're gonna get the job.'

"I turned around and said, 'Oh, wonderful. I get to play myself. What a good choice,' and walked out of the room. Then I saw all the girls that were there to read for my part and I got angry that he would dare read anybody else to do me!"

Not everyone could audition at the theater at that time. Sammy Williams was out on tour with the national company of *Seesaw*, which Michael had formed shortly after the show closed on Broadway. While in Philadelphia, Sammy received a phone call in his hotel room at three o'clock in the morning. It was Michael—whose nocturnal hours and enthusiasm led him to telephone friends and associates at all hours of the night—asking him to come into the city that weekend. Michael didn't go into details, so Sammy guessed that he would be auditioning for the Tommy Tune role in *Seesaw*, which would afford him the chance to move up from the chorus when Tune left the show.

But when he arrived in New York it turned out to be a new project that he had heard very little about since that time months earlier when he had attended the all-night meeting. Michael wanted him to read for the role that would be based on Nick Dante's story.

Before the audition, however, they met some of Michael's friends for brunch, and then attended a matinee performance of the New York City Ballet, which featured an all Jerome Robbins program. It was Robbins, the undisputed genius of musical theater with his productions of *Gypsy, West Side Story, Fiddler on the Roof,* and dozens more—as well as numerous ballets for the Balanchine company, of which he was associate artistic director—whom Michael had always admired and after whose career he wanted to pattern his own.

During the course of their day together Michael questioned Sammy about his own life experiences. Finally he asked Sammy to read aloud from the transcript of Nick Dante's story.

To date, Sammy's entire acting career consisted of the words he had shouted in *Applause:* "Margo! Margo!" He had no experience as an actor. He looked over the pages without an actor's tools. He read Nick Dante's dialogue aloud just as he would have read anything else. It was without emphasis, without inflection, and without meaning.

Michael stopped him. He told Sammy to look over the monologue once more and went out of the room.

When he returned, Sammy read through the material again. There was no change. Michael must have wondered what he had gotten himself into.

It was precisely at that point that Michael Bennett demonstrated the qualities that separate the great directors from the pack. Most would have wound things up with a quick "Thank you." Michael only asked Sammy to read the material over a few times and remember the story. Again he left the room. When he returned he asked Sammy simply to tell Nick Dante's story in his own words.

Dante's story had been one of a traumatic childhood, of feeling painfully out of place among his contemporaries. His discovery of being different, of being gay, and of being confronted with this by taunting schoolchildren at a time when he was barely beginning to understand it himself had been a source of great unhappiness. He had been afraid even to raise his hand in school for fear of being laughed at.

Sammy started to tell this story. When he arrived at the part about Dante's high school career, he burst into tears. Extemporaneously telling the story, instead of reading it, had brought it into focus for the dancer. It struck very close to home. His own life, his own hidden pain, flashed into his memory and he cried uncontrollably.

Michael held and comforted Sammy, brought him a box of Kleenex, and helped him pull himself together. But each time Sammy would begin again, the material would overwhelm him, and he would burst into tears.

Then Michael called Marvin Hamlisch to tell him there was somebody he wanted Marvin to meet. Michael and Sammy rode in a cab over to Hamlisch's apartment. Sammy was now doubly affected, by the monologue and by the heady atmosphere of star director and star composer into which he had been plunged with little warning. In the taxi Michael asked him what he wanted to do with his career. At twenty-five Sammy had still not given it much thought. He knew only dancing and, from years of being laughed at, had no thoughts of opening his mouth, even onstage. On the other hand, he now knew the business well enough to realize he did not want to end up an aging chorus boy, either. He knew that one day he would have to stop dancing. Michael said to him quietly: "You'll act first. Just trust me."

At Marvin's apartment Michael asked Sammy to tell them Dante' story, but once again the paraphrased monologue was difficult for Sammy to get through. Marvin was very gracious and asked Sammy to sing. The Academy Award-winning composer played a tune and Sammy sang along. They talked into the night

. . . .

at Marvin's house. The next day Sammy returned to the national company of *Seesaw*. He didn't hear anything for months.

Although Sammy went back to his tour not knowing if he had the part, Michael didn't look any further. He had found a depth of emotion in the young dancer he could draw on for his show.

Three months later, in another city, Michael appeared at the road company's opening night party. While there, he invited Sammy to join his project at an unspecified date in the future. Sammy agreed.

Then, some weeks later, at three o'clock in the morning on a Thursday, the telephone rang once more in Sammy's hotel room. It was Michael. His office had made arrangements for Sammy to be back in New York on Sunday. That Saturday would be his last day with the national company of *Seesaw*.

Steve Anthony—who had participated in the original group meeting as well—was also on tour with *Seesaw*. Michael had choreographed a special number for Steve and Sammy to do with Lucie Arnaz.

"We were in Chicago," Anthony remembers, "and the stage manager called me into the office and said, 'Michael called, and Sammy's going back to New York to start a workshop. I think you should know, since you dance with him.' I said, 'Oh, okay.' So then I'm thinking to myself: 'Well, that's real nice for Sammy but why didn't I get a call?' "

What Michael was searching for was a chorus line that, when each of its participants was examined separately, could turn into a cast of principal actors. Each dancer had to exhibit some special personality trait that Michael and his writers could fasten on. Not all of the dancers present at the original meetings were able to communicate that at an audition. Between Jacki and Trish Garland, the two close and competitive sisters, only Trish demonstrated the dynamic quality Michael was looking for.

In New York, she auditioned with a ballad. Then Marvin asked her to repeat the same song as an up-tempo number.

"But this is the only way I worked on it," she replied.

"He gave me the beat and made me do it up-tempo. I didn't know what I was doing. Then they had me read. It was just a piece of paper with this monologue on it. My nerves affect my motor movement. I couldn't stop my legs' shaking. My hands—I couldn't stop them. I just kept going, and at the end of it I said, 'You guys could afford to get maybe a little heavier paper.' And everybody broke up. That was the winning moment."

Jacki didn't do as well. On tour with Ann Miller in *Anything Goes*, she had to make a trip into the city to audition. "I felt insecure and I didn't feel support. They didn't even ask me to read, so I felt like they didn't even want me to do it from the beginning. I never really had a good rapport. I don't think Michael really trusted me or respected me. I don't think he really knew me. Or even cared."

Another girl from the midnight meeting, Renee Baughman, didn't sing well at all, and was a cinch not to get the show. But Michael was attracted to her charm, her exposed nerve, her dancing. He cast her and the writers planned a song about how badly she sang.

To audition for your own life story and not get cast was possibly the most frustrating aspect of the process. Mitzi Hamilton was doing *Pippin* at the time of the auditions and had fallen in love. Between the show and the affair, she had no time for taking dance class. "I was playing 'Falling in Love Again' and having a wonderful time. The tryouts came up and I was unprepared and gave a very bad audition."

Michon Peacock also felt she did poorly, even reading lines of her own making. It was doubly frustrating because less than a week earlier she had sung the same song for Bob Fosse and it had gone over well. He had asked her to understudy Chita Rivera in a new Broadway musical he was developing called *Chicago*.

Chris Chadman was in bed with hepatitis when he got his call from Michael. He had finished two years in *Pippin* and was about to go into rehearsal for *Chicago*, which Fosse had invited him to join as well. Chris told Michael he was very sick.

"Get in a cab—don't worry about it," Michael said.

"I'm in bed with hepatitis," Chris reiterated.

"Get in a cab and come over," Michael insisted.

Chris went.

"Meanwhile, I'm dying with hepatitis. I'm thinking, 'Michael, why are you doing this to me?' More: 'Asshole, why are you here? You're dying. 'Cause you're stupid and you want to work. And you'll die to get a job.' So I sang my song. Then he said to me:

'Sing 'Santa Claus Is Coming to Town' as a striptease.' I went, 'What? Really?' He said, 'Yeah.' I went, 'Really?' He said, 'Yes.' I said, 'Me? Why do you want me to do this?' All I remember is that it came out like Mae West: 'Oooh, Ya bedda not cah-ry. . . ."

Chris got the job. "I said, 'I can't do it. I'm sick. And I'm probably gonna do this other show.' Then he called me up twice to say 'You're sure?' I said, 'Yeah, I'm sure.' And he said, 'Well, we'll hold your place for a while. Maybe you'll get better.' "

Chris got better, but he started *Chicago* for Fosse, as did Michon. Then *Chicago* was postponed for four months when Fosse suffered a heart attack, a story played out in his autobiographical film, *All That Jazz.* (In real life, the choreographer recovered and soon they were back in rehearsal.)

Those dancers from the original meeting who had been chosen by Michael to go on with the project waited for rehearsals to begin. Meanwhile, Michael continued to seek other dancers to fill out his cast.

Ron Kuhlman, tall and handsome, first auditioned for Michael Bennett as a replacement for the Broadway company of *Follies.* He attempted a double pirouette in stocking feet on a raked stage and fell directly on his ass in front of the choreographer. "I just picked myself up and went out the door without even listening for my number." But this time he read well from a long monologue based on the life of Andy Bew, with whom he shared all-American good looks and a jock dancing style. "I was excited because of the people involved. My last audition—there had been several—was a Friday and I was about to go away on this bike hike for a couple of weeks. I wanted to know right then what they were thinking, so I said, 'If you're not going to use me, you can tell me now, because that way I can leave.' And they said, 'I think you better stick around till Monday.' "

After college Cameron "Rick" Mason spent three months in Paris dancing in the nightclub act of Sylvie Varten, a French Ann-Margret. On his way back he stopped off in New York and saw his first Broadway musical, *Pippin.* "I couldn't believe it! I knew this was home. So I sold everything and came back to New York, January 17, 1973, with seventy five dollars—and it was freezing.

"For the first time in my life I felt energized. The hustling and the bustling. I liked it. I never had those feelings before. It was like an excitement and I was willing to take it on. I was gonna give it a couple of punches if it gave me a couple of punches, but I was willing."

Rick has a boyish charm and a terrific jazz technique. He got a call to audition. After he had sung the only song he knew all the way through, and waited for a conference to take place at the back of the theater, Michael came onstage and said, "Fine, you'll do." Rick didn't at that point have any idea what he "would do" at.

Robert LuPone's agent sent him to audition for Michael Bennett. Unprepared to sing, Robert simply launched into a song he and the piano player both knew, "Once in Love with Amy," making up for his lack of preparation with a surfeit of nervous energy.

Michael was sitting high in the bleachers and he put up his hand and said, "Calm, calm, calm."

Robert stopped, realizing it was perfect direction.

They called him back to dance, but he didn't show up. He was no longer going to dance auditions because he didn't want to be a chorus boy. A week after the dance call at which he failed to appear, they called him again and asked him to come in once more, this time to read for a role.

When he showed up at the studio prepared to audition one more time, he found himself in a group of some twenty people.

Michael stepped forward and said to them all: "Welcome to the cast of *A Chorus Line*."

CHAPTER V
. . . .
First Workshop

August 4, 1974. The company standing around Michael that first morning resembled the group Michael, Tony, and Michon had put together just six and a half months earlier for the midnight meeting. There was the same tense excitement of people about to tumble over the threshold into an uncharted experience. But this time they were on more familiar ground: first day of rehearsals for a new musical. For the initial meeting, they could not prepare; they had prepared for *this* moment all their professional lives. Everyone felt a quiet confidence in having been chosen, though they were almost totally in the dark about the project itself. One dancer recalls: "I didn't know anything other than the fact it had this silly name."

Several, like LuPone, had come prepared to audition again and went onstage only to be told they had the job. Trish Garland was shocked. "You mean we don't have to do any more?" But what more was there to do? They had sung and danced for Michael and the authors; they had read; they had exposed their lives.

They found themselves among friends and acquaintances. Some they knew only by reputation. Rick Mason: "I worked with Wayne before. Candy was in Milliken with me that year, and I'd heard of Thommie Walsh before, that he was a holy terror. I adore him but he's got a mouth like a viper."

These dancers had signed on for a six-week term: Renee Baughman, Carole "Kelly" Bishop, Pamela Blair, Candy Brown, Wayne Cilento, Trish Garland, Ron Kuhlman, Baayork Lee, Priscilla Lopez, Robert LuPone, Cameron "Rick" Mason, Donna McKechnie, Michel Stuart, Thommie Walsh, Sammy Williams. And Tony Stevens.

When Michael first asked Tony to be a part of the workshop, Tony talked it over with Michon and declined. "We felt that he needed distance from us," Michon recalls, and Tony was holding out for choreography jobs, trying not to perform. But the transition to choreographer was difficult and Tony was broke and out of work. When another dancer dropped out at the last minute, Michael called Tony again and this time he agreed.

For most new Broadway musicals, the first day of rehearsal follows a fairly standard procedure. Cast members receive individual lead sheets for their songs and complete scripts which the authors have been working on for a year or more. The sets and costumes have been designed. The pressure is already mounting. The first deadline is in sight. The out-of-town previews, to which tickets have already been sold, is only a short time away. Changes are still possible, but only within the strictly limited framework established by the producer and his budget.

In Russia at the beginning of this century, Konstantin Stanislavsky led the Moscow Art Theater into a new and unorthodox approach to rehearsals. Bearing in mind that the system was state-supported and required fewer kopeks, it went like this: They rehearsed until they were ready. Months at a time. They experimented with clothes until the cast was comfortable, and did the same with sets. The actors experimented with their characters and the basic script material until it became their own. By the time they opened, the actor and the character were one. The quintessential performance.

Now Michael prepared to do the same, but he would go Stanislavsky one better. Lacking a Chekhov, he would begin with an incomplete manuscript, and work through the process until he arrived at a play. In this way, not only actor and character but the basic material as well—the eventual book, music, and lyrics—would be flawlessly integrated.

But Michael never consciously attempted to mimic Stanislavsky's experiments at the Moscow Art Theater. He simply had the artist's urge to experiment, his own personal success to risk, the confidence to leap into uncharted waters, and the arrogance to ask others to follow.

Michael also had a basic instinct, a fine and sentimental

feeling for the material that had surfaced through his early probing. Each dancer was given material transcribed from the interviews. Of those who had been a part of the meetings, some were
given material from their own lives; some were given material
from others'.

Before Michael could turn it all into a musical, he would
require a framework. In what way could the dancers deliver such
straightforward, first-person material? A series of monologues was
limiting and would grow tiresome.

The initial idea was very surrealistic. Dante and Michael had
the dancers summoned to the theater and a disembodied voice
began asking questions. The dancers would not know why they
were there. Nor would the audience. All very Pirandello-ish. But
Bob Avian said, "It's an audition." He said it over and over again
until he won his point and Michael and Dante agreed. The framework would be an audition.

In 1968, Michael had staged the musical numbers for *Promises,
Promises*. The final chorus audition had been seven hours long.
Ballet dancing, tap dancing, jazz dancing, improvisation, panto-
mime, songs, and reading for parts. He was going after specifics.
He didn't want a chorus; he wanted a group of individuals who
could work together.

Just as Michael had done then, so he would do now. Everyone
agreed that the show would be structured around an audition for a
director and his assistant casting a new musical. The play about
that musical would begin with the final dance auditions. It would
end with eight getting the job. This would provide plenty of
opportunity for dance and establish the dancers as individuals. In
the desperation of their wanting and needing the job, in the
agony of their vulnerability and their fear of rejection, they would
draw the audience deeper and deeper into the performers' lives.

In a process of life imitating art imitating life, Michael began
the workshop playing the role of the director. The director announced to the dancers and the audience that he was looking for a
chorus of individual personalities and asked each dancer to talk
about herself or himself.

From then on Michael would take dramatic license: The dancers would talk, sing, and dance themselves into more revelations
than would ever happen in a real audition.

In order to coax the audience into the traditional suspension of disbelief, Michael would experiment with and ultimately adopt an additional technique. When the dancers looked away from the director, they would be entertaining private thoughts. Anything that seemed inappropriate as a public confession would simply become a private one. By shifting back and forth between the two, they would encourage the audience to accept both.

For six weeks Michael led the cast through improvisations based on two themes: the audition and the dancer's life. They tried everything in that first workshop. Working from their monologues, they began to create characters that they could make their own. They played with the drama of what would happen at an audition and they did a great amount of dancing.

Several scenes were created around individual relationships among the dancers. LuPone as Al, a macho heterosexual, and Michel Stuart as Greg, an East Side homosexual, worked on an argument that resulted in a fist fight. This contretemps was based on an experience Chris Chadman had related at the midnight meeting.

In the early 1960s, the High School of Performing Arts had very few male dancers enrolled. One of them, a straight dancer with a sizable chip on his shoulder, probably felt a good deal of pressure to be macho; he beat up Chris, a short, slight boy. "He would have killed me if somebody hadn't broken it up," Chris recalled. At the time, Chris was devastated. Later he realized it was more the other boy's problem than his own.

Donna and Kelly, each playing an older chorus girl, had several short scenes together. For one, they sat on folding chairs at the side, watching the audition, talking about all the years spent in the theater.

"Look at so and so—she thinks she's hot shit," Kelly began.

"Yeah," Donna replied.

"It's heartbreaking, isn't it?"

There was a pause; then Donna said, "Fucking show business," and walked away.

Individually the dancers were encouraged to find their own characters through a combination of themselves and their material. Thommie Walsh had some funny stories of his childhood— being shut into his high school locker by bullies, pretending he had polio to avoid athletics—which had entertained the group at their first meeting and now entertained the cast. Kelly's character, the sassy adult chorus girl, developed out of herself and four dancers she had worked with. The result was the humorous, blatant, sarcastic Sheila, sophisticated and sexy, who had a co-quettish sparring relationship with the director.

Candy told of being an Air Force brat and of getting her first job in *Hello, Dolly!*

Ron Kuhlman told Andy Bew's story of watching his mother drown.

Creating a character then called Maggie, Donna McKechnie talked about her own childhood.

Additional material was brought into play as Michael put the cast through some of the same talk sessions that had created the original body of material.

The full effect of these stories was four hours of turgid melodrama. Michael called it the "Towering Inferno," each character in turn leaping out of the burning building of his or her life.

Since the show they were ostensibly auditioning for would require only eight dancers, they played out the final elimination scene each day. Michael would play the scene with different dancers being chosen, and they never knew until that moment what his decision would be. In a way, he was forcing them to audition continually, as if at the end of every day he would grade their performance in rehearsal by selecting those who would stay and those who would go.

By now, Michael and the songwriters had identified sections of material that would be turned into musical numbers. If a picture is worth a thousand words, a song is worth many pages of dialogue. No musical can have fifteen leads. The process of distributing the material had already begun. Hamlisch and Kleban had started attending rehearsals and were conducting their own interviews as well as sifting through the transcribed material. The first song they wrote was "Sing!" for Renee Baughman—which they had planned from the moment she auditioned for them. (Coincidentally, Renee, a Buddhist, had chanted to have her own song.) They also created a song called "Résumé" for the opening, and "One" which would be performed by the dancers to back up the leading lady in the musical for which they all were auditioning.

In theatrical wisdom and jargon, a musical comedy must have an "eleven o'clock number." This would be a 1930s-style dance sequence, "One," in which the dancers would prove to the director their ability to frame a star. Michael first attempted to stage this number using a woman from the audience. Like Dolly Levi's waiters and Auntie Mame's southern gentlemen, the chorus line would so flatter this ordinary woman with their dancing that she would appear to possess all the attributes of the great leading ladies. She would do virtually nothing. The nearest boys would guide her, and the sweeping patterns and dance steps would all point to her. Since the audience would know that the "star" was one of their own, they would come to understand the truth behind the star performances they had so often applauded. The flattery that Michael Bennett had fashioned for Katharine Hepburn in *Coco*, for Alexis Smith in *Follies*, and for Michele Lee in *Seesaw*, would be created this time for an ordinary, unskilled, and uncoached civilian. His dancers would dance for her, guide her around the stage, sing for her, smile for her.

That the so-called back-up dancers did all the work and didn't need the star after all was a theme Michael had toyed with for years. He himself had been a Broadway dancer, in *Bajour*, *Here's Love*, and *Subways Are for Sleeping*, and had done his share of supporting these ladies.

Had this number worked, it might have become one of the most audacious numbers ever staged on Broadway. It would also have been a perfect metaphor for the show. However, that device was abandoned as the musical took shape.

How each character would be expressed through song was a constant subject of discussion among the writers. The dancers were pulled out of rehearsal and taken down to the greenroom for a talk with Kleban and Hamlisch, who probed their stories in more detail. One of the show's most memorable songs, "At the Ballet," was created at this time from Kelly's and Donna's childhood experiences.

The experiment continued. There were various versions of each song, none of which seemed to work. There was an opening number, which worked conceptually, followed by a number of true but melodramatic monologues, which did not. Hours of material, four songs, and fifteen slowly solidifying characters still remained largely unformed. In the six weeks of work Michael had moved carefully, if spasmodically, in a positive direction. Most important, he had created an environment conducive to creativity, experimentation, and risk-taking.

By this time the company had built up an unprecedented sense of trust. Focused around Michael, that trust in one another enabled the dancers to let out their innermost feelings in seeking the material from their own lives that would best give expression to his vision of the play. This gave freedom to the creative process and placed the emotional emphasis on the process rather than on the result. As one dancer described it: "There was no bullshit."

There was another element that went unarticulated but was nonetheless felt by all. For the first time in their careers, these dancers were given the chance to make a real creative contribution to an evolving musical, the subject of which was personal and dear to them. Donna spoke for all when she described the experience as the opportunity to "stand up and be counted."

But another side of the experience began to manifest itself as well. The natural rivalry between dancers, which had been held in abeyance during the meetings and early rehearsals, now began to reappear. Competition for the largest roles, the best material, and, most of all, for Michael's attention, began to develop. At first the dancers only sensed the change. Then, as the days went by, they began to understand it. Michael looked to the individual dancers, the improvisations, and the rehearsal sessions as the source of his show. Those who most captured his attention, whether on the stage or off, would inevitably be given more to do.

For Trish Garland, the workshop became excruciatingly painful. "Some people became real overt, always on, and those people for the most part got more material. Everybody was into themselves; everybody was real selfish. I mean everybody. So there wasn't a lot of laughter. There wasn't a lot of spontaneity. A lot of people had been in therapy. I hadn't, so this was really difficult for me. My tendency was to go into my shell. I was trying, but it was very difficult and I started withdrawing more and more. So what happened is that they started taking away my lines. I came in one day and I heard other people saying my lines and I hadn't been told. That was devastating to me. All these things kept putting me further and further away. I wasn't sure whether I wanted to continue. I really didn't know if I had the capacity to do this. It was just too painful to me. I would go home and cry. I'd just be bawling my eyes out and not be able to talk to anybody because it was something that was going on inside of me and I couldn't really figure it out."

Sammy Williams had worries also. In his last performance on the road with *Seesaw* he had worked hard to give his best dance performance to date, and had sprained his back. During the first workshop he could not dance. Michael encouraged him just to concentrate on getting well, but Sammy knew that if he couldn't get up there and dance, he would lose his job.

For the first three weeks of rehearsal Michael virtually ignored Sammy, seldom talking to him and offering little acting direction. He did ask Sammy once or twice to "Get your hand off your hip. Don't stand like that." All of the dancers were under intense pressure to prove themselves as actors to a demanding director, and Sammy grew more and more anxious.

Finally Michael rehearsed his monologue. The pain of Nick's story came through vividly, and Sammy's reading was honest.

At last Michael drew Sammy aside, put his arm around him, and congratulated him. Michael's intention had been to put Sammy in touch with that part of himself that would be most useful when he expressed the sentiments of Nick Dante's story. That was Michael's genius, and his danger, as a director. He did it with almost all the dancers, and many of them recall those early rehearsals as emotionally wrenching.

Michael's approach with Donna was to create a distance between her and the rest of the cast that would later become part of her performance. He started right at the beginning, when he swept into the first meeting with Donna on his arm, arriving an hour late. The other cast members realized that while they had to compete for Michael's attention in order to bolster their roles, she did not. For years she had been his favorite dancer and he would find an important place for her before the show coalesced.

"All of a sudden we're competing," says Donna, "and I felt uncomfortable with that. It was uncomfortable for a long time. I learned to live with it, but I felt very misunderstood. The configurations of it were that I was not a member of the line in the play or in real life. I wasn't chummy. They had their friendships, and like kids at school, everybody kind of found security in each other. I thought maybe they thought I was aloof, but I couldn't 'get down,' as it were. I was always the last person to know what was going on in the company anyway. It was that way in school, too. I always found out that people were having sex and I never knew it!

"My most painful feeling was wanting to belong and feeling alienated. The need to be accepted and recognized among my peers. Because of the very nature of the show and my role in it, just the opposite was happening."

Looking back on Michael's treatment of the dancers, a pattern emerges. For Michael, there was no separation between rehearsals and real life. Using his unerring instinct for people, he manipulated each of the dancers, intensifying in them those feelings that would be of most use to the drama.

Already a smaller circle within the company of dancers had developed. Priscilla, Thommie, Kelly, Pam. Some spent time with Michael after rehearsal and others did not. Donna did on occasion, but not when the others were there. She and Michael had a very exclusive relationship, and Michael was intent on keeping her apart in order to create and define her role of the star who couldn't go back to the chorus.

Actors in general are at the mercy of a director for guidance—unlike dancers, who can check technical details of line and execution in the mirror. The actor's craft is too subtle for mirrors, and requires feedback from the director. In their long days together, all the dancers developed a reliance on Michael. They constantly sought his approval and his friendship. The soul-searching improvisations they did made them all the more vulnerable.

Michael turned this to his advantage, creating an environment in which the dancers were encouraged to reveal themselves, and one in which experimentation, improvisation, and small failures would lead to scenes he could use. In turn, the dancers grew close to him and trusted him implicitly.

On the final day of the six-week workshop, the company ran through all the material they had developed thus far. As they were rehearsing "One," Michael, dancing with them, suddenly collapsed to the floor. He seemed seriously injured. Concerned, the dancers tried to help. Several ran to the phone while others stood around, anxiously waiting for direction. Only the stage manager and Bob Avian knew Michael was faking. The scene that resulted from Michael's carefully planned hoax was eventually inserted into the show and precipitated the question: "What do you do when you can't dance anymore?"

Many of the dancers began to feel manipulated. They had been on a performer's high, but now felt used and betrayed. For Michael, it was all worth it.

As the six-week workshop ended, a solid foundation had been established. It was by no means a show yet, but there were several songs and a good deal of usable biographical material.

And some dark clouds had begun to gather.

CHAPTER VI

· · · · · · · · · · · · · · · · · · · ·

Hiatus

In the fall of 1974, Michael was asked to direct the Broadway premiere of a new Neil Simon comedy, *God's Favorite*. Mike Nichols had staged many of Simon's early plays, but his involvement with films was making him increasingly unavailable. The writer and his producer were searching for a replacement. For Michael to be awarded the opportunity meant that he had arrived as a director as surely as he had arrived as a choreographer a few years before. He accepted the job.

The hiatus would do his downtown project good. The first phase of the workshop had been worthwhile. A lot of the material had proven useful and the basic concept of the audition had worked. Michael had pulled an enormous amount from the fifteen dancers and had experimented with "the line" itself, the horizontal downstage formation from which the dancers would face the director and the audience.

Yet he was still a long way from a show. He knew that in its present form the material could not hold the interest of an audience; the connecting tissues were nonexistent; there were only four songs; no single character leapt out at the audience; the show lacked humor; and Donna, for whom he had so much hope, had not yet found a real character or a place in the show.

During the layoff Dante went to Las Vegas as a dancer in Cyd Charisse's nightclub act. While there he worked on the script but couldn't accomplish much and began to experience self-doubt.

Back in New York, Michael called on author James Kirkwood to join the creative team. Kirkwood had never written a musical but he had several plays and novels to his credit. Michael phoned Dante, informed him that he was bringing in Jimmy Kirkwood to

help write the book, and hung up. While Dante did not appreciate the manner in which Michael handled the situation, he knew if
he could put his own ego aside, a remarkable opportunity still
existed for him.

Kirkwood had written one of Dante's favorite novels, *Good
Times/Bad Times,* and his presence would relieve Dante of some of
the pressure that had been building on him. While Dante was in
effect being replaced by a more experienced writer, Michael still
wanted Dante's cooperation and the various monologues and ideas
he had compiled so far. So Dante went to meet Kirkwood with
enthusiasm. Though Kirkwood and Bennett were initially uncomfortable with the three-way collaboration, Dante's continuing effort and good will were instrumental in making it work.

During the winter interval, Michael was occupied with *God's
Favorite.* The Simon play went smoothly but suffered from classic
second-act troubles and never met with the success of his other
plays. By January 1975, Michael was ready to continue his workshop. His first job was to reassemble the cast, most of whom had
sought other employment during the hiatus.

Kelly Bishop had disappeared. "We did the first workshop.
They said, 'Okay, everybody wait and we're going to get some
money together and do another workshop.' And I thought, 'Wait?
What is this *wait?* I'm going to sit and do nothing in my life?' I'd
been in the business long enough by then to know how long it can
take to get money. Somebody says, 'We'll let you know in two weeks,'
and in four weeks you're still waiting and in six weeks they aren't
sure and by ten they say it fell through. So I was just taking care
of myself." After two industrial shows it was the middle of winter and
her unemployment benefits ran out. She was offered the role of one
of the girlfriends in a national tour of *Irene.* She didn't like the
show and she really didn't want to do it, but she felt she had no
choice. She signed a six-month contract. Three weeks later she
heard that more auditions were being held for Michael's project and
she was crestfallen. Unable to leave *Irene,* she resigned herself to the
circumstances. Then Michael phoned her and said, "What are you
doing there? How long is your contract, and why didn't you tell me?"

"I told him I had one week of unemployment left when I took
the job, and it was the dead of winter and Christmas was in two
weeks and I had to work."

"I would've lent you the money," he said.

"We've had this argument before. I don't want you to lend me the money. I want to make the money."

"Let me see what I can do," he said.

A week later Kelly was out of her contract. It cost Michael some money and it cost him a favor, but he had reclaimed her for the second workshop. "Talk about a B-movie story," she says. "It was a fabulous feeling to have Michael Bennett pull me out of Detroit and back to Broadway."

Trish Garland had taken a trip to Spain and Morocco. When she returned to the city she attended a Buddhist meeting with Nick Dante and other Broadway gypsies, and there heard that Michael had been looking for her. He wanted her to know that she could either stay with the show—knowing she would have a small part—or she could leave. The choice was hers. Her first reaction was: "I don't know if I want to do this anyway. What did I want it for if it kept hurting me? So I made a decision that I would chant about the problem half an hour a day."

In the end Michael's office simply called her to go back into the workshop, and she went.

Just before the second workshop got under way, Bob Fosse offered Candy Brown a job in his musical *Chicago*.

"It was a very hard decision," she recalls, "and it mostly came down to economics. I didn't know what Michael's workshop was gonna do. And we weren't getting much money. I'd already been in two shows for Bob and he was tried, true, and tested. I felt a little bit of allegiance to Bobby, although I'm sure he wouldn't have felt I owed him anything. I liked working with him. Now with Michael, on the other hand, you always got the feeling he's scrutinizing you. As a dancer, you go through so much trauma at auditions you shouldn't have to feel that you're still auditioning or still under some sort of pressure once you've got the job and you're at work. I just never felt comfortable with Michael. I didn't trust him. Plus he's sort of cliquish. He had this little group of friends that visited his house." So Candy decided to go with *Chicago*. "I don't think Michael ever really forgave me for it. That's just a gut feeling. Nothing he ever said or did. He was just that kind of person." Candy had to be replaced.

*   *

At the same time Candy Brown declined to continue with the project, Ron Dennis found himself auditioning for Michael, who was looking to add a few more dancers to the line. Ron had come to New York from a small community on the east side of Dayton, Ohio, and had auditioned for Michael Bennett several times in the past. He was a short, wildly energetic young black performer who had been dancing for several years. Michael had seen him in shows and at auditions, but they had never worked together. He was invited to a callback.

In the by now time-honored tradition of the show's auditions, he and the others were asked to talk about their lives. "Some of the people at that last callback really laid out some heavy stories about the hurt of studying dance and all that, and I felt too much joy dancing to care about all that other bullshit."

But Michael was impressed with his enthusiasm, and during Ron's audition turned to his collaborators and said, "Why does the part have to be a girl? Why can't it be a guy? He's got all the qualities Candy had. His story is very similar to Candy's—a black all-American dancer. I want this guy."

The ebullient, feisty dancer became a part of the company. "I was just glad to be a black person in that show. At least they hired one."

Just at the end of the first workshop the songwriters had created "At the Ballet." Though the lure of the ballet studio as a safe, warm, loving substitute for a volatile or arid home life originated with Donna and Kelly, the experience had been duplicated in a dozen stories. And perhaps that was just the point. In a key song the writers had found a universal metaphor, a theme that many people, even outside the dance world, would relate to: everything always being beautiful at the ballet.

To perform this song two more voices in addition to Kelly's would be needed. Michael decided to add two new characters to the line. Though Donna had been called Maggie for the first six weeks, her character would now take the name Cassie Ferguson. Her early childhood material would stay with the former character, and a new actress would be brought in to play the role of Maggie.

The third voice and second new character would be "Bebe Nichols from Boston, home of the baked beans, and here I am!"

Just prior to the second workshop, Michael held massive public auditions for the first time. Two of the dancers he found there would take on these roles.

Kay Cole had been a child actress with a natural talent for dancing who had hit the road in her pre-teens; Jane Robertson had been Miss Dance of Oklahoma. Though neither had worked for Michael, Jane had danced for Tony Stevens in *Rachel*, and Michael had heard Kay's clear, beautiful voice in the recent Sammy Cahn songbook on Broadway, *Words and Music*.

Michael's auditions mirrored the structure of the show. There were the ballet and jazz dancing with eliminations after each, singing, and more eliminations. Then the unexpected personal interviews. Callbacks, and the whole long ordeal would be repeated. From hundreds of singers and dancers who had seen the advertisement in the trade papers, and dozens who were known to Michael's office and had been specifically invited, only a handful would remain standing on the floor of the Public Theater by late afternoon on the last day. It was a wet, cold January day. The city had laid out an array of its finest talents for Michael to choose from.

In addition to increasing by two the size of his cast, he was in need of seven more dancers who would be in the opening number. From the auditions he chose:

Chuck Cissel, a good-looking, suave black dancer and rhythm-and-blues singer from Tulsa, Oklahoma.

Donna Drake, a small brunette dancer fresh from school in North Carolina who had been downtown trying out for another show, saw the auditions under way, and worked her way in.

Carolyn Kirsch, an experienced gypsy who began her career in 1963 in *How to Succeed in Business Without Really Trying* and had gone on to dance in a host of Broadway musicals, including *Promises, Promises* and *Coco* for Michael.

Nancy Lane, a slender, pretty, dark-haired girl with an outsize nose and sense of humor, from New Jersey.

Leland Schwantes, a graduate of the North Carolina School of the Arts and two-and-a-half years of touring the world with the Alvin Ailey company.

Michael Serrecchia, an Italian boy from Brooklyn who had begun to dance at the suggestion of a physical therapist.

Crissy Wilzak, short, well-built, with the straight blonde hair and freckles of a California girl, who had outlasted the firings in her first musical, *Seesaw*.

These dancers would be seen auditioning for the musical in the opening number and then be cut. This would allow Michael to demonstrate the ruthlessness of the theater—something no one there needed to be taught—and with it, begin to build audience empathy. The eliminated dancers would also understudy the others, for Michael now had a clearer vision, and he knew this "project" would soon become a show.

The first workshop had begun in the middle of the New York summer, when dancers' muscles are easily warmed up. The work had taken place not at the Shakespeare Festival's plant but at the American Theater Laboratory, a dance studio owned by Jerome Robbins on West Nineteenth Street. (It had once been used, coincidentally enough, for a two-year experimental workshop Robbins had conducted, bringing together actors, singers, and dancers and utilizing the Actors Studio technique he had studied.) Now Michael Bennett returned to the studio to begin the second phase of his workshop. He intended this phase to lead directly to a new musical.

Returning with Michael would be fourteen of the fifteen original dancers and the two new dancers, Kay Cole and Jane Robertson. Candy Brown had been replaced by Ron Dennis as the black, all-American, would-be kindergarten teacher. The line from left to right: Ron Kuhlman (as Don), Kay Cole (Maggie), Wayne Cilento (Mike), Baayork Lee (Connie), Michel Stuart (Greg), Donna McKechnie (Cassie), Carole "Kelly" Bishop (Sheila), Thomas J. "Thommie" Walsh (Bobby), Jane Robertson (Bebe), Patricia "Trish" Garland (Judy), Ronald Dennis (Richie), Robert LuPone (Al), Renee Baughman (Kristine), Cameron "Rick" Mason (Mark), Pamela Blair (Val), Sammy Williams (Paul), and Priscilla Lopez (Diana).

Tony Stevens returned as Larry, the director's assistant.

To cast the role of Zach, the director, a role Michael himself had been playing until now, he stepped outside the small world of gypsies he had been dealing with and sought an established actor. The role of Zach would be the fulcrum. Zach would run the audition and thus power the show. Just as a director with jobs to hand out commands an audition, he would have to take command of the stage. Michael seriously considered Christopher Walken, an intense, good-looking actor with a background in dance. But he decided on a tall, strikingly handsome actor with clear blue eyes, dark hair, and a Barrymoresque flair for the stage.

Barry Bostwick had a variety of credits including a brilliantly comic *tour de force* as Danny in the original stage musical *Grease*, and the ineffectual Brad in the cult film *Rocky Horror Picture Show*.

Michael made Barry the offer while Barry was in California doing a movie for television. Though Michael offered little money for an unformed role in an off-Broadway workshop, Barry accepted, under two conditions.

First, he wanted to be free to leave if the character didn't develop into a large enough part. Second, he wanted to be allowed in on all meetings Michael held with the writers and production staff. He justified this condition as a need for background information on the character of the director. Another motivation was self-education.

"At that point in my life," Bostwick remembers, "I wasn't sure that I just wanted to perform. I was developing a couple of shows on my own to produce, and I wanted to use the experience of the workshop to learn how a show is put together from the beginning. So I made a deal with Michael that I would work with him for a month if he would allow me in on certain creative meetings where actors don't usually go."

It was agreed. The final role was cast. Barry flew to New York and the company reassembled to begin the second workshop.

CHAPTER VII

· · · · · · · · · · · · · · · · · ·

Second Workshop

The auditions for new cast members had continued right up until the day before the second workshop began. Some of the returning dancers had waited months to pick up where they had left off, while the dancers just hired knew little about the mysterious project.

Chuck Cissel remembers what it was like that first week of rehearsals. "All we had was each other. We had no songs—we had the opening number and maybe a couple more."

Michael said to the cast: "Listen, we're going to need each other to get through this."

The company read over the material as it had been sifted down from the first workshop. Kirkwood and Dante had assembled a more detailed script. A lot of the original characters had been split into parts, their stories spread out among others.

The first read-through lasted four hours. The play was so heavy it could have passed for Russian drama. Tony Steven recalls that "for a long time it was sad and depressing. A *long* time. It just happened that way. It meant so much to everybody who was doing it that we had a tendency to play it serious and heavy, because it was all real—it was true. The material was all the juicy, meaty stuff and very little of the humorous stuff."

When Crissy Wilzak heard the show for the first time, she found it "a big cry from the beginning to the end. Everybody had this huge sob story to tell."

After the read-through the new people were asked to introduce themselves, and they all spoke at length about their lives.

Michael Serrecchia told about not being able to walk until the age of thirteen. "It was a skin disease. I had no skin on my legs and feet. It would grow in patches and the flesh would get infected and I'd get blood poisoning. It was really disgusting. Also a very smelly ordeal—all that exposed flesh all the time. We couldn't afford a wheelchair so I just lay down a lot, and if I had to go someplace my mama carried me. Gave the woman four hernias, thank you." When he was thirteen the skin finally began to grow and stick. He began to walk. "So, as Dolly Levi says, I joined the human race at a late date."

Learning to walk at thirteen was a balancing act from one foot to the other. "I used to live in fear of doorways. I couldn't navigate myself through them. I was given tap lessons to improve my coordination. In my first tap lesson I had to hold on to the barre with both hands—white-knuckle time—and the teacher said, 'Shuffle ball change, shuffle ball change, ball change,' and this look of panic went over my face and I said, 'Shuffle what?' Jimmy Kirkwood laughed about that for two years."

A new Trish Garland returned to the second workshop. She was nervous but determined to assert herself. "I'll never forget. We had to talk about our holiday. So names are being called and my name isn't being called and I'm just trying to listen. I'm chanting *Nam Myoho Renge Kyo* to myself and watching and listening to everybody and it's getting longer and longer and there are more people now. This time it was the regular group there, but also all the creative staff and the understudies. So finally they call my name and I get up and I just start talking and everybody started laughing. Nobody laughed in the first workshop, mind you. There was no humor anywhere. Everybody laughed and I looked at Michael and he had this huge smile on his face, and from that moment on, everything completely changed for me."

Michael was smiling because a dancer had broken through her natural reserve to express the unique individual he had known was there. Introverted Trish had been the last one to come forward with a character. In the first workshop Michael had reduced her part. Now he began to build it. "I got all the lines that didn't work. That's why my part is so non sequitur. 'Oh, it doesn't work? Give it to Trish—she'll make it work.' I had changed what we call in Buddhism 'poison' into medicine. I could have left the show. My innate nature would've led me to leave, to say 'Fuck you. I

don't want to do this. I can't deal with it.' Then I would've slit my
wrists later, but my good fortune—and I thank Nicholas and
Michon [fellow Buddhists]—is that I didn't give up."

As rehearsals progressed, the talking ended. More and more
effort was poured into the dances, the songs, and the scenes.
Improvisations and experiments revolved around chosen themes.
Each day, the songwriters arrived with material to be learned. The
opening number, the audition, would be based on a new song that
replaced "Résumé," titled "I Hope I Get It." The dancers would all
be put through tough ballet and jazz combinations for the director. Michael would teach the combination and then he and Wayne,
the best dancers with similar styles, would do it for the cast, with
Michael challenging Wayne for technical supremacy. They would
kill themselves to perform it, and the other dancers would see
how it should be done.

For less-experienced dancers, not hired for their technique,
this could be intimidating. Ron Kuhlman found it especially difficult.

"We came back for the second workshop—that's when Michael and Bob had the beginning of the opening number—and
they showed it to us. The double pirouette and the jump and all,
and it was 'Oh, my God!' We got up there and I was so nervous I
couldn't even do a single pirouette, and that was in a group. Then
Michael made me stand out in front of everybody and do a
pirouette. Well, I was totally mortified. I could hardly stand up,
let alone turn on one foot. A lot of times people would pick up
the combinations just like that, and hours after everybody had it
I'd be out there trying to learn the thing, going over the steps. It
was terror, believe me. I had to work real hard to get up to their
level of dancing."

Secretly, Michael never expected everybody to dance at the
same level. He wanted the audition to have the look of authentic-
ity to it. In an audition some dancers pick up quickly and dance
with calm confidence; others ask a million questions and dance
out of nervous energy. Some know the director already; some are
in awe; some can't even remember the number they've been
assigned. There are good dancers, mediocre dancers, and poor
dancers. And there are plenty of bad habits. Michael had seen it
all before. Now he arranged it so the audience would see it too.

As they worked on the opening, the smaller roles developed, each based on a single character trait. Michael Serrecchia, who learned to walk as a teenager, still had a bad habit of dancing with his head down until he learned the steps. They were running the opening series of steps and Michael corrected Serrecchia.

"Okay, Serrecchia, pick your head up," Michael yelled. "Pick your head up!"

Then Michael realized it would work for the show. He turned to the authors and said, "Put that in!" Serrecchia became the Boy in the Headband and it turned into three major laughs.

Chuck Cissel developed a character for the "audition" that reflected how he felt about being a black dancer in a predominantly white theater world. His first Broadway audition had been for *Follies*. Chuck was one among seven dancers left at the very end. Michael had said, "I can choose six."

"The other six were white," Chuck recalls. "Guess who got cut? After I ranted and raved up and down, Michael told me that since *Follies* was a period piece, it would not be proper for this little black face to be onstage dancing. I was terribly hurt because I had outdanced all of those guys and then outsang them and outread them. When he got ready to choose everybody, he couldn't look at me. I was very, very upset."

The next time he saw Michael was at the Public Theater auditions. "When I walked in that door I must admit I had *a lot* of attitude. I said, 'Isn't this funny? We meet again, Michael.' He remembered right off. So I auditioned, cool; I brought my band down there; I did four numbers. I gave a concert. Then I danced. They began to tell me what my role would be in the show. So I told them: 'Look, I'll think about it, okay?' They called and said, 'Listen, we really want you.' I said, 'I'll think about it.' So I went about my business. Then I thought about it." Chuck decided it was something he ought to be involved with, and finally agreed. For the opening number he brought his own attitude.

"When we go to auditions and we are better, a lot of times we are not chosen because of our color. I was giving black people something to relate to. Every dancer who came to the show said, 'Right on.' Michael liked it, too, because it did give Zach something to play with. It's: 'I know this step. Don't tell me what to do.' "

Michael had given everybody names. He said to Chuck: "Your name will be Freddy."

"No, my name will not be Freddy. My name will be Butch."

"Why Butch?"

"I don't like Freddy, and Butch is a stronger name. Butch is my favorite cousin's name, and my mother's name is Burton."

Michael knew when he was licked. Chuck's character became Butch Burton.

Crissy Wilzak became Vicki Vickers, the beautiful, sexy dancer with no ballet training. Zach would ask her during the combination if she had any ballet, and she would answer no. Then he would tell her to stop dancing. She would get through the jazz all right, but only if someone danced in front for her to follow. "Whenever I would go on [as an understudy] for somebody, Zach would still ask *me* that question, so I'd be cut out of the ballet number anyway. Just so I wouldn't have to pretend I was graceful."

The remainder of the show was being assembled slowly. During the process, Barry Bostwick grew uncomfortable. "We did a certain amount of improvisation in and around the germ of a scene," Barry describes. "Bobby breaks his ankle or whatever and we all sit around: 'What would you say?'

" 'Oh, I would say this.'

" 'What would you do?'

" 'Well, I'd get on the phone and get a doctor down here.'

"That sort of stuff. I felt the rehearsal process was extremely self-indulgent, in that the time wasn't being used as wisely as I thought it should've been. I never said anything about it, but there were just too many hours spent with people on the floor with script pages being ripped out, and lines being thrown here, and Michael going: 'Umm, Bobby, why don't you take this line, and, uh, no, give it to, uh, no . . .' That sort of indecision—on-the-feet, shooting-from-the-hip stuff. Maybe it's part of the way he works, that makes his work brilliant. To me it was a big fucking waste of time."

Many of the characters still had long, serious monologues. Ron Kuhlman told the story of "his" (Andy Bew's) mother's drowning in Chicago. Michael Serrecchia remembers the first run-through as "four and a half hours of sheer desperation. No music, no dancing. I remember going home after the first run-through and saying this is the longest, saddest thing I've ever seen in my life."

As time went on, most found the work satisfying and creative, yet they had no idea where it was going or what the overall dramatic intentions were. And there were some terrible days. Almost everybody had an emotional breakdown at one time or another. "We all were seeking something. We were breaking ground in a lot of ways," Kay Cole remembers. "It was a very psychological experience. We worked our asses off."

No popular play had ever been assembled in this fashion. No group of actors, much less dancers, had ever been asked to improvise so much material out of the fabric of their own, and fellow dancers', lives. Never had a show been assembled so laboriously, oftentimes in a seemingly haphazard way.

Michael was putting himself into the show, not as the director-choreographer he had come to be, but as the young gypsy he had once been. The seventeen dancers all became part of his own autobiography, and several characters—Mark, Mike, Don, Bobby—contain specifics drawn from his real life (Bobby: "To commit suicide in Buffalo is redundant"). In the end, all of *A Chorus Line* is true. Every speech is drawn from the real life of one of the participants in the meetings and workshops. Because he was ultimately responsible for organizing and selecting the material, however, all of it was sifted through Michael's perceptions and his experience as a chorus boy in the theater.

Yet his fantasy, his alter ego, is Zach. The demagogic director-choreographer, omniscient, powerful, mysterious, is the role he created from his vision of himself.

At one run-through about three weeks into the workshop, Barry Bostwick got so involved in what was happening on the stage that he was moved to tears. He found himself playing the scenes following "At the Ballet" teary-eyed, and ended up dealing with the show in a different way, on a more human level. Afterward he got a lot of strong notes from Michael, saying "No, that's totally wrong. Stay totally detached from their lives."

Michael withdrew that portion of the character's humanity from the show when he called on Barry Bostwick to remain uninvolved with the emotion-racked stories that resulted from Zach's probing.

Through the month, Barry's role stayed fairly static and low-key, which was not suitable to an actor on the verge of stardom. "Part of the frustration was that my character wasn't directly involved with those people on that stage. When so much of the rehearsal time was spent on them, and I saw very little time being spent on my character, I kept pushing Michael, saying, 'Well, when are we going to get to Zach? Our agreement was that we were going to develop a character based on what you do—you or a choreographer like you.' And as the weeks went on I realized that he was developing in his own mind a scenario which was going to make his character a presence in the audience. Just a presence. Just somebody who would pose a question and not be involved.

"He should have at least glamorized his life, exposed something that would be engaging to me as an artist and to the audience. All the conversations I had with him, nights sitting around bullshitting over drinks and dinner, I could never get him to commit himself to that, and in fact, by the end of the month I think I became a real thorn in his side, something he just didn't want to deal with anymore.

"We grew apart, and he said to me at one point: 'I see you sitting over there in the bleachers judging me and I can't take that when I come to work in the morning.' I was looking to him for the character, but he was seeing that I was judging his work and it made him nervous. He didn't realize that I was going to do it to the extent that I was doing it because I was committed and dedicated to my work. I had to really try to fathom out the heart of that character. The only place I could look was to him."

How much Zach would reveal of himself to the audience, and concomitantly how much Michael was willing to expose of himself, were only part of Barry's search for the substance of his character. The other part was *how* Zach was going to be revealed. How much singing, dancing, and dialogue would he have? These were prime concerns for Barry, who didn't want to overextend himself as a dancer, or limit himself as an actor, and had no interest in doing a part in which he didn't express himself musically. Especially in a musical.

As the month went on, Barry felt more and more confident in his dancing. He worked with Bob Avian and gradually mastered whatever choreography was assigned to him. Most of the real dancing fell to the dancers as a matter of course. Zach's relationship with Cassie was still undeveloped. Hamlisch and Kleban were supposed to write a song for Zach, a soliloquy in which he would stand center stage, alone, and sing his emotional condition. This was to happen following the accident scene when the character Paul was carried offstage. In early run-throughs, Zach was left onstage alone for a moment while the authors considered what he could express in music. But unlike the rest of the roles, there was no real-life counterpoint developed for Zach, and Michael was unwilling to make his own contribution. After a couple of run-throughs the authors decided he would remain silent. The yet-to-be-written sequence was cut and Zach simply returned to the audience after packing Paul off to the hospital.

At that point Michael said to the actor point-blank: "Listen, Barry, this guy's not really going to sing. This guy's not really going to do any dancing. He's going to be a presence in the audience which is basically there to motivate their lives."

"It seems like a cop-out from your standpoint," Barry replied, "but I don't have the vision of the whole piece that you have. I don't have that. I don't see what you see at this moment, because I haven't been involved with the creative aspect of the project for the last two-and-a-half weeks."

Barry had joined the workshop on the condition that he could sit in on the behind-the-scenes making of the musical. During the first week or two, as the show was being pieced together, he attended three or four creative meetings. He went to Hamlisch's house to hear some new music; he sat with the staff as they discussed production design. Although he did not say anything during the meetings, afterward he let Michael know his thoughts, and Michael was open to questions and suggestions from him. However, very early on, it became apparent that this arrangement was a problem for the creators. They were unaccustomed to having an actor looking over their shoulder and they viewed it as an intrusion. Michael began keeping Barry at arm's length. He was no longer welcome at the meetings. It was a disappointment for Barry, who wanted to learn producing firsthand.

By the end of the month it was mutually and amicably decided that Barry would leave the workshop. Michael said, "Barry, this is not going to utilize the things that you are capable of doing right now in your career."

"In a way he probably guided the situation into getting rid of me," Barry realizes. "Into making me unhappy enough to say I can't take it anymore. Psychologically I'm sure that's what happened. He didn't want to deal with me anymore, so he made it as difficult as possible for me to be there. His vision was not my vision and I understood that. That's why we parted in a friendly manner. Because by that point it was just business. It wasn't productive for me as an actor.

"He knew he was in for trouble if I stayed around, because I knew they were going into six more weeks and I wouldn't let up on him and I would be unhappy and I wouldn't have accepted the final draft as it was. And Michael, being the kind of person he is, being on top of the pyramid, didn't want anyone who could even grab at his socks, and I felt like I could at least get to his tennis shoes and maybe pull a little bit of humanity and a little bit of emotion out of him. And that was a big threat to him.

"In fact he said to me at one point that a problem in *Company* [which Bennett had choregraphed] was that the guy who played Bobby, Dean Jones, was always unsatisfied with the direction in which the part was going and that he was a strong enough star and a strong enough personality to fight him on it and he became a pain in the ass."

Michael sensed that Barry's ego was strong enough to create the same problem, and for Barry, "It was head on head the whole time. I felt that there was a great clash of ego, in that he wanted to sublimate me. That was the battle. It was a big mind game for him. I felt, the whole month, it was the hardest battle, emotionally and intellectually, I'd ever been in. He's devious. And he's highly intelligent, brilliant at his work, and he gets and uses information about you that he's culled from you by his own ways. I don't know how to say it. Probably all the great directors have been like that. They have found ways to get information from the person, emotional, physical, intellectual information, then turned around and either showed it to him or used it on him or used it against him to pull a performance out of him *or* to keep him in his place. And in a way I find that Michael used the information he got for all of those reasons. To get a great performance, but also to keep the actors in their place, and I was not willing to be put in that position, so it became a real battle. But I wasn't the only one fighting it. He was fighting that battle with everybody there, but fortunately for him he had cast a lot of people whom he'd already done battle with before. They'd already lost. I was a fresh opponent, and my ego is such that I wasn't willing to lose, and ultimately I would've lost if I had stayed."

Barry saw Michael as a convoluted man. "That kind of brilliance—there's always a dark side to it. His need for control sometimes overshadowed and destroyed some of the best sides of his talent, I think. I thought that it was a fabulous piece of theater. And I was sad to leave it from that standpoint."

For four days they rehearsed the show without a Zach. Robert LuPone had been playing the role of Al. Now he talked Michael into letting him take over the role of the director.

"At first," LuPone says, "he did not want to give it to me because he did not know or trust me as an actor. I wanted to prove that I could do it. We talked. I went to his apartment to read. I kept saying 'I can do it. I can do it.' Michael takes chances. Ultimately he gave me that chance."

In fact, Robert LuPone was one of the few cast members who had seriously studied acting in the city and could approach a role with more than instinct. At the beginning of the workshop he and Michael got along very well. Michael liked LuPone's strong, masculine stage presence for the role of the cocky, one-dimensional Al. But now LuPone's demeanor would have to change. He would have to be more subtle. The boisterously confident Al would have to become the powerful, manipulating director. His pantherlike grace and the sandy, Mephisthophelean beard he grew to play the part completed the picture. LuPone became the play's quiet engine. He gave up the role of the boy and took on the role of the man.

Only this man conceived, wrote, and was directing and choreographing the show. "The minute I got Zach," LuPone now realizes, "was when my troubles started."

At first Michael played the role while LuPone watched. "I read the newspaper and he rehearsed. Basically, Michael directs by playing all the roles. That's how he finds out the information for himself." One dancer, who came in fresh for the second workshop, didn't know what was real and what wasn't real, couldn't tell the rehearsal from the show from the show-within-the-show they were auditioning for.

When LuPone finally took over the role, he found himself at odds with the director he was playing. Not, as in Bostwick's case, because he wanted the role expanded, but because Michael, knowing he would be taken for the director, microscopically scrutinized LuPone's performance.

The first time LuPone and Donna rehearsed the Cassie–Zach scene, they simply ran through it twice. The scene called for Zach to fend off Cassie's desire to confront their shared past, and then to deal with his own failure in their relationship. Michael was willing to provide material for his musical from his own experience, but he was reticent about confronting it outright. A dichotomy arose from this conflict, in which the truth was presented on the stage, but Michael himself was unwilling to face his own private issues during the rehearsal process. His personal compromise was to give LuPone no direction or feedback.

"I was in a paper bag, trying to find my way out. I'd say, 'Well, I don't think the guy would do this,' only to find out months later that Michael had lived it the night before." Although LuPone never clearly understood the Zach–Cassie relationship, he later discovered that Michael had been in several relationships not unlike the one LuPone was playing out as Zach with Cassie.

To make matters worse, while Michael encouraged the rest of his cast to experiment, he denied the actor playing Zach this freedom. Once, during a preview, LuPone chose to play Zach gay, and Bob Avian had to restrain Michael from physically attacking LuPone after the performance. Michael didn't talk to LuPone for two weeks following the incident.

Michael knew who he was, and was comfortable with it. Unlike some gay theater people from earlier generations, he made no attempt to disguise his homosexuality. But he refused to give Zach, his alter ego, that kind of public exposure.

"He could not understand me or appreciate me," LuPone complains. "I drove Michael nuts and Michael drove me nuts. I wanted to walk over and punch him. It was that simple. I'm telling you, nobody won and nobody lost, but it was war, absolute war. Now I'm at a point in my life that I would never put up with that kind of direction. I'd quit the second day. But I took it because I thought, 'He's the director.' I'm talking from a clarity now I didn't have then. I was manipulated and didn't know it, and now that could never happen to me and I thank Michael for that. I can tell you that I never got the feeling that Michael protected the actor. For two years Michael Bennett and I were gladiators and that's it. Nobody won and nobody lost and we both can't stand each other. On the best day, we have respect for each other."

With LuPone playing Zach, Michael needed to find a new Al. He auditioned actor-singer Scott Allen, who had worked with Nick Dante in a dinner-theater production of *Fiddler on the Roof*. "I went and I met Michael and Bob Avian and all those people," Scott recalls. "I sang and I danced a little. I was scared about dancing anyway, so it could have been Balanchine sitting there and it wouldn't have made any difference. Singing I'm very comfortable with—he liked my singing. He said, 'You're not a dancer. You're a singer.' I said, 'Yeah, I know. I'm not trying to pull the wool over your eyes. Nick told me to come down. Here I am." A week later they called and asked Scott to take over the role.

By the time he arrived, the company had already learned a number of dances, and Scott, with little training as a dancer, had to struggle to keep up. "I'm standing there thinking, 'Jesus Christ, here we go. I'm gonna be fired any minute.' " After a week he caught the flu and went home sick. That night in bed he got a call from Michael.

"Listen, I don't want to fire you," Michael explained, "but I want to take you out of the part and put your understudy in, and make you the understudy."

So that's what happened. Scott's lack of experience and ballet training became the basis for his own new role in the opening, Wrong Arms Roy. He understudied Al, and his understudy, Don Percassi, took over the role.

For Don Percassi—a short, dark, muscular Italian with a Lebanese nose, boundless energy, and a rapid-fire infectious laugh—singing and dancing are just what he always did. "I'm not gonna tell you my first show, 'cause it dates me!" Don first met Michael Bennett and Bob Avian when he was doing *West Side Story* in London and they were in the European touring company; Jerry Robbins took both companies to dinner in Paris. He met Michael again when he worked for him in *Coco*, the musical Michael staged starring Katharine Hepburn as Coco Chanel.

"I knew he was a genius," Don recalls. "I told what's her name, the Venezuelan girl—she's a choreographer now—Graciela Daniele. Graciela and I used to lie on the floor and laugh all the time. She used to do 'six o'clock,' where she could put her leg up on the wall and stand like that, and I told her to marry me. Ha! Ha! Ha! Ha! We used to laugh all the time. I told her, I said, 'This kid's a genius.' 'Cause I'd worked with Jerry Robbins, Leonard Bernstein. I worked with people, and I know that he had that same thing that Robbins had. It's a little glint behind the eye. Sometimes he would come in and stuff would come spewing out; some days, nothing."

Don was doing the warm-up for *Money Maze*, a game show on ABC. "We'd come in and we'd play the game, warm up the audience. Leland Schwantes was working there, too, and he was already doing the workshop. He told me they needed somebody to understudy, so I went down there, auditioned, and was hired."

LuPone had been playing Al, and Barry Bostwick had been playing Zach when Don was hired to cover Al and Mike. "So I didn't have to talk about all that stuff. *Ha! Ha! Ha! Ha!* I just told them this is me—take me as I am. I ain't gonna tell you no stories. I had a great childhood. I said I can't tell you anything depressing. I had everything I wanted.

"There was a lot of crying when I came in. A lot of crying. What they took out they could make into another show. I mean it was one big Italian epic. But I was used to it—that's my life. I called my mother up once and I said, 'This is really weird. We sing for three hours, we dance for three hours, then we cry for three hours. This has got to be a Sicilian musical!'

"First of all, I thought, 'These people are brilliant. What the fuck am I doing here?' I'm going, 'Oh, Jesus, I hope he never gets sick.' *Ha! Ha! Ha! Ha!*"

Don Percassi inherited the role of Al when Michael felt Scott Allen wasn't dancing well enough. Don thought that "they just had nobody else and time was getting short and so they said, 'Well, we gotta use him.' *Ha! Ha! Ha! Ha!*" Don's self-effacing humor belies the fact that he was enormously successful in the role.

Because Don was uncomfortable with some aspects of the character, Michael simply adapted it to him. The fight scene between Al and Greg was cut. "I had to throw Michel Stuart on the floor and beat him up. When I did that, they all laughed. I mean, it just wasn't me.

"The only time I used to feel comfortable was when Marvin Hamlisch—the Great Marvola, we called him—when the Great Marvola used to come in wearing his double-knit suits. He'd wear them up to here. So anyway, we used to get around the piano and he used to create the music on us. I loved that. He was actually tailoring it to us."

For Don the entire experience was a joy. For others who felt the pressure more intensely, Don could usually be relied on to lighten the mood.

Once Michael had straightened out the Zach and Al casting, he was confronted with a second problem. Until now, Zach's assistant, Larry, had been played by Tony Stevens. Tony had enjoyed doing the first workshop and had been happy to return for the second, but Fosse had asked Tony to assist him on *Chicago*, which was just then going back into rehearsals after a four-month layoff. That was a big step toward what Tony really wanted to do, and he chose to be Fosse's real-life assistant rather than to act the assistant in Michael's show.

For the dancer whose own frustrations had been instrumental in getting the fast-evolving musical started, it was a moment of ambivalence. "I knew that whether I was there or not it didn't make much of a difference. I knew I would share in the experience whether I was onstage or not, because it was my life. I don't have any regrets about leaving."

Michael respected Tony's ambitions to choreograph, and throughout the first workshop only Tony was permitted to sit out front with him and watch the staging develop. In addition, he had discussed aspects of the show with Tony and kept him informed about what he was trying to do. Now that Tony had a real career opportunity ahead of him, Michael was sympathetic and encouraged him to take it.

When Michael took over the material, he was openly gracious to Tony and Michon. After all, it had begun with their efforts, with an idea they had brought to him. So far each had received a dollar. Now, if Michael felt any twinge of guilt, with Tony gone there were no longer any reminders.

When Tony left to join Fosse (and Michon Peacock, Chris Chadman, and Candy Brown) in *Chicago*, the role of Larry became available.

Michael offered it to the understudy Leland Schwantes. But when Leland first joined Michael's project, it had been with the understanding that he was committed to another show, still raising money, an off-Broadway musical called *A Matter of Time*. Leland had joined the *Chorus Line* project with the caveat that should *Time* go into rehearsal, he would be able to go back to it. At just this point, that show was capitalized.

Leland opted for *A Matter of Time* and he left with no hard feelings on either side. His job as understudy, and even the role of Larry, was not crucial and he would not be difficult to replace.

Another principal, however, was also scheduled to join the cast of *A Matter of Time*, though Michael and Leland were unaware of it. Jane Robertson, playing Bebe, was one of the three dancers doing "At the Ballet," probably the only completely successful sequence at this point.

She was unhappy with her role, and felt loyal to the group of friends from *Time* who had worked to mount their own new musical. As for Michael: "I barely knew the man. I don't think he was comfortable with me. I found it difficult to please him and I wasn't in his tight little group that went out smoking and drinking and carousing. I was there to do a job. I couldn't play his games. I'm not good at those kinds of head trips."

Jane was terrified to tell Michael that she was quitting the workshop. "I did it at the end of one of the rehearsals and he was not nice. He said sarcastically, 'I hope it's a big hit.' He was like 'How dare you.' You could tell he was hurt. I had not told him going in, because I felt it might affect the way he worked with me. I thought for sure I'd get attitude the whole time. But then we didn't have a close relationship, so I didn't feel that I should tell him."

Below: *Michael directing the line.*

Bottom: *Michael directs "And..."*

Top: *Michael discusses a scene with Kay Cole; in background, Bob Avian with Ron Kuhlman.*

Above: *Michael and Marvin Hamlisch at work.*

The Finale.

Above: Cameron (Rick) Mason, Wayne Cilento, Michel Stuart, and Thommie Walsh (from left to right) audition with the ballet combination. All four make the cut.

Below: Cassie confronts Zach about their past.

The line: (from left to right) Ron Kuhlman as Don, Kay Cole as Maggie, Wayne Cilento as Mike, Baayork Lee as Connie.

Michel Stuart as Greg, Donna McKechnie as Cassie, Carole (Kelly) Bishop as Sheila, Thomas (Thommie) J. Walsh as Bobby, Nancy Lane as Bebe.

Patricia Garland as Judy, Ronald Dennis as Richie, Don Percassi as Al, Renee Baughman as Kristine.

Pamela Blair as Val, Cameron (Rick) Mason as Mark, Sammy Williams as Paul,
Priscilla Lopez as Diana. (Not pictured: Robert LuPone as Zach, the director, and Clive
Clerk as Larry, his assistant.)

Left: *Sammy Williams as Paul introduces himself to the director.*

Right: *Wayne Cilento as Mike tries to prove he can do anything in "I Can Do That."*

Donna McKechnie steps out alone in "The Music and the Mirror."

The authors: (front row, left to right) James Kirkwood, Michael Bennett, Nicholas Dante; (back row, left to right) Edward Kleban and Marvin Hamlisch.

Michael takes a bow as A Chorus Line *becomes the longest-running Broadway show of all time.*

Michael directs Donna and other members of the cast in preparation for the 3,389th gala performance.

Onstage during 3,389: Donna leads all of the Cassies through "The Music and the Mirror."

Michael could teach a new Zach or Larry the role easily, but for him the show was the line, the seventeen dancers who were onstage virtually the entire time. They were a picture puzzle in both the physical and emotional senses. They had all come so far together. They had relationships, vignettes, attitudes that had not developed out of the script but out of their own lives through the rehearsal process. The script was only a vague blueprint for the life that existed on the stage.

For one piece of that puzzle to drop out now was frustrating for Michael, who, in spite of a talented professional staff, carried an enormous workload and made all the decisions himself. For Jane, the hardest part was dealing with friends in the business who disapproved.

But Jane was adamant. She had what she felt was a very small role, while others were developing larger roles and being pampered by Michael. The concept of the line also frustrated her. "If I could have gone into the dressing room [while others were onstage] I probably could have dealt with it, but I had to stand out there and back up these people that I knew I could do as well as, but I wasn't given the chance. I found it very unsatisfying. It was hard for me to stand on line and watch other people." She left the show.

The musical that took both Leland Schwantes and Jane Robertson away from Michael's project closed off-Broadway in one night.

For a month, Nancy Lane, the Jewish girl from New Jersey, had understudied Priscilla Lopez as Diana Morales and Jane Robertson as Bebe Nichols. "I wanted to do Morales. I couldn't understand why they couldn't see me as a Puerto Rican! Jane told Michael she was leaving and Michael was so pissed. 'Get out! Get out! Why didn't you tell me? You ruined everything!' Because by then it was a family.

"I went to him and said, 'Can I audition for the part?' I was real timid. But I knew I was better than she was. See, I didn't know any of these people 'cause I wasn't a gypsy. They were all like hardened criminals to me, all these gypsies—oh, God—and I was this little girl from New Jersey saying, 'Okay, I can do that.' Scared to shit. I was so scared I didn't ever talk to anybody."

When the role of Bebe became available, Nancy auditioned for

Michael. "And afterward he said, 'I knew you could do it. Oh, yeah, you'll be great.' I got the part."

Nancy brought to rehearsals a fresh, new character that was badly needed. "I love to make people laugh. My mom and dad are *real* funny people. They're real pissers. They always tell jokes and they're the life of the party, the lampshade on the head. It's what I do best, what I like to do the most. I used to watch Ed Sullivan and say, 'But, Mom, I can do that!' I'd perform for everybody. Always. When we were little, my sister and I used to perform as a sister team for the Salvation Army and old-age homes and stuff.

"We lived in New Jersey and went into the city to see shows all the time. We used to go to Rockefeller Center to see the skaters and we used to go to Radio City. The Jewish family: 'Come on, darling, we'll go to New York. We'll go have Chinese food!'

"I wanted to go to New York and study for the theater but my mother had other ideas. 'Oh, no. The girl's gonna get an education. You have to have something to fall back on. How can you get a husband without an education?' So I applied to *one* college and, my luck, I got accepted! It was in Richmond, Virginia, of all places. I got accepted as a 'Recreational Leadership major' but they had a great theater department. So at registration, there was this social director person there, I went over and said, 'Ah, excuse me, there's some mistake. See, I should be in the theater department.'

"My parents had a heart attack. They said, 'We're not paying for this. We're not paying for you to be an acting major.' But they did and I was, for two years."

The role of Bebe Nichols was changed to Bebe Benzenheimer and Nancy fit it like a glove. The old theater adage—there are no small parts, only small actors—could not have been better applied. Though the role did not expand, in Nancy's hands it blossomed. She sang her portion of "At the Ballet" with touching simplicity and her one-liners got enormous laughs.

Now there were three female roles with overlapping characteristics. Kristine, who is nervous because she can't sing; Judy, who is nervous because she is scatterbrained; and Bebe, who covers up her nerves with chutzpah. These roles could have been interchangeable unless each actress was able to bring something distinct and unique to her character. Renee Baughman, Trish Garland, and now Nancy Lane did just that.

And Michael saw an improvement he had not anticipated. The project had been lacking in humor. At the beginning, Michael was not concerned with whether the show was funny. But as the material took shape, it was preponderantly grim. When Nancy joined the line, he had his *tummler.*

Nancy's move from understudy to principal was easier onstage than off. The youngest of the crowd of experienced gypsies and on the outside of Michael's inner circle, she tried hard to fit in. But Michael wanted to draw on her youth and inexperience ("Don't tell me Broadway's dying, 'cause I just got here!") to create her character, and kept her on the periphery of his social circle.

"I did the show when I was twenty-four and I was the baby. I wasn't friends with anybody. They didn't like me. I wanted so much to be friends with Priscilla Lopez and Kelly Bishop and Renee Baughman and Trish Garland and all those girls who were gypsies. I always wanted so much to be a part of the group, but they never made any attempt.

"I love directors," she says. "I admire them enormously. I think they have the worst jobs, 'cause they're the mediators, they're the mother, they're the father, they're the boss. I really respect them. But Michael was a different breed. Michael was just a different kind of person. I really can't excuse his abusiveness. Terrible. The whole experience. Putting us through what he put us through. Getting crazy, really getting crazy, yelling and screaming. There was no need to. We would have produced for him no matter what, because we were in it so far by then. He was a *meshuggener.*

"Michael is very talented and very crazy. I didn't talk to the man once. When I first got the job as Bebe, I was young and I was real aggressive and I really would do anything for Michael.

"There was a big blowup. I was having a lot of problems with people in the company. We were blocking stuff in front of the mirrors and I was so diligent about being where I was supposed to be and doing it exactly the way I was supposed to do it, and everybody else was fucking around. They knew Michael and they were friends and they were all probably loaded at the time. Michael always was and I didn't know it. He just really blew up at me one day. He humiliated me in front of the company, yelling at me and making me cry. I ran out of rehearsal crying. Sammy said, 'Oh, Nancy, don't worry. He does that all the time.' I was fine after that. I still wasn't friends with anybody but I was okay."

It was curious how Michael's personal treatment of the individual dancers forced them into a position that paralleled their roles. Whatever he brought out of them—fear, insecurity, anxiety, alienation, anger, or bitterness—enhanced their performance. This was a technique Michael inherited, and refined, from Jerome Robbins, who would humiliate dancers, pit them against one another, and delight in strife within the company.

Auditions are the most degrading portion of the actor's life. They are constant and unavoidable. Michael's show was in part framed by an audition, and by encouraging competition throughout the rehearsal process, he never gave his actors relief from the unbalanced, off-center, tense, and nervous-feeling auditions engender. That feeling was not acted. It was real.

While in search of a replacement for Tony Stevens, Michael ran into Clive Clerk unexpectedly. The two had worked together in Toronto when Michael was sixteen and Clive was fourteen. Born Clive Wilson in Trinidad, he had danced during his teen years in Toronto and New York, then in 1963 had gone to Hollywood to act and had been away from dance for ten years. Reaching a point where the actor's life was not enough for him, he went back to school, and was in New York studying at the Art Students League when he met Michael at a party at Jimmy Kirkwood's house and was invited to sit in on a rehearsal.

"Needless to say," Clive explains, "I had watched Michael on the TV every year picking up his Tonys. We reminisced about the past and then Michael told me about the show. I mean it was a Judy Garland musical: 'We're putting on this show in the barn' type of thing. 'We're having a run-through tomorrow, as luck would have it. Why don't you drop in?' "

So Clive went downtown to the studio, bearing in mind that because "this little off-Broadway show" wasn't going out of town, he could do it and still continue his studies at the League. It would be a nice interlude. He found more than he bargained for.

"I thought it was the most exciting thing I had ever seen. I remember the jazz combination. I remember there were these little bleachers and just these dancers, these beautiful, beautiful people coming at me. And piano and drums, and just the energy in the room was the most extraordinary feeling. My God, it was like coming home again. From the beginning of the show, right through the opening number and the beginning of the line, it just blew me away. It just brought back my whole childhood as a dancer in theater. I had stopped because of some—I think now, in retrospect—unfortunate considerations I had. I really loved dancing; I just had the feeling that I wasn't going to make a career as a dancer. I suppose I had set my sights somewhere else and at times I almost wished that I had really hung in there and gotten more enjoyment out of it. Seeing this brought back all those old feelings and I wanted to get up and dance again. So I said right there, 'Oh, yeah, I'd love to be in your show, Mr. Bennett.'

"As I got involved, it became more and more exciting. As the charley horses diminished and I got more familiar with what was going on, it just became a joyous experience. It all came back to me.

"There was also a feeling of honesty that I had not experienced in any other area of show business before, certainly not in L.A. doing movies and television. It was like being able to breathe easily. To be able to be yourself. That's what was being generated on that stage. Between that freedom of spirit and the physical workout and actually dancing again, I was just alive. I loved it. I thought, 'Well, I don't care if I pick up a brush ever again.' "

Clive was a complete stranger to everyone there except Michael. As Larry, the director's assistant, he was not involved in the soul-searching or the audition. "I wasn't liked by some people who had problems about the fact that I was there. I wasn't really a gypsy, and it was difficult and I had my feelings hurt a bit by some degree of alienation. Then there were others who were just terrific."

Now, a month into the second workshop, Michael had a complete cast: Robert LuPone and Clive Clerk as Zach and Larry; Nancy Lane as Bebe; Don Percassi as Al. To replace Nancy Lane and Leland Schwantes as understudies, Michael added two more dancers: Carole Schweid, a vivacious, dark-haired, ethnic girl who had grown up commuting to the theater from New Jersey; and Brandt Edwards, a lanky boy off a farm two miles outside Byhalia, Mississippi, half an hour from Memphis.

. . . .

Brandt was the last person hired into the original cast. Michael and the Shakespeare Festival planned to add another six weeks to the original four of the second workshop, and this time, because the production was nearing performances, Michael wanted no more defections. The entire company was put under contract. They were in for the duration.

The pressure mounted. Until this moment the project had been in workshop. To any outsider wandering into the room—producers, theater owners, staff, friends, any of whom might generate word-of-mouth publicity that flows like an underground river in the New York theater—there was an invisible sign announcing: "This is just an experiment."

But the time had now come when the workshop had to either deliver a show or disband. The creators couldn't go on mulling over the material indefinitely. Decisions had to be made.

CHAPTER VIII
....
Rehearsals

J oseph Papp never liked musical comedy. Those slickly entertaining boy-meets-girl song-and-dance shows that were put
together by uptown producers for Long Island theater parties
had no appeal for him. Papp began his producing career with classic
dramatic literature, and when he added original plays to his
mandate they were in the same serious mold.

Papp did produce an innovative new musical in 1968. A couple
of unknowns brought him a lengthy antiwar manuscript consisting
largely of swearwords and buzzwords from the hippie generation.
It was a paean to the flower children, it would *feature* flower
children, it was structurally haphazard, and it had no discernible
plot. When Papp realized it was relevant, unformed, experimental,
and could be played in almost any sequential order, he produced it.

A composer who had been knocking around off-Broadway
because he wrote contemporary music, for which there was no
market as yet on Broadway, was brought to the project. He wrote
an infectious, rhythmic score, the first-ever rock score for a
musical comedy. A collection of young men and women, who also
lived outside the mainstream because they lacked technique, were
gathered to perform the material. What they didn't lack was vocal
talent, athletic ability, and enthusiasm. The resulting show was
still something of a sprawling mess.

At this point Papp turned it over to another producer, who
presented it at a nightclub called Cheetah. It was reworked by
a second director, whose personal style gave the musical an
astoundingly fresh look. From there it was moved to the Biltmore
Theatre on Broadway, where it was greeted with amusement,
misunderstanding, and ennui.

Then *Life* magazine published photographs of its first-act finale, in which the cast appeared nude, and the Michael Butler–Tom O'Horgan production of *Hair* became one of the legendary musicals of the twentieth century.

So when Michael Bennett, a Tony Award-winning Broadway Baby and the golden boy of director-choreographers approached Papp with twenty-four hours of tape recordings containing intensely personal stories by Broadway dancers at an encounter session, it seemed made to order.

But as the musical lost its free-form structure, as the singing and dancing gained in emotional power and Broadway slickness, Joe Papp's interest declined.

Michael had let Clive Clerk in on the fact that he was having problems with his producer. "I recall a time when Papp was going to pull out. If one night Michael and Bob had said, 'Oh, let's forget it,' that would've been it. Or if suddenly there wasn't any money, it just could've all gone by the boards. But it was destined to be."

Perhaps destiny was less a part of it than Michael's overwhelming drive and ambition. Carole Schweid thinks that "Michael knew from the first day where it was all going. I have no doubt about that. This is his trip from maybe when he was five. This is the one." Dancing, choreographing, directing, writing, producing. It did seem as if the ladder was always leading up.

Michael's momentum, and the enthusiasm of his staunch supporter Bernard Gersten, Papp's closest business associate and a longtime fan of musicals, were overwhelming influences. Papp agreed to continue with the project. Instead of disbanding, the "workshop" would now become "rehearsals," and six weeks later, public previews would commence in the Festival's Newman Theater. That meant a show had to be ready.

The opening number, "I Hope I Get It," always worked. It was written and rewritten, staged and restaged, rehearsed and re-rehearsed, but from the beginning it was a powerful, exciting sequence. Everyone felt it. When rehearsals formally began, the opening was solidified. Brandt Edwards was put in as Tom: "When I went into the show I could barely do a double pirouette, so we didn't have to worry about me looking too good and getting cut." Carole Schweid was put in as another of the dancers who would be eliminated. Michael staged and tightened the natural circumstances of an audition into twenty minutes. He directed the dancers so viewers would understand the tension, competition, humor, and desires an audition elicits, as well as the process itself. He overlaid the physical activity with lyrics that exposed the characters' inner thoughts. He focused the choreography carefully—a process by which the audience is subtly guided to look where the director wants it to look and thus learn what the authors want it to know—until there were levels within levels.

After the first elimination was reached, the seventeen dancers remaining onstage stood at attention in a single line, displacing their faces with their photographs, the actor's indispensable calling card. The look was stunning.

There is a moment in the theater when the audience feels a chill down the back of its collective neck. It is a moment the peripatetic theatergoer hopes for, waits months or seasons for, and never fails to recognize. It is The Spellbinder. It happens in *A Chorus Line* at the climax of the relentless, surging opening, when the dancers chosen for the final round of auditions step into the line.

Then Larry collects the photos and résumés and the frozen line of stiff bodies shifts murkily into a live lineup of hot, sweaty dancers, nervous and anxious, then shifts again into a frozen tableau of seventeen individuals, all silently telling the audience a great deal about themselves merely from the physical poses they strike. This is the motif Michael repeats throughout the show. It is The Chorus Line, and the first time it happens is no more or less effective than the last. It would become a theater landmark for all time.

To arrive at this tableau, Michael began by saying, "Okay, everybody stand onstage however you are most comfortable. Now strike a pose."

Michael went down the line and worked with each dancer, until a logo pose was created which was the perfect physical expression of each character. Michael edited, adjusted, made sure no two were alike. Each dancer introduces himself. The show moves on.

*   *

For the next sequence—Sammy Williams's real-life story of watching his sister dance, the songwriters had created the number "I Can Do That." It was given to Wayne Cilento as the aggressive Mike Costa (né Costafalone). It was meant only as a brief song and tap dance to break the ice before the serious material got underway. Michael promised that more substantial material would be created for Wayne later in the show.

Some comic relief was needed next, so Thommie Walsh stepped forward as Bobby, the class clown, with a monologue about his own childhood—the stories he had told at the original meeting. Zach, sensing the comedian in Bobby, pointedly asks him if he is going to deliver a comic routine. The performer denies it, then goes on to do exactly that.

Within this monologue Michael wanted a song. He knew it wasn't a good idea to go too long without music in a musical and he had already begun to suspect that the structure of the play could not be based on a string of long monologues. The song was called "Confidence," and was written for the two ethnic minorities standing on opposite sides of the line, Ron Dennis as Richie and Baayork Lee as Connie Wong. In it, Richie sings about what he has that the others lack ("Confidence, it's written plain all over me"), and Connie sings that she has it, too, and that she can pass for an adult or child, a black or an Oriental ("I've passed for Ethel Merman's little girlie; I've also done a year or two in *Purlie*"). In the last chorus they alternate lines, both believing that Zach is not going to cast more than one minority, and thus each seeing the other as his or her principal competition. The zinger at the end of the song is that these two completely confident dancers are really "very, very . . . insecure!"

Ultimately, the cheerful little tune was too much of a traditional musical comedy number, out of keeping with the serious tone Michael was establishing, and the lyrics were too hip. Much to Ron and Baayork's disappointment, "Confidence" was jettisoned.

"Nobody tells you a fucking thing," Ron says, "and you're left in the dark. I think just as human beings, and as common respect to artists, you should get some explanation. Someone should say, 'Relax, it's not gonna work. We're gonna give you something else.'

No. 'We're cutting it.' That was it." The song was replaced with "And," a simple, melodic lyric that depicted the inner thought shared by the whole line: What stories from their past should they tell Zach? What does he want?

Here Michael established a technique that would emphasize the difference between dialogue spoken to Zach and the characters' inner thoughts, a device he would use throughout the show. For personal thoughts, actors would look up and away from Zach. Eventually these lines would be said or sung in a direct blue spotlight, which came to be known as the "thought" light.

The first third of the musical was completed. They had reached what Michael wanted to be a high point, or the nine o'clock number. (Shows used to begin at eight-thirty, and musical comedy formulas—where and when it was necessary to knock 'em dead—evolved accordingly.) The number would be "At the Ballet," and it was to become his favorite in the show—where, for Michael, the show started.

That song had been written for Kelly Bishop in the first workshop and would now be expanded to include Kay Cole as Maggie and Nancy Lane as Bebe. And here the unusual nature of the work Michael was forging would be most clear. The song, the dialogue, and dance would be artfully blended and the result would be a single, seamless sequence. Each performer would have material from the transcripts. Kelly would have her own story; Kay would have Donna McKechnie's; Nancy would have Michon Peacock's and others'. The lyrics would be passed from one to the other. At the climax the entire cast would pantomime the classic ballet class variations, including a section of barre.

Kelly's part was already written because she had done the initial workshop. The Bebe section was written for Jane Robertson, but many in the cast felt that it had never worked well for her. Jane simply never liked saying that she was not a pretty girl. Nancy's sense of humor about all things, herself included, brought the material alive. "It was part Donna McKechnie, part Kelly Bishop. I really related to it because it was me, too. The ballet part—oh boy, the ballet part really hit home. I felt great when I was a kid and I was dancing. The best in the world.

"Bebe was me actually. My mother always said I'd be very

attractive—I mean the whole family had honkers, these huge noses. I was attractive, but I wasn't pretty, ever."

Kay Cole describes how they "sat around a piano one day, just the three of us with Marvin, Michael, and Ed, and he just sort of tinkled and we sang and he said, 'Why don't you try this?' and 'Why don't you try that?' The arrangement evolved very naturally, as all of Marvin's music did for the show." The whole "Ballet" sequence would ultimately flow naturally from actress to actress to dance.

The roles of Al and Kristine were based on Steve Boockvor and Denise Pence Boockvor, the married couple who had attended the initial group meeting. In an early version of the play, Zach called Al aside, brought up some earlier disagreement between them from another show, and eliminated him in the middle of the audition. In response, uncharacteristically dropping his arrogant, tough-guy act, Al begged Zach to let him stay for his wife's sake, claiming Kristine was far too nervous to continue doing her best without his support. In reality, he didn't want to lose face with his wife.

In another scene, Greg taunted Al about their experience together at the High School of Performing Arts. Al lost his temper in defense of his own masculinity. It became clear that he had difficulty dealing with the open homosexuality so prevalent in his profession and considered the gay men around him a threat.

These scenes did not contain the kind of drama consistent with the rest of the show. Little by little it was becoming evident that the material was at its most powerful and eloquent when it was presentational, with Zach confronting the dancers as they faced the audience, in both the literal and the metaphysical sense. Dramatizing relationships between the dancers onstage was proving ineffective. Scenes like these became exercises that enriched the subtext, but were eliminated almost entirely from the evolving script. Since Don Percassi wasn't completely comfortable with the original Steve Boockvor prototype anyway, and Michael was tailoring the show for this particular cast, both scenes were cut.

Early on, the authors created a song for Renee Baughman about her inability to sing. It had been structured so that the rest of the company finished her sentences. One afternoon they were to rehearse this sequence, but everyone except Al and Kristine had wandered off. Don Percassi wanted to get on with the rehearsal and Michael and Bob asked, "Where is everyone?"

At which point Don said, "I know all the parts. I'll just sing the parts for Renee. Let her do the damn thing and let's get the hell out of here."

"I wanted to go have tea," Don explains. "Eleven o'clock in the morning, I haven't had my tea, and everybody's crying already. We had had one of those emotional mornings."

Renee did her song, Don sang all the responses, and Michael stood up and said, "That's it. That's the number."

It stayed that way. The company vocals were saved for only the final few bars, and the number became primarily a husband-and-wife-duet.

Michael initially wanted to interview every character on the line, but time simply would not allow it, and not all of the long monologues originally drawn for every character had enough dramatic power to stand alone. The problem became how to deal with the dancers who didn't have a song or monologue of their own, and it was solved by "the Montage."

No sequence in the show better demonstrates the craft of Michael Bennett than that woven around the song "Hello Twelve, Hello Thirteen, Hello Love," better known to the dancers as "the Montage." Totaling nearly thirty minutes and anchoring the center of the two-hour-and-twenty-minute intermissionless musical, "the Montage" is made up of half a dozen separate but integrated sections.

During rehearsals, Nick Dante recalled how at the original talk session he had sat listening to someone tell his story, and it had triggered thoughts of his own. Now he went back to the transcripts and collected a number of lines of dialogue that revolved around similar subjects. He went home and put a piece of paper into his typewriter sideways. Forming two columns, he transcribed a monologue from one of the principal characters down the first column. When he reached a line that might trigger the thought process of another character, he transcribed that second character's thought in the parallel column. While the second character spoke, the first would continue in pantomime. He brought the idea to Michael with the caveat that lighting would play a crucial part. It was a powerful ballet of words, and for a time they considered staging it without music. (At one point further back, Michael had even discussed the project as a play with dancing but no songs at all, and always considered it not "a musical" but "a play about a musical.")

Then Hamlisch and Kleban began setting Nick's idea to music and lyrics. Trish Garland recalls working with Marvin Hamlisch: "He did 'Hello Twelve, Hello Thirteen' literally on the spot. All the harmonies. You're going, 'Wait a minute, don't you go home and prepare, maybe show us it's a little tougher for you?' You were watching creative genius, and you were doing it all the time."

This collection of remarks on similar themes was strung together, written into recitative, distributed among many voices, and staged. At one point the litany of individual woes and memories overlap one another until there is a virtual cacophony; then everyone drops out except Paul. Through his single voice the audience is reminded of the dancer's initial problem: What should I say when he calls on me?

Staging this complicated, multileveled number was a long, arduous process of experimentation that was sometimes exhilarating, sometimes frustrating. As an understudy, Scott Allen observed the whole thing. "In the beginning, I wasn't very impressed with what was going on. I thought, 'This is a lot of bullshit. What are these people doing? These are supposed to be *the* dancers and we can't even get these steps together.' Everybody was fumbling and falling all over themselves. They were just creating things. They would do it and then throw it out. Mostly the thing that I remember is the chaos onstage of trying to get these dances together. 'I can't go through there!' 'We can't fit this way!' It was a lot of jumbo."

Yet Crissy Wilzak, another understudy, felt that "you could see some of the stuff we were doing was a little dumb, but you always knew that stuff was going to be thrown out because Michael's such a wise man. After I had seen what he did for *Seesaw*—how he molded this piece of stuff that he didn't even really care about—I had absolutely no qualms that he could take a project that was entirely his own and make it a phenomenon. I said, 'If he's working with something that's his own, forget it. This is going to be something.'

"There was something I do remember about Michael that happened in *Seesaw* and happened also here. If he was in a mood where he didn't want to work or choregraph, he just wouldn't for that day. He said during the Richie segment, 'I'm tired of choreographing. Here's the music—you all go off into singles or pairs and make up steps for me. I don't want to do it.' He took much of mine. It was rock and roll, and watching *American Bandstand*, I always knew the latest and the greatest steps, so when he asked us to make up these rock and roll steps, I just thought, 'Oh ho ho!' I went up and designed steps and he used them. I just love those steps, and as a matter of fact, I even wrote the background music. He said, 'Now, Crissy, we need some background music.' He took me and Chuck Cissel and said, 'This is the music. We need some background stuff.' I go, 'Well, how about singing 'Shit, Richie, Shit, Richie,' and just keep going.' "

Michael was not afraid of not knowing what he was going to do. He was the choreographer who could come in and say, "Now, I don't know what we're going to do here. Okay, you think of a step and you think of a step." He wasn't afraid of just letting people contribute. It was one of Michael's talents that he could utilize everyone's ideas as needed. "The Montage"—a flurry of rock and roll activity that became as intricate as a Swiss watch— grew out of the mix of numerous dancers' contributions and Michael's painstaking process of selection.

Ultimately "the Montage" would be made up of five distinct sections, three of which would grow out of Dante's original collection of thought lines on similar themes, which Kleban would transform into lyrics. One of these became the "Mother" sequence, a lilting lullaby for Maggie about her mother counterpointed against eight smaller childhood memories of parents distributed among the other singers. The other two sequences would be based on the "Hello Twelve, Hello Thirteen" theme and were written around the principal obsession of adolescence: sex. They progressed through "goodbye, thirteen" to "goodbye, seventeen" and culminated in "hello, love." This included the "nervous breakdown" sequence, in which all of the dancers spend sixteen bars of music in an extemporaneous, though carefully choreographed, screaming fit.

Sandwiched between the first and second sections of "the

Montage" was a song written for Diana. At one of the meetings, Priscilla Lopez had talked about a teacher at the High School of Performing Arts who had given her a hard time in acting class. From that material Hamlisch and Kleban fashioned the song "Nothing," in which Diana recounts the teacher's insistence that she didn't have the talent to be an actress, that she couldn't feel enough in improv class, and when she heard of his death, she in turn could feel no grief for him. The teacher—who was notorious among the school's graduates and instantly recognizable when the show opened—was given the anonymity of a name change.

Between the second and third sections of "the Montage," Richie was supposed to have his moment in the sun. The authors had reserved a space for him there, but they didn't know how they were going to use it. Time was growing short. Just about a week before previews, Michael got together with Bobby Thomas, the rehearsal drummer, and began scat-singing from material that Candy Brown had contributed.

Candy, whose family traveled around with her Air Force dad, was very sheltered. "Everything was just hunky-dory," she recalls, "so I was petrified to graduate from high school. I didn't know how to act out in the real world. So I went to college. I was in the chorus, the band, cheerleader, student council, vice-president of the junior class—you name it and I did it. I was originally going to be a kindergarten teacher. That was soft and nice again, but that's when I got my eyes opened, 'cause there were people from all over the world at college and I learned everybody didn't take piano lessons, everybody wasn't a Brownie, everybody didn't go to dancing school. And I thought, 'Man, I gotta get outta here. I'm gonna be too scared to leave this kind of environment.' That's why I really left school, 'cause I said, 'Nobody's gonna hand you a scholarship to life.' "

The character of Richie became a combination of Candy's and Ron Dennis's personalities. Michael called Ron into the room where he'd been working with the understudies. They had been doing background for the number that Michael was singing a cappella, in a Joe Cocker-ish style. Michael knew what kind of black sound and feeling he wanted but he couldn't sing it. They put it down on tape in a rough form and Ron took it home and, using his experience in the black gospel show *Don't Bother*

Me, I Can't Cope, went to work on it. It became "Gimme the Ball."

"My upstairs neighbor was rehearsing some ladies for his act in my living room. It was hysterical. He would come back and listen to what I was doing and say, 'That's good, that's good.' Then he'd go back and work with his group. Then come back: 'Oh, that's great!' My thought process for that song was, I wanted to do an Aretha Franklin sort of vocal and run with it. I wanted those kinds of highs and lows that she does."

And so "the Montage" was pieced together, then fitted around "Nothing" and "Gimme the Ball." The dancers who had yet to have stories of their own were slowly incorporated into "the Montage" with shorter monologues set to recitative music.

Michael insisted each turn be strictly in keeping with the realistic, documentary approach he had established. Ron Kuhlman: "Whenever we had trouble with one of the monologues he would say, 'Be yourself more.' That's a little ambiguous, because sometimes it's difficult to do. I tried to be myself and then he'd come back with the same note and I'd be very frustrated. I'd go, 'Oh, God, I'm not being myself. Who am I being?' Anyhow, I'd know what he was trying to say, but it sometimes didn't help the dancers to give him what he wanted. Sometimes he would want something other than themselves or more than themselves."

What Michael demanded from his dancers was a new, higher level of acting. Since everything they were creating came out of their own, true experiences, the show was developing into a type of docudrama. To benefit from this without becoming melodramatic, it was imperative that each performance be as raw and truthful as possible. To that end Michael pushed each dancer to shed the performer's outer act—the gimmicks, the *sell*—in favor of honesty. Since many people take up acting in order to hide themselves behind the roles they're playing, Michael had to work hard to coax each dancer into that open a performance.

With "the Montage," a *rising line of dramatic action* was beginning to develop. The material is essentially structured as a revue: a plotless collection of seventeen stories revolving around central themes. It lacks the series of inevitable scenes, each falling hard upon the next until a climax is reached, that has been traditional to dramatic structure since Aeschylus. By using the idea of an audition, Michael had tied the material together and given it a framework. Now he *strung* it together by placing it in chronological order. The first story is Mike's number, "I Can Do That." Mike says he was four when he went to dancing school with his sister. Bobby is next, with his monologue about grammar school, followed by "At the Ballet," the years for a dancer which would generally follow. Most of what is talked about before "the Montage" is preadolescent memories. Most of what is talked about after "the Montage" concerns professional careers in New York. "The Montage" bridges the gap, and itself moves from "hello, twelve" years old to "goodbye, seventeen" years old to "hello, love." In short, Michael, in passing the story from dancer to dancer chronologically, told the story of a typical dancer's life, thus giving the material the impression of a plot.

By the time each section was worked out, "the Montage" resembled a jigsaw puzzle in a jumble. Fitting the pieces together took more days of trial and error. Weeks passed. The cast had been working continuously for three months. The winter ice had melted off the street. The steam on the windows, caused by the cold air on the outside and the hot, sweat-drenched air on the inside, had abated. The cast was tired and, after so unusually long and difficult a rehearsal period, becoming anxious.

Michael was struggling with another serious problem. His star dancer, whose story was schedule to follow "the Montage," had an underdefined role and no number.

Donna McKechnie and Michael Bennett first met in the mid-sixties when they were both dancers on the musical television show *Hullabaloo*. They did not know each other well, and Michael kept very much to himself. Donna was amazed to meet someone as young as Michael who already knew he wanted to be a choreographer. When Michael choreographed one of the television episodes, he included a short dance for Donna. Through dancing, they came to respect and admire each other.

Their bond was also based on similar backgrounds. Both had difficult childhoods. Both found an identity in dance. Both were oldest children in their respective families, with the same number of years between themselves and their younger siblings.

The next three times Donna and Michael worked together

were quite by coincidence. For *A Joyful Noise*—the summer stock tryout of a new musical—Michael choreographed his first original musical and Donna played opposite John Raitt. Michael knew the script was an inferior one, and determined to establish his reputation with several big dance numbers. It was Donna's first leading role. The musical was a disaster. Michael's work was impressive, but Donna was watching from the sidelines. Michael perceptively understood the situation and said to her, "Look, you've got to dance. You've got to do something." He choreographed a little piece for her, but by then it was too late. Donna was unhappy in the part and realized she lacked both the experience and the ability to assert herself. She left the show and was replaced by Susan Watson. The production moved to Broadway and flopped. Only Michael's dance numbers stood out.

That was 1966. Michael continued to choreograph, including industrials and *Henry, Sweet Henry* on Broadway; he doctored *How Now, Dow Jones* and the off-Broadway *Your Own Thing*. Then David Merrick asked him to stage the musical numbers for *Promises, Promises*.

Michael's approach on *Promises* was to do *no* dancing unless it was entirely real, in character, and naturalistic. Even in his early career he had begun to develop a trademark he would retain for a lifetime: the fullest integration of the various elements that form the musical theater. Throughout theater history, including even the landmark dance musical *Oklahoma!*, the choreographer and the dancers rehearsed in one place while the director, writers, and actors rehearsed in another. (At one point during *Oklahoma!'s* rehearsals, someone said to the director: "You better take a look in the basement. Agnes De Mille is doing some unusual things.") With *West Side Story*, Jerome Robbins furthered the dramatic function of dance numbers in musicals, and they were no longer seen as filler. Still, few shows managed to integrate dance into the dramatic text. In *Promises, Promises*, a show about office shenanigans, Michael had material and collaborators of intelligence and he launched himself and the theater into a new era.* The dancing, and all the musical staging, grew out of the script and the

---

Promises, Promises was produced by David Merrick, with a book by Neil Simon, music by Burt Bacharach, lyrics by Hal David, and was directed by Robert Moore.

characters. Not just because they *could* dance, but because they *would*.

For the *Promises* song "I Like Basketball," a big dance number was anticipated. Costumes for basketball players and cheerleaders were planned. It seemed like an ideal opportunity to bring on the chorus, at least to a director of the sixties. But Michael was a director for the seventies. To him, there was no chorus, only a collection of characters who worked in the office. He had cast his dancers as actors with this in mind. On the street in front of Madison Square Garden, chorus boys and girls in jerseys and miniskirts simply did not suddenly appear, the way they did in countless musicals until *West Side Story.* (And often still do.) Against the opposition of his older and more powerful collaborators, he staged the number as a solo, using only the lead character's enthusiasm for basketball and a rolled-up raincoat for the ball. To anyone mired in the formula musicals epitomized by a movie mogul's opinion of *Oklahoma!*—"No girls, no jokes, no chance"—the stage appeared frighteningly bare. But for the audience it was hugely successful. To the credit of his partners, the number stayed in. It was Michael's first real battle to increase realism in musical staging, and he won.

Donna was cast as one of three secretaries in that show. Each secretary had a subplot and together they sang "Tick Tock Goes the Clock," about getting married, then went into a short dance. Out of town the show played a half hour too long, and Donna found herself in Washington, D.C., with an expendable role in an overlong show.

Michael staged a dance number for the three secretaries called "Turkey-Lurkey Time," which closed the first act. Sticking to his concept of realism, he first choreographed little more than what would actually take place during an office party. Everyone pushed the desks together, and the secretaries climbed up and executed a cute, simple sequence of steps.

The number was *too* realistic. It was boring. The first-act curtain came down to no applause at all. The audience sat stone-faced.

Michael walked backstage and said, "All right. They want a dance number. They'll get a dance number."

He rechoreographed the dance, inventing a tricky, hip, generic signature step and building a fluid jazz number around it which climaxed in a rousing group number led by Donna. The number drew enthusiastic applause. And Donna's job was saved.

In Donna, Michael had discovered the essential choreographer's tool: a great solo dancer. In a group of dancers, Donna stood out. She possessed that unique blend of talent, skill, and personality. Her performance in *Promises* was a victory for them both. It stopped the show on Broadway and again in London.

In 1970, Harold Prince produced *Company*, a musical about modern relationships. He told Michael Bennett he had gotten Donna McKechnie signed up and he told Donna McKechnie he had Michael Bennett. Eager to work together again, they both agreed to do the show.

For *Company*, Michael planned a solo dance for Donna on the subject of sex, but here was another show that had its share of out-of-town problems prior to success on Broadway. With it, Michael as choreographer and Hal Prince as director took another step closer to integration. In *Company*, the principal actors *were* the chorus. Donna played one of the central figure's three girlfriends. Michael created a flashy dance number for her called "Tick Tock," in which she wore nothing but a slip.

"He approached me about doing it topless," she recalls. "I was so embarrassed about being thought of as a prude, I gave some artistic reasons. 'Oh, the mystery. You can't give them all of it. We must stimulate their imagination.' My instinct was right. What is it that Eglevsky said about dance nudity? With the male, it never stops on the beat."

Out of town, Hal Prince wanted to drop the number. "No one understands the brutality of show business unless they do a musical that's in trouble out of town," explains Donna.

Half an hour before a performance in Boston, Donna and Michael, Prince and composer Stephen Sondheim stood on the stage behind the curtain as the audience filed in. Prince wanted the number cut and that was final. It had no connection with anything; it came out of left field.

Donna would never forget the scene. "Every once in a while I speak up for myself. This was one of those moments. I looked at Hal and said, 'You can't cut that—the show needs it.' I can't believe I'm saying this. I'm pitching to Hal Prince about what his show needs. I said, 'Look, people don't understand why it's there, so make it connect with something.' I kept throwing the ball at them and they kept throwing it back. And Hal intermittently kept saying, 'Donna, it's fifteen minutes to curtain. We'll talk about this later. Just go and get your makeup on.' I said, 'Hal, I'm not leaving this spot until you tell me that you're going to solve this problem and keep that dance number in.' And he said, 'Donna, it's five minutes.' I was thinking fast. I said, 'Look, you can reprise a song that Bobby sings. I could be every girl in his life.' And Stephen Sondheim said, 'I want no reprises in this show.'* And Hal Prince said, 'Donna, please go and dress,' and I said, 'I'm not leaving,' and he said, 'All right, all right! We'll fix it!' And I went, 'Thank you,' and I walked up and got dressed. I don't know who that person was, but it worked."

Michael got the film composer David Shire, who happened to be on his honeymoon in Boston, to write a dance arrangement. They were in the theater from noon to midnight. They reconstructed the number, music and dance, and put into it the sounds of love from the previous bedroom scene, including "I love you" at a climactic point. The audience got the connection and the number stayed in. For Michael and Donna it was their second resounding success together. *Company* was the most brilliantly staged and integrated musical of the decade. Donna danced "Tick Tock" triumphantly on Broadway, in Hollywood, and in London.

Michael had choreographed solo dances for Donna in *Hullabaloo*, *A Joyful Noise*, *Promises, Promises*, and *Company*. Their working method was deeply collaborative. Simply put, his choreography made her look good and she in turn made his choreography look good. What's more, he did not stop with the steps but directed his dances. They were little scenes, building, talking to the audience, exploiting character nuances, and thus were more gratifying to perform. The two had a rare artistic partnership.

From the beginning of his latest project, Michael intended for Donna to take on a substantial role. She was to be not one of the

---

*George S. Kaufman set this precedent with *Guys and Dolls*. Until that time, most second acts were a musical reprise of the first. When Kaufman said to Frank Loesser, "If you reprise your songs, I'll reprise the jokes," a new era was begun.

gypsies but a woman who had made it out of the chorus into featured parts. She was back because that career had not panned out. She was broke and needed to return to her dancer roots.

Typically, Michael began with some basic truths. Donna had been featured in, and had stopped, two Broadway shows. But by 1973 her career had not progressed past those successes. She had tried Hollywood but failed to make a name for herself. She was a dancer and throughout her life had returned to dancing for financial and spiritual resuscitation.

Michael left Donna totally alone, giving her freedom to work. "It showed me that he had great trust. I knew Michael and Bob from other shows and we had that particular relationship. It was very respectful. You can imagine how after the fact people would say, 'Well, you and Michael . . .' It wasn't that way. Nevertheless, I think Michael had a real intent to find the right spot for me. I wasn't just one of the kids, either. I never felt like I quite fit in. I had a different way of working. I never thought of myself as being a chorus dancer. So I kind of stood apart. And Michael kept me apart, too. I didn't have a lot of the relationships that everybody had with each other, those get-down relationships, from dressing rooms and different shows. I didn't get into it.

"I felt that people respected me, but what I didn't like was that I was put up a little bit. When you're a shy person at school, you want to be part of a group. In rehearsal, it was like seeing all of my age-old dilemmas reenacted in a group situation."

To begin with, Donna McKechnie as Cassie Ferguson did not dance in the opening number with everybody else. After it was over and they reached the line, she made a late entrance in high heels, a silver lamé jump suit, and a fur chubby, sweeping in like Lauren Bacall and interrupting the audition with "Oh, hi, how are you? Does anyone have change for a ten? There's a cab out there." There was a lot of dialogue in which she indicated that her agent had sent her over for a leading role by mistake, but as long as she was there, what the hell, she might as well audition. Whatever quiet desperation she was suffering, she covered with a display of bravado that would outshine Carol Channing making an entrance at Sardi's. It became clear that she and Zach had been lovers, and the more she denied a desire for special treatment, the more it was obvious she expected exactly that. He invited her to change her clothes ("Right here?") and dance with the chorus boys and girls. She just happened to have a bright-red leotard in her handbag, so she joined the line.

Her principal moment would come following "the Montage." The company was granted a break, and Cassie stayed to speak with Zach. The truth surfaced. She needed work, and what she did best was dance. A dancer does not want to wait tables, and a dancer does not want to teach.

Over the months there were five revisions of Cassie's song, and more than a few members of the company felt the earlier versions were superior to the one that was finally used. Originally the number was called "Inside the Music."

It was a beautiful song: "Inside the music, there is a dancer. . . ." Many dancers who heard it still think it has a prettier melody. The songwriters tailored it for Donna's three-octave range, and it was a bit too glittery. It was thoughtful, lovely, and Donna could act it—put the need, the yearning into it—but it was too introspective and it was hard for her to be assertive with the material. Ultimately, it didn't say enough. It didn't reach out.

The songwriters wrote her a stronger, more aggressive plea, "The Music and the Mirror." If the melody was narrower, the rhythm was stronger, the lyrics were beltable. The song allowed Donna to present her character at her most desperate, most vulnerable, and weakest.

"My image was of a little ant who has this big face. I felt like someone who has nothing. Who feels herself against it totally. The fight-or-flight feeling. That was the situation and when someone feels that weak, that frightened, instead of running they go, 'God damn it.' That was the feeling—the more powerful, the more committed I was to that, the better it worked and the more they loved it. I was portraying a character who was totally desperate and it was the last battle of her life. It was the most desperate fight imaginable for this woman."

If that song was one of the last to be set, the dance portion that accompanied it took even longer. This was not unusual for Donna and Michael, who in the past had found the dance sequences to be their greatest obstacle, and one that often required some false starts. To create a dance is to work with something that cannot be intellectualized, a feeling for the music and the rhythm that satisfies the moment's dramatic intent.

The first day they began this work, Michael was on edge. Although the cast didn't know it at the time, Michael was spending his evenings in a desperate fight to save the show.

Joe Papp wanted to open the show at Lincoln Center's Vivian Beaumont Theater, instead of downtown at the Shakespeare Festival. Michael knew this meant disaster. The downtown Newman was a proscenium theater, while the Beaumont's design incorporated a thrust stage facing a cavernous house. It was a white elephant of a theater; it had killed a number of shows and at least three attempts to sustain acting companies. Michael knew better than anyone that the delicacy of the drama would be overwhelmed on this stage, and the starkness of the production would be softened by the elegant decor. Almost more devastating to Michael was what the change implied: Papp had lost faith in Michael's workshop.

But Michael's tenacity overrode all obstacles. He never gave up on his vision. He secretly went to the Shubert Organization and offered them the production. Enthusiastic about the show, they promised him their support and a theater. Papp, unwilling to lose the show, acceded to Michael's demands: *A Chorus Line* would open downtown, as planned.

Fighting these battles after rehearsals left Michael tired and morose just at the time he and Donna set to work on her dance. But rather than ask for help or sympathy from his friends, he became the petulant boy. During one rehearsal, Donna, Bob Avian, and rehearsal drummer Bobby Thomas remained in front of the mirrors while everyone else went on a break. Michael, slumped in the house, said to Donna: "Okay, do something."

Donna began searching for steps. Bobby Thomas played rhythms. Bob Avian followed along. Donna, unaware of Michael's preoccupations, began to question if this was how he expected the dance to come together. "But I had to remember that in years past, there was a liberty Michael would take with me that he would never take with anybody else. On the one hand I felt special about it. At the same time I wanted to say, 'Get your ass up here!' "

Everyone left the rehearsal unhappy and frustrated. Bob Avian went to Michael and confronted him. It was one of the few times in their long collaboration he voiced any criticism of Michael.

Michael took the rebuke and the next day went to work in earnest.

At last it began to come together. But the number remained stubbornly problematical. It wasn't quite working, and no one could figure out why. It was all one feeling, all mad dancing. Donna felt as if she were hitting the audience over the head with it. It was the eleventh hour. This was *the* dance number of the show, the number that was going to say something about dance, and it suffered from overkill.

Michael called a production meeting specifically to deal with the dance. Marvin Hamlisch, Bob Avian, Bobby Thomas, Donna, and Michael all gathered at his apartment after rehearsal.

They talked about the subtext of the dance, trying to refine it. Then Donna had a thought: "Look, why don't we just stop the rhythm and do a slow four." Bobby Thomas beat it out on the piano cover while Hamlisch enthusiastically followed. Michael was intrigued.

Avian suggested another change in rhythm, and Michael said, "Yeah, and then we'll bring the mirrors in and then . . ." All of a sudden, after weeks of frustration, everything seemed to fall into place. Bobby Thomas invented changing rhythms to match each subtext, and pounded them out for Michael, refining them at the drums the next day.

It was only the most recent contribution from Thomas, who had been the drummer on all Michael's shows. "Bobby," Michael often said, "was the man who made me dance."

The dance music and steps were altered to encompass several different moods a dancer might go through, each section expressing a separate need or feeling from Cassie's soul as a dancer. The changing rhythm of each new sequence gave the number the variety it needed, and allowed it to build more deliberately toward the climax.

"My feeling to change the rhythm," Donna recalls, "wasn't just to do it arbitrarily. It had to do with my instinctive feeling. As an actress, when you fulfill one emotion completely you don't stay there—you go to another. The narcissistic thing came out of it. Then came another—the eroticism."

At the climactic point of the number, several of the boys stepped out from behind the mirrors and danced along with her.

Michael used the real dancers here—Thommie Walsh, Wayne Cilento, Rick Mason, Michel Stuart, and Michael Serrecchia—not as themselves but as Cassie's nightclub backup. The section had evolved in fact from work Michael had been doing with Lucie Arnaz for the national company of *Seesaw*. The number built phenomenally as all of them threw their arms forward in a climactic statement of the needs of a dancer.

Following the dance, Zach confronted Cassie with their working relationship. He could not accept her coming back to dance in the chorus. He saw her as a failure, but the failure was his own as well, since he had choreographed her successes.

This material reflected Donna's own life. Michael had coached and coaxed Donna into Broadway fame; then she had tried Hollywood and failed. To get back to New York she borrowed money from her father for the first time in her life. On her return, before this project began, she was out of work, had no vision of what her career could be, and was turning thirty.

Donna remembers vacuuming her apartment and feeling sorry for herself, being depressed and feeling reclusive.

"I'm watching *Jeopardy* on television and *I'm one of the answers!* In this game show! And I'm going, 'Boo hoo, boo hoo, I'm a celebrity and I don't even know it!' But I didn't think that I was a celebrity. I just thought, 'I feel like shit.' I saw the irony of it. I saw the futility of my situation."

Jimmy Kirkwood had created a dramatic monologue for Cassie out of Donna's own experience, though embellishing it considerably. Cassie began describing an afternoon when she was supposed to go to an audition and vacuumed the floor instead. The agent called to ask where she was. She continued vacuuming. The cat bothered her and she picked it up by the tail and threw it out the window. She began screaming and vacuuming and screaming and vacuuming and ended up in the hospital with a nervous breakdown.

The Kirkwood imagination was more melodramatic than documentary and didn't really fit the tone of the play. In this case the truth, if less strange, was more effective than the fiction. Donna had undergone intense frustration, and returned to the city to find renewal. Though the climax of her self-pity may have been touched off by the comical coincidence of hearing her own name as a celebrity answer on a daytime quiz program, she did not undergo

· 113

a nervous breakdown. With the help of a psychiatrist she had been seeing for years to deal with her childhood, she was able to draw out of herself a strength and commitment that enabled her to go on.

In attempting to restore her flagging career she had returned to New York, but never to the ranks of the chorus via the cattle-call scene. However, another dancer Michael and Avian knew did go that route. They told Donna the story: A successful girl dancer in New York who had worked for Michael and Bob went to Hollywood and appeared in *The Fortune Cookie* with Jack Lemmon. It looked as if her career was going to flourish, but it did not, so she returned to New York and showed up at a Milliken Breakfast Show audition in front of Michael Bennett. One night after rehearsals Michael and Avian were talking over their past, and Michael remembered how he had felt at the time. He had said to her, "I can't hire you. It's my problem. I can't work with you. I can't look at you in rehearsals after knowing what you've done. To me it's a step backwards."

She said, "Well, that's not my problem. I need this job."

And he said, "I'm sorry."

Out of those memories came the "We can't go back" dialogue.

In getting to the core of her character, Donna admits that she had a hard time breaking through. But for over a year prior to rehearsals, she had been studying acting with Warren Robertson. His exercises in sensory recall enabled her to find the emotions she needed. Now she took Cassie's scenes to the class, and worked on the problems. "You cannot do that kind of sensory work," she says, "without using yourself. But I also used every dancer behind the scenes. I had a lot of support by knowing that I was representing a whole particular humanity in show business. I don't think I could've done it with that conviction if I was just speaking about Donna McKechnie. The people I've known, the fears, the heartbreak. When you love putting on shows and you love being in shows and then you go to auditions and you see the pain that people endure. Year after year I've seen people get lower and lower and sink into the ground. I think that I had enough of that experience, enough of seeing it, being around it, and having it myself. I knew what the hell I was talking about because I'd seen it. If I couldn't reveal true feelings in a play about this business, what could I do? I mean if I couldn't do it here, I couldn't ever do it."

Later in the show Zach and Cassie continue their confrontation. In the second scene it comes out that they had more than a working relationship—they had been living together. She accuses him of being so driven and ambitious that when he was working on a show without her she disappeared from his life. She walked out on him, but she accuses him of hardly noticing. Though Zach is by now established as no more than the domineering master of ceremonies, and the audience is barely following him enough to notice, there is a burst of feeling from him that is revealing, not only about the character, but about Michael. He is a workaholic. He wants to rise to the very top of the business, and that business and his art are the only really fulfilling things in his life. No woman can compete with that.

And no man. In an early draft of the script Cassie also accuses him of having a love affair with a man. Zach admits it is true and thus is clearly, though inconsequentially, identified as a bisexual. But Michael decided not to use that angle and the references were eliminated. It was not a play about Zach, and Michael's initial impulse to keep the director firmly in an emotionless background never weakened.

Following that second scene, Cassie picked up her bag and ran out of the audition.

The only monologue that remained in its original length and seriousness was in the hands of a young dancer acting for the first time. Following Donna's sequence, Sammy Williams as Paul would step out and present Nick Dante's story.

By now the seven-page monologues the characters had begun with had all been jettisoned or turned into song. Except one. While the Paul monologue had been edited down to three full pages, it remained the same in substance, and became one of the single most powerful monologues in theater literature, covering the subject of homosexuality with as little stereotyping and as much humanity as had ever been presented.

The lack of a song, however, was a major concern to Sammy in the beginning. During rehearsals the creators had told Sammy that he would get a song, but the song never materialized. Other cast members had songs and dances, and he was angry for a while that he didn't get one.

Dante, on the other hand, was thrilled that they couldn't turn his life into musical comedy.

As part of their audition, the applicants would be put through two more dance variations: a thirties routine and a tap routine. The first variation was the choreography and lyric to the song "One." The dancers were asked to do this in a clean, impersonal style. This routine was performed by the dancers so many times and in so many combinations that it was permanently imprinted on the audience. Michael the choreographer always knew that if you did something enough times the audience would applaud. But more than looking for applause, he wanted to demonstrate vividly the intricacies of choreography.

Michael's earlier plan, to use a member of the audience, was abandoned. While he never had much trouble controlling his own minions, an audience member might prove too unpredictable.

The last dance sequence would be the tap number. The whole routine was choreographed and rehearsed to "Tea for Two," then handed over to the music department. Hamlisch wrote a simple melody to replace the classic, complete with "breaks." For the spaces, the authors created a line of dialogue for the inner thoughts of each of several characters, all around the theme of how exhausting the audition was becoming. The company danced it together, then in four smaller groups.

Like everything else, it was a product of the trial-and-error rehearsals Michael conducted.

"The scene happened on our feet," says Clive Clerk, who had by now stepped into the role of Zach's assistant, Larry. "It was out of an improv session. Bob Avian came up on the stage. We were at the Newman Theater. He got up and went through how he would conduct a tap audition, and as he did I was writing things down, and at the end we handed it over to a writer and had a script made out of it."

Clive was the only dancer present who did not want his role enlarged. "There was never a great deal of chatter about the part of Larry. Larry is one of those dinner-is-served parts. Which was just fine with me."

*   *

For the climactic ballad, Hamlisch and Kleban did their home-work. Carole Schweid remembers "the day Marvin came in with 'What I Did for Love,' trailing the lead sheet behind him in the wind." It was more than the songwriters' attempt at a hit tune, although it succeeded there as well. The song revealed why the dancers subjected themselves time and again to the kind of thing the audience had just witnessed.

Michael decided against an ordinary curtain call to follow the final elimination scene, which was still changing daily. Instead he planned a grand finale. He brought the show—for which the dancers had been auditioning—onto the stage. Every cast member would enter and dance in a version of "One." The chorus line would emerge as the star, and Michael would have proven his point. If the finale could bowl the audience over, the synergy would be clear. The sum of the parts had made the whole greater.

The climax reassembled the chorus line in its classic mold. After getting to know all the dancers intimately, the audience would finally be confronted with the dancers as they were por-trayed in other shows. They would wear matching costumes, matching top hats, matching smiles, and perform matching chore-ography in a cold, robot-like manner, which Michael associated with the mechanical characters in Fritz Lang's film *Metropolis*. In a conversation he had with his friend George Furth, Michael de-scribed how he hoped the number would affect the audience.

"It will be the end of chorus lines as we know them," Michael rhapsodized. "The audience will be horrified at how the chorus line robs the dancers of their personality. We will do every kind of chorus line, and the audience will be appalled at the inhumanity of it. They won't be able to applaud—they'll be speechless!"

"Will there be kicks?" inquired Furth.

"Of course."

"Then," Furth ventured, "they'll applaud."

"Not if I do it right!" Michael answered.

As the time for performances approached, Michael increased his meetings with the designers Tharon Musser (lights), Theoni

V. Aldredge (costumes), and Robin Wagner (set). It was time to add production elements.

Aldredge had been visiting the studio to study the dancers' own rehearsal clothes. Don Percassi recalls of his costume: "That's what I wore to rehearsal. I always wore a hat 'cause my hair always looks like this. That was my TKTS T-shirt. I still have the original one in my trunk, without the sleeves. I cut the sleeves out of them all, 'cause they bother me." And Clive "had a pair of dance pants and a top like that. Actually it was kelly green and had a white number on it." Aldredge assembled the costumes by balancing theatrical needs for individuality with the real clothes of the dancers.

Wagner began with Michael's long-ago idea of a show that takes place completely in a rehearsal room. They first discussed a bare stage as it is used for an audition. Then, in a step that actually went backwards toward less, rather than forward toward more, they eliminated the look of an empty theater or room by covering the walls with plain black drapes and painting the floor black. Upstage, Michael had three requirements: 1) A continuation of the black box; 2) mirrors from the original rehearsal hall idea; and 3) the backdrop for the final number—a piece of the set from the show for which the dancers were auditioning. These three requirements were combined brilliantly by the use of the most ancient set device in theater history: the two-thousand-year-old Greek *periaktoi*, the triangular box that revolves to present any one of its three sides. The simplicity of the idea is deceptive. The circular movement of the revolving backdrops was so fresh, after decades of walls flying in and out vertically and horizontally, that it ended up playing a significant part in the flow of the show.

Wagner believes that the only essential element in the scene design is the white line on the floor upon which the dancers stand. It has a remarkably metaphoric look, and represents the title as well as the whole theme of the play. Unfortunately, only those people in the balcony seats know it even exists.

The simplicity of the sets and costumes left lighting designer Tharon Musser with a major assignment. Because black does not reflect light or alter its color, the black box that framed the work space allowed her great artistic freedom. Using many more instruments than usual to compensate for the lack of elaborate design in the other departments, she created a wide variety of isolating light focuses, sometimes pinpointing actors in the dark space and at other times flooding the stage with changing patterns in a kaleidoscopic array. She used as her principal theme the harsh white light of an audition, taking theatrical license to expand on that, and returning to her main theme when the dancers returned to the line. The blue "thought" light accented the moments of an actor's private thoughts. The number and intricate timing of the light cues, synchronized as most of them were to the music, required better control than was possible with the old stagehand-and-dimmer-switch technique. Musser installed the first computer-ized light board on Broadway. The only detriment to the whole panoply of theatrical effect was that the harsh white front lights for the central motif made the girls' legs appear flatter and wider, adding ten pounds of unwanted weight. For a female dancer, that could be a psychological catastrophe.

Many musicals have failed because the audience left the the-ater with nothing to hum but the scenery. The look of this show would be deceiving. Behind its simplicity stands an enormous achievement: The physical elements augment the drama.

As the musical sequences were locked in, the piano arrange-ments went out to be orchestrated. Because a specific sound was required for each number and because the constant changes and last-minute decisions made time short, three orchestrators were employed: Bill Byers, Hershy Kay, and Jonathan Tunick. The show begins with a single, tacky rehearsal piano and, using the same theatrical license that Tharon Musser employed to go beyond the plain white work lights, eventually takes in a wide array of sound appropriate to each song and dance. The Newman Theater has no orchestra pit, so the entire eighteen pieces were crammed backstage and piped out to the audience over speakers. There were times when the actors literally had to climb over the musi-cians to make their entrances and exits.

As the first public performance approached, the question of whether the show would actually work loomed over the entire company. Excitement and apprehension mounted to an almost intolerable pitch. Their whole lives were consumed by the show.

Nancy Lane remembers rehearsing eight hours a day, every

day. "That's all we knew. We didn't even know how good the show was. Honest to God we didn't. Marvin Hamlisch would be there, and Ed Kleban and Joe Papp would come to rehearsal, Bernie Gersten, all those guys, and they'd say, 'Looks good, looks good.' And we didn't know. It was all the same to us—it was all so much the same." The dancers were too close to the material to judge it.

Yet there was an undeniable energy arising from the show. That many dancers, that much exciting dance, that much honest, invigorating, tuneful music, had their effect on even the casual observer.

Ron Dennis recalls how "every now and then people would come in and watch, and they'd go out sort of smiling and not wanting to smile and let you know they were smiling because they liked it. They couldn't help themselves. You got a sort of energy about it that I can't really put into words. It's something you feel. There would be people coming in and out, watching the rehearsals, and you would know when they were with you—you could feel it."

For some time Michael had kept Papp out of the theater. Finally he invited him to a rehearsal, a run-through that made Papp a believer at last. He turned to Michael and said, "It's the greatest thing I've ever seen."

But Michael, ever the perfectionist, was hoping for criticism and was startled by Papp's reaction.

"Get out of here," he said jokingly. "Who needs you? What good is an unqualified rave?" He had purposely kept Papp out of rehearsals for a few weeks in order to get a fresh perspective. But the show was solidifying, and even Papp supported it now.

The line between actors and characters had completely disappeared. Each dancer presented a story that was drawn from true life. Some were telling their own stories; some were telling other people's; other stories were composites drawn from the original meeting, interviews, and improvisatory rehearsals. The question of who contributed what material to which character would clatter along the gypsy grapevine for years. More than one dancer would lay claim to various ideas. Michael and the authors had collated the material in such a way as to make each character consistent.

They had been helped in this by the performers. Each actor

had come to play himself or herself—the most difficult of acting exercises.

But no matter where the stories had originated, they belonged now to the seventeen chorus line dancers. Stripped of scenery and costumes, stripped of stereotypical musical-comedy characters and the star they usually danced behind, the dancers stood alone, with only the reality of the lives they were to portray. Whether they were talking about themselves—as Donna, Kelly, Priscilla, and Thommie sometimes were—or talking about others, like Sammy (Nick), Wayne (Sammy), and Kay (Donna), no longer mattered. They played themselves onstage, and their own mannerisms and actions, relationships and nuances would forever be the model. When the cast took the stage for the first time, there had never been a more *original* original cast.

Trish Garland "can remember the first night of previews. We were all very concerned that they were going to critique our lives. If they didn't like the show, they were saying they don't like our lives. Well, that's a very hard thing to deal with. We didn't know if it was good or not. Nobody knew and anybody who says that we did is lying. Thommie Walsh said, 'I will be so embarrassed if my friends come here and they throw things at me. I will be so embarrassed if this is a flop.' "

But there was one thing upon which everybody agreed. Crissy Wilzak: "You were just sitting on this volcano ready to erupt."

CHAPTER IX

· · · · · · · · · · · · · · · · · · ·

Downtown

As the cast put on their costumes and warmed up, they had a million things running through their minds. They had to remember lines, lyrics, staging, harmony, dance steps, and multiple last-minute changes. They had to play the show for a large audience for the first time and, everyone hoped, accommodate laughs and applause in their timing. They had to rise above their nerves, yet use that nervous energy to demonstrate the anxiety provoked by an audition. Ordinary tension was higher because of the nature of the material, and the seventeen dancers were all playing much larger and more special roles than they had ever played before.

On April 23, 1975, at eight o'clock, none of the dancers were as ready as they would have liked to have been, but they stepped out onstage in front of a paying audience at the New York Shakespeare Festival's 299-seat Estelle R. Newman Theater anyway.

The first preview of a new musical is seen by friends, family, agents, theater businessmen, and musical comedy mavens. This by no means defines the audience as a group of well-wishers, and that first performance was not without problems. The *periaktoi* units were not yet ready, so the upstage mirrors were draped with black curtains when they were not being used. The finale had no backdrop. The Zach–Cassie scenes, played onstage alone, seemed endless, as were the numerous repetitions of the musical number "One," which seemed to run on and on to no purpose.

Yet in spite of all the problems, there was a positive response. On a gut level the show reached out and grabbed the audience. Nobody had ever seen anything like it before. By the finale, they were completely absorbed, and they roared their appreciation.

It was a beginning. Word of mouth began to build. After a week of previews the whole city was buzzing about the show.

But the show was, for all practical purposes, still in rough shape. Not only were the design elements incomplete, but the play needed changes and improvements.

The company had worked intensely for a long period of time and lately had been wondering when it was all going to end. The success of the first preview gave them a fresh sense of excitement. Then Michael said, "Okay, now we have a hit and we have four weeks before we open and we're gonna rehearse every day." The dancers heaved a collective sigh and thought, "Oh, no, not again. Not another four weeks."

Just at this time the annual Milliken industrial show came around. The show paid handsomely, was very prestigious, and took place only in the early mornings. Dancers could keep the clothes they modeled, as well as a handsome bonus over a substantial salary, and perks included food at rehearsal and limousines for the gypsies who had to race to their own Broadway matinees later in the day. Rick, Thommie, Wayne, and Baayork were offered the show, and Michael allowed them to accept.

They rehearsed from nine to one on Milliken, then ran downtown to *Chorus Line* rehearsals for the afternoon, had a dinner break, then did the show. Soon Michael was regretting the time they were putting in on the industrial, and began giving them a lot of flak. He didn't want the dancers to split their time, yet most of them needed the money. He began calling rehearsals too early, knowing that the Milliken dancers would be unable to make it.

Michael did not want to share his dancers. One day at the Milliken rehearsal the door opened and Michael and Bob walked in uninvited. Michael confronted the Milliken choreographer with "I need these kids." The kids went with him to rehearse.

As they progress, musical-comedy rehearsals tend to get physically harder. There may be a lot of sitting around when the material is being formed and discussed and the combinations are being developed, but once the show is on its feet, there is always too much to do. In addition, changes going into the show are rehearsed during the day, but not necessarily put in that same night. And there may be more than one attempt at making a number or scene right. The performance can be to the actor like a Chinese menu: one from column A, three from column B, two from yesterday's version, with today's ending. At the same time, as the deadline of the critical opening approaches, dances, music, and dialogue that have been finalized must be rehearsed again and again until they are absolutely right.

Wayne Cilento recalls: "We were a mess downtown. We were so sick. We all had colds. We were all dying. We were all run-down, I guess. Everyone was sick. We couldn't breathe, we couldn't sing, nothing. It was awful. They were shooting us up with B-twelve and C shots every night before the show. We had vaporizers in the rooms. I danced like shit down there, but it was gut level. It was all honest, gut level emotion. We were scared to death, all of us, and that's exactly what an audition should be, and it was brilliant."

Everyone had his own way of coping. One actor remembers Michael saying "Okay, everybody, take your Valium."

Though Michael was not speaking literally, by 1975 drugs had been around the dance world for a long time and he did not discourage their use.

The changes began. Cassie's late entrance, breaking into the line after the opening audition, was a disaster. It made her a hateful character.

It lasted one night. After the first performance Donna and Michael were at a bar across the street discussing the show. She said to him: "You're giving me an entrance and you're trying to make me a star . . . and you're killing me." The entrance was forestalling any sympathy the audience might have felt for her. His desire was to make her come off in the best possible way, but it wasn't working. There could be no star in that show. It would unbalance it, and distort its real meaning.

So it was agreed that since Cassie had decided to attend the audition, she would have had to come to terms with herself in advance. Forgetting her pride, she had to line up quietly along with everyone else and take her chances. The next day Donna was put into the opening. Since it was already tightly staged for twelve girls and twelve boys, this forced Carole Schweid out. "My first note session was doomed from the beginning," Carole moans. "Donna went into my spot and I was out of the opening."

"I Can Do That" was originally intended to be an icebreaker, and Wayne Cilento was supposed to have another number within the Montage to exploit his character, but in rehearsals no one ever got around to writing it. Then, the first time he performed "I Can Do That" he stopped the show. Still Michael wasn't completely satisfied.

Wayne's number had been established early in the process. By the time Michael finished the rest of the show, he went back and looked at "I Can Do That."

"That number stinks," he said to Wayne. "We have to change it."

It was now only two weeks before the official opening. Wayne estimates he had been doing the number for six months.

For two weeks he did a different version every night. They rehearsed during the day; then Wayne performed the new version that night. Michael hated it. He did another number the next day; Wayne did the new number that night. Michael hated it. Then "I Can Do That" went into the middle of "And." Then they put it in another position. One day they wrote a new number about "Joanne," a little girl, based on Wayne's childhood: "I lived in a neighborhood where there were no boys my age. Just a couple of girls. Joanne was my little friend. We hung out together. It was about how I was in love with her and she took me to dancing school. We used to eat cookies and watch *The Mickey Mouse Club* on TV."

Finally, after near daily attempts to find another version of "I Can Do That," or another song for Wayne, Michael came back to him and said, "We're going back to 'I Can Do That.' "

"But I thought you said it stunk?" Wayne replied.

"It's terrific. It'll be fine."

Wayne never got his second number.

The show was working, but there were precious few light moments. From that original read-through of Chekhovian sobriety, the material had become shorter, tighter, and more musical.

It had not become too much funnier. What Michael wanted now—and the songwriters were behind him—was jokes. Since neither Nick Dante nor Jimmy Kirkwood was providing them, he brought in a third author.

Neil Simon has been known as "Doc" for as long as Broadway can remember. Simon always claims in interviews that the nickname stuck from childhood, when he was given a toy stethoscope. This may be so, but "Doc" Simon, in addition to writing a play and a screenplay every year since he stopped whispering jokes into Mel Brooks's ear for Sid Caesar in *Your Show of Shows*, once doctored plays and musicals in hotel rooms from Boston to Philadelphia. An old friend of Michael's, he came downtown and he brought his jokes with him. New material began appearing for Pam Blair, Thommie Walsh, and Kelly Bishop.

Kelly's role as Sheila had solidified by the second workshop. It was working well, and finally Michael began skipping over her first sequence of dialogue during run-throughs and moving on to sections of the show that needed more work. She had grown comfortable in the part and when previews began, audiences rewarded her with regular laughs on her several one-liners. Then, in previews just prior to the opening, a page of new dialogue appeared for Kelly, as well as for Pam and Thommie. Michael came in with Kelly's opening sequence entirely rewritten. Kelly read the lines and instinctively didn't like them. They took Sheila to a more superficial level, giving her cracks like—in answer to Zach's query "Why did you start dancing?"—"Beats working in a luncheonette." But Kelly trusted Michael completely and saw no reason not to try out the new material. Besides, others had gotten new pages as well. That night, with her newly memorized lines, she took her place as usual.

It was a disaster. The new lines did not go over. The character Kelly had created became colder and less sympathetic. Later in the show, lines that had always gotten laughs did not work nearly as well. Had she not finally sung "At the Ballet," Kelly is sure the audience would have wanted to stone her.

Walking offstage, her eyeballs rolling, Kelly returned to the dressing room. She didn't say a word, a sure sign that she was angry. The dressing room was silent. The other dancers glanced at her mournfully. Finally she announced to anyone listening: "I have said those lines for the first and last time."

"What will you do if Michael approves the new material and insists it stays in?" one of the dancers asked.

"If it stays, I go."

Michael walked into the room, making his usual rounds for notes. As it happened, both Thommie's Bobby monologue and Pam's "Tits and Ass" introduction had gone exceedingly well. The new jokes lightened the material and solicited major laughs from the audience. Michael encouraged the performers and locked both of the new sequences in. Then he turned to Kelly. There was silence in the room. Kelly waited.

"You, I fucked," he said. "It goes back to last night."

"Oh, thank God you said that," she sighed with relief. "Michael, I don't know what I would have done if you had said you liked it. I was ready to walk out."

"No. It goes back to just the way it was."

Michael had brought in Neil Simon and inserted the new jokes in total secrecy, without a word to his own authors. According to Nick Dante: "Jimmy Kirkwood and I went to rehearsal one day and there were about eight new lines in the show that neither of us recognized. I always assumed that Michael wrote them, because Michael could be very funny and often came up with wonderful lines. I didn't find out until about four years after the show opened that Neil Simon wrote them. I never knew."

It is unlikely that in the history of the American musical theater there has ever been or will be a dance number as long and hard as "The Music and the Mirror." In previews, Donna continued to work to absorb it all and build stamina. It was a struggle to perform it every night and rehearse all day. The boys, who joined her fresh for the last sequence, forced her to become aware of her spacing at the climactic and most difficult part.

"Michael called me one night," she remembers, "and Bob was on the extension, and he said, 'What's wrong with you? Why aren't you dancing?' And this is after a period of leaving me completely alone. I mean, never 'Good morning, hi, how are you?' This was the first phone call in weeks. And I said, 'Well, I'm trying. I'm doing the best I can.' I felt really bad because I knew that I wasn't dancing it the way that I could, but he had me in front of the fellas. We had marks to hit and I never felt the freedom. I'm

· 127

trying to stay within certain areas. I said, 'I'm trying to stay on my marks.' He said, 'Oh, that's the reason.' "

The next morning the boys were cut from the number.

Rick Mason will never forget it. "As I walked in I saw Wayne and Thommie. I remember looking at their faces and I knew something was up, because I think the rumor had started a day or two before. I just kept saying, 'No, it's not gonna happen, it's not gonna happen.' And they said it happened. I was crushed. It looked very Vegas and I understood that afterward, but it was the only thing I had in the show. The one thing I thought I could really give."

Wayne Cilento felt: "We were too good. We were better than her. We were taking the moment away from her. We were too strong. Because we were better than her, she never did the dance once until we were cut. Then she finally got through the dance. I think she was not making the number work so he would say it doesn't work."

Donna never asked Michael to take the boys out of the number, and she never said she couldn't dance it with anyone else onstage. But the next day she walked in to find the change had been made. "I was hated," she felt. "I feel really bad that Rick felt that way. I'm not sorry it worked out the way it did, but I'm sorry if feelings were that bruised about it."

Donna was not the type to try to manipulate the situation by cruising through the dance until the choreographer was forced to see things her way. The boys didn't fit because suddenly five characters from the line were backing a star—just what the show was *not* about.

Michael had given himself an almost insoluble problem. Since the number was a long solo at a crucial spot for a star dancer, it had to stop the show. But its theme—the dancer's need to work, dancing out of that desperation—was not an easy one to visualize. To Wayne Cilento: "It was great when we were in it. I hate it now. I think it's just a marathon with no steps. Donna just made it work because of who Donna is."

"I think he did it for a purpose," Wayne continues. "I think he didn't want that number to stop the show. I think he passed the point where it could've stopped the show. After the mirrors went up and she ran around for another couple of eights, it shoulda stopped, and it went beyond that. I think what he was saying is that she was a fucking horse and she was gonna get through it. She was persistent to work, and that's what Cassie is about. I think probably he was right. Because you sympathize with her. I think it was part of the plan to sympathize with her toward the end of the number, that she was getting nowhere. In actuality the number went nowhere, and that's where she was—nowhere. And it does work."

In fact, "The Music and the Mirror" is Michael's most complex dance. Michael turned to Cassie's motivation for choreography, and set a number that *looked as if Cassie were making it up as she went along.* That's the reason many steps are repeated four times. In improvisation, the dancer will tend to experiment with something, like it, then repeat it until it's comfortable. For Michael, good choreography was never superficial steps, and here he settled on steps the dancer/actress could use to play the multiple beats of her dramatic subtext. But if not acted well, the choreography could not stand up. And if the audience is not drawn into the emotion as well as the choreography, they become lost.

Michael's constant direction to Donna was: "Less is more." It had been a favorite expression of his since they first began working together. Donna's extraordinary technique as a dancer allowed her to dazzle the audience, but gradually, in a process of refinement, he would trim away, encouraging subtleties.

Finally the number worked for Donna. But for the boys, it was hard to lose the thing they did best: dance.

Rick Mason was especially hurt. "Here I felt that I had something to offer but it wasn't being used. It was a phenomenal number. I used to dance the fuck out of that dance. And I never got a compliment. I never got anything from Michael about how I was doing. I had never worked with Michael before. I needed desperately to have some feedback, because I needed to know if I was doing a halfway decent job."

The character of Mark was one of the hardest characters to play because he didn't get a lot to say. He didn't have a long monologue. Rick worked to make him believable through his reactions, because that was the only way the audience was going to get to know him. "During rehearsals Wayne got two versions of his song," Rick recalls. "Thommie got six versions of his monologue. I never got one word changed. I was given it and that was it. It was shitty compared to these things they were getting, I thought. This was my problem and it was frustrating because I kept saying to myself, 'Well, what am I doing wrong? I can sing just as well as Thommie or Wayne. I can dance just as well as they can. I'm a little bit better-looking than them.' I knew it was my first exposure; I couldn't be greedy, but at the same time I never understood why I wasn't given more. That was the start of it, but things grew from that.

"Michael picked five and he was going to stick with his five. Basically they were Priscilla, Pam, Donna, Kelly, and Sammy. They got the meaty roles and they always got the publicity. Those five, along with Thommie and Wayne, were the big problems in the company in the sense of ego. Their ego. I wish I was able to say to Michael: 'Hey, give me a chance! I want you to see this.' Thommie and Wayne could do that. They could say, 'Michael, it's not working for me. I can't say this, Michael.'

"I got very bitter to a lot of the kids in the cast because of their friendship with Michael. I got bitter toward Clive because of his friendship. He had known Michael from Toronto. Here I was, working so hard and not making waves. I never complained about my song or anything and here were others constantly complaining. Constantly saying, 'I want to do this. I can't do this.' Or 'Why should I have to do this?' I couldn't do that and I kept saying to myself, 'God, is that what I have to do to get what I want?' I can't do that. I'm not a complainer. I want to work hard.

"Every one of them got what they wanted. Every one of them got the exposure. Although Pam was not happy with it. Pam acted neurotic. I don't know how many times I got gum thrown in my hand right before her monologue because she had to have her mouth fresh."

Rick developed an anger toward the others, who were getting attention he felt he deserved. "I started to hate every one of them," he admits. "I took my stuff. I was a good little boy and I said it and that was it. That's why I got mad at myself. For not having enough guts.

"I can't change myself if that's what it takes. I would have forsaken a lot of me. I would have to become that pusher, because the business is a pushy business. You will get pushed off if you don't keep pushing. It's an ass-kissing, backbiting business and I'm not good at it. I wasn't good at it with Michael.

"I remember one day in rehearsal we were doing a version of something, and I had a line and Michael yelled, 'If you don't say it louder I'll take it away from you!' Not, 'Rick, a little louder please, because we're having trouble hearing you.' No. 'If you don't say it louder I'm gonna take it away from you.' I felt this small. So I was inhibited by Michael, very much so. I wanted desperately to be able to talk with him.

"I could never talk to him. I so much wanted to be able to just say good morning and feel good. I remember walking into the studio. I would walk through the door and I was fine until I was in the room, and then I was in a wave of depression. It was overpowering. I used to come home and cry."

If Michael chose to talk to you, and he needed to get something out of you, he did. If he didn't, you were on your own. Scott Allen remembers Rick Mason "in tears many, many times. He would just lie on the floor in the theater and start crying, thinking, 'What am I doing wrong? Why doesn't he talk to me? He hates me.' "

Rick was perfect as the baby-faced Mark, who was new to auditions. Consequently Michael had little to say to him. It was frustrating for Rick, but Michael had the problems of the show on his mind, so Rick was left on his own a good deal of the time. "I was having a rough time one week," Rick recalls. "I was being short with everybody. Carolyn Kirsch said something like 'Why the hell are you on the rag?' Michael overheard her and pulled me away from everyone and asked me what was wrong. I said, 'Michael, I have an ego just like every one of these kids in this company. Sometimes it needs a little petting or it needs a little boost just to keep it going. I've never gotten that.' And he said, 'My God, I didn't know that you had that problem to deal with. I didn't think you would need that.'

"I bought it. I thought to myself, 'Well, jeez, I must be proving myself.' But it was a bunch of bullshit. He was basically pacifying me. Now I can look back on what he said and laugh, because he really did a number on me.

"One night Michael called every one of us to tell us how terrific we were. This may sound funny, but you have to remember the position we were all in—every one of us was so excited thinking he called us up. We all went to work the next day and found out everyone got called. The impact went totally down the tubes."

Donna McKechnie knew Michael's way of working better than anyone. She recognized his unique brand of seduction and wanted no part of it. It was his way of being in control. "I didn't like it then and I don't like it now. I don't like the insinuation of it. I sound so prudish but I'd worked with Frank Loesser, Bob Fosse, Abe Burrows, and they didn't cross over lines. They showed a respect for the work and the job. Not to say they didn't take chorus girls out from time to time. But there was less manipulation and less insinuation. It wasn't so incestuous. I sensed that was going on in the show a lot. It made me uncomfortable and I avoided it like the plague. I believed in Michael so much. I had worked with him successfully, and over the last two years he had given me a lot of hope by letting me know he was thinking of me for a show. So I was totally devoted to his ideas and I was totally supportive. If I didn't like the way he was doing things I'd maybe turn my head to it. Turn a blind eye."

Meanwhile word was mounting on the street that the show downtown was very special. The opportunity for career advancement could not have been far from the thoughts of any one of the seventeen line dancers as the official opening approached. Because the show was still in transition, it was always possible that a role might suddenly expand or contract. Everything was up to Michael.

Michael had been father and mother, guide, guardian, and God to each of them for so long that their dependence on him was total. The sun rose and set on what he said and did each day. For theater people in rehearsal, no other life existed anyway. Michael made no compromises, bones, or apologies. His ambition was greater than theirs. When you worked for Michael, you worked his way.

He knew most of the time exactly what he wanted and how to get it. Crissy Wilzak says he "just had this . . . thing about him. When he called 'places,' *nobody* thought about diddling around for two seconds. He had this iron hand over everybody that was just amazing. I was scared of him. He just had that air about him. Knew exactly what he wanted and he knew how to dig, how to say something to get you going, to get you to do something. But he wasn't kind about it. He'd just do anything to get you to do what he wanted you to do. Even if it was kinda mean. I'll never forget one time when Michael was at one of our understudy rehearsals, one of the girls who understudied Kristine, she had a great voice and she said, 'Oh, Michael, I just can't get into this part. I just hate to tell people that I can't sing.' He looked at her and he said, 'Well then, you'll never be an actress.' Boy did she love that number after that."

Robert LuPone, from his position as "director," watched the show coalesce.

"Where did the acting of the piece come from? I'm telling you, the best ensemble I've ever seen. Where did that come from? Fear. That was the result of his kind of direction. It forced the group to act as one. I think that ensemble reality is what made the show work. But I mean *every arm* was in one place. Every emotion was felt down the line. It didn't come from acting necessarily. It came from total abject fear of Michael Bennett."

One night in performance, after "At the Ballet," the dancers moved back into line. Wayne Cilento wiped sweat out of his eye. During notes that night Michael screamed at him.

"You ruined the whole number! You ruined the whole fucking show!

"You exaggerate so much," Wayne shot back. "Why the hell are you exaggerating?"

Michael backed off and said, "Oh, you know me, I always exaggerate." But Wayne and everyone else present would think twice the next time they went to wipe the sweat out of their eyes.

In part, doing the show was traumatic for many of the dancers because they were being asked to do things, as actors, that most actors would have found challenging. Because the show was drawing excited audiences in previews, everyone was feeling the additional pressure of success. Then there was the competition between dancers for the limelight. All this started to have a detrimental effect on the company.

Clive Clerk, older and more experienced, could see the tension rising. "I had a feeling for the problems that a lot of the kids were having," he observed. "So and so was doing this. So and so wasn't, and I was promised this, and this was taken away from me. And the need to be a star, to shine, to get somewhere through the show. This was their chance and there was such a desperation on the part of several people. I wasn't feeling any of that. I wanted to get nowhere from this show.

"It was a joy for me. I'm the kind of performer who loves the rehearsal more than the performance. And that rehearsal period was incredible."

Don Percassi, who had already been in *High Spirits, Walking Happy, Mack and Mabel, Sugar, Molly, Lolita My Love, Love Match,* and *Hot September,* was another lucky one who never went through any of the traumas. "The experience was a good one for me. I was coming from years of doing shows. It was just another show. I never expected anything out of it. I never expected to be made a star. I just expected to work and I expected it to run. God knows I was getting older and I couldn't be choosy. *Ha! Ha! Ha! Ha!* I could be choosy but I'm trying to say that it was a nice little step up from a chorus part.

"I let stuff pass over me which I might have taken seriously. Like Michael screaming and stuff. 'Cause if I had to take that stuff seriously I'd probably be out of the business. I'd probably be crying somewhere in some hotel room. But Gower [Champion] screamed at me. Gower screamed at me all the time. There's always a victim, right? Don't be the victim. Michael used to scream and yell at me and make fun of me and everything. He used to holler at me all the time.

"I could only do what I could do. Like I said, I came used to being battered around for many years because of my personality. Michael had not discovered anything new. *Ha! Ha! Ha! Ha!* He used to pick on me terribly, really yell at me and scream, but I'd had people yelling and screaming at me for twenty years before I got there. Jerry [Robbins] used to throw things at me. I think it's because I'm too crazy. Like I got caught in the curtain one night. Before we had the *periaktoi* we just had mirrors and they would draw the curtain across the back of the stage. Well, I walked back too far and then the curtains came and covered me up and I thought I died. I said, 'I have died onstage.' And Baayork had to crawl onstage on her hands and knees and look for my feet so she could drag me off from underneath the curtain. So she came, and she went underneath the curtain, and she and Ron Kuhlman, they're pulling me out and I'm in tears. I thought I died. I said,

'This is death here. I have died and I have gone to theater heaven.'
I didn't know where I was.

"I don't do it on purpose. I don't see too good very quickly
when they change from dark to light. That's why Michael used to
get mad at me all the time. I was always bumping into walls, and
he told me once he was gonna fire me unless I got contact lenses.
My sight thing always was a problem. Once I got into the black I
didn't know where the hell I was. It takes a few minutes. That's
why I got this scar here, from smashing into something when I
couldn't see the light change. I got thrown against a brick wall
one night. I was on the end of the line in the finale and we had
the speed thing around—the grapevine circle—and they let go of
me and I went right up against the brick wall. I went down just
like in the movies and I just crawled offstage, 'cause I couldn't see
anything."

The rehearsal period, which now included eight preview performances a week, continued. Michael was tightening the show.
Early previews sometimes resembled a French farce, with actors
entering and leaving the stage too often. Michael reduced this to
one unobtrusive exit for Priscilla's song about her high school
acting class, and a realistic rest period for the dancers during
Donna's number and Sammy's monologue. This left all the dancers
onstage for the majority of the show, which made for a more
unified dramatic impression.

Next, Michael placed the second Zach/Cassie confrontation
downstage in front of the dancers as they continued to practice
the "One" chorus, then blended the two together. Ron Kuhlman
recalls a rehearsal after they had done the first preview: "We were
rehearsing and changing and changing and changing. It was the
scene where Cassie and Zach were in front of the whole group as
we were saying 'Left, right, left, right,' and they say, 'You left. I
didn't leave. You left.' And he said, 'Okay, now, say it now,' and I
thought, 'Oh God, that's great.' I guess it affected me so much
because I was just back there kind of listening, wondering what he
was going to do with this, and when he did, I thought, 'Oh, that's
brilliant.' A lot of things like that happened in the course of the
show."

With less than two weeks to go before opening, Michael

· 135

pointed out to Marvin Hamlisch and Ed Kleban that the song "Tits and Ass" wasn't getting nearly the laughs it ought to, and if nothing happened soon, he would cut it and ask for another one. Hamlisch and Kleban, who had been entering the theater through the stage door, decided to enter with the audience for the next performance, in the hope that this would give them a new perspective on the problem. They read the program for the first time and noticed that by calling the number "Tits and Ass" they gave away the principal joke in advance. The program was changed. Ever since, the song has been called "Dance: Ten; Looks: Three" —and the audience laughs aloud when it hears the lyrics.

For months a proper ending for Cassie had eluded them. With Cassie grabbing her dance bag and leaving in the middle of the audition, too much of the show was over. "The audience got the feeling that I was going to go home and kill myself. Put my head in the oven. So we couldn't leave it that way." In the next version, she stayed to the final elimination but did not get the job. "We were standing in line and he didn't give it to me and I left. I did that for a week and it was just horrible. I leave and everybody's a loser. I'm a loser, he's a loser—everybody ends up being a loser."

Michael resisted giving Cassie the job because he knew that in Zach's position, he wouldn't. Michael said to Donna: "Quite honestly, in a real situation I would not hire you. I couldn't handle it."

Marsha Mason, the stage and film actress then married to Neil Simon, campaigned for Cassie to get the job. She had been studying the through-line for Cassie and knew that nothing else would work. She felt that the audience, as well as those younger dancers who might be in the same position one day, all needed to believe they could go home again. The change was made and Cassie got the job in the final scene. Michael and Donna were satisfied they had deviated from the truth for a good cause. Donna was especially happy. She felt strongly that "you have the responsibility to give people hope if you're gonna do theater."

As the musical took final shape, preview audiences responded with standing ovations, and favorable opinion spread rapidly by word of mouth. Backstage there was a sense of "I don't know what this is going to be, but it's not going to be just another show."

Everybody was on a high. Even in previews, the show was the hottest ticket in town. Bernie Gersten was the ambassador of *A Chorus Line* and its biggest promoter. There were baskets of fruit and champagne. Every weekend was a party, and celebrities came backstage every night. Groucho Marx came back twice and on opening night sent a cake with a toy duck sitting on it. Decorating the cake was a leg with a hammer tied around it—"Break a leg." Diana Ross, unable to get a ticket at the last minute, was willing to sit on the aisle steps. Ingrid Bergman came, Ann-Margret came, and Katherine Hepburn came. Crissy Wilzak had always admired Hepburn and was the first one out of the dressing room after the performance the night she was there. Hepburn was standing in the greenroom alone with Michael, and he said, "Katherine Hepburn, I'd like you to meet Crissy Wilzak."

Crissy was suddenly thrilled, standing for a moment in unabashed adoration. She carried her happiness for days and days.

Then, on May 21, 1975, the show held its official off-Broadway opening. Nobody could have predicted the magnitude with which the show would hit. The press gave it unanimous raves.

In *Variety*, Hobe wrote:

> The problem is to find superlatives to convey something of the enjoyment and excitement of *A Chorus Line*. . . . It is one of the best musicals in recent years. . . . The musical has just about everything. The basic idea is original, the story is engrossing, funny and frequently touching, and the characters are identifiable, colorful and unpretentiously gallant. There is spectacular dancing, enjoyable music, lively pace, brilliant scenery, costumes and lighting, plus a finale that brought the consistently responsive opening night audience to its feet, cheering. . . . *A Chorus Line* is not merely the best New York show of the season, but the best in many seasons.

The Village Voice review stated: "Bennett's devotion to the myth of Broadway has enabled him to sculpt possibly the most effective Broadway musical since *Gypsy*. . . . *A Chorus Line* is the best commerical musical in years."

The Christian Science Monitor said: "*A Chorus Line* would be superior entertainment in any season: original, full of style and flair, at times quite breathtaking and essentially very touching . . . genuine show business, with verve, sentimentality (and passing vulgarity)."

Martin Gottfried in the *New York Post* wrote:

> . . . a dazzling show: driving, compassionate and finally thrilling. It is a major event in the development of the American musical theater. . . . The show is a pyrotechnical exercise in theater choreography. . . . Bennett's work as director and dance master is simply awesome, doubtless helped by his assistant Bob Avian. . . . At a time when producers are taking choruses out of their musicals for the sake of economy, director Michael Bennett has taken everything else out.

And Clive Barnes in *The New York Times* wrote:

> The conservative word for *A Chorus Line* might be tremendous, or perhaps terrific. . . . From opening to the stupendous closing chorus . . . his choreography and direction burn up superlatives as if they were inflammable. . . . It is a show that must dance, jog and whirl its way into the history of the musical theater. . . . The reception was so shattering that it is surprising if by the time you read this, the New York Shakespeare Festival has got a Newman Theater still standing in its Public Theater complex on Lafayette Street.

Eerily prophetic, *The Village Voice* also said: "*A Chorus Line* is, in effect, the last Broadway musical."

Never in the history of the theater had an off-Broadway show garnered such praise and attention. Over the next month the cast was featured in every major magazine, and in December Donna made the cover of *Newsweek*. The impact on the cast was enormous.

For the rest of the summer the dancers continued to play the show to accolades. The stories that had been told in the privacy of a rehearsal room so long ago now became a matter of public record.

For Donna McKechnie, the whole feeling of the show every

night was enriching because of the autobiographical material. When her mother saw the show, Donna warned her in advance: "We all told things about our lives. You might hear something you recognize here and there." But Donna's mother was "pleased and proud," Donna says. "I think the recognition I received was more important than what I revealed in terms of her personal life." Her father also came to see the show at the Public Theater and afterward couldn't find words to express how he felt. Then, one week before she appeared as Cassie on the cover of *Newsweek* magazine, he died. "My first thought when I saw the cover . . ." Donna said. "Well, it kind of took the oomph out of it. I was very unresolved about my dad. I had a hard time communicating with him, reaching him, as he did with me, but I was so eager to please him that I thought, 'This is what I'd like him to see.' I was still looking for validation from him, because he never liked the fact that I was in show business. He had a lot of contempt for it."

Kelly Bishop's mother also came to see the show, all excited about "my daughter on Broadway." Kelly took her aside beforehand and said, "Now you have to understand, it's very theatricalized."

"I knew that she'd know the stories," Kelly recalls. "I mean, we were there together. But I wanted her to understand that I didn't hate her. I was a little concerned. By then my father had died."

Sammy's monologue was so powerful that Michael did not want Nick Dante's parents to see the show until after it had opened. He feared they might have a negative reaction to seeing their son's story exposed, and this might upset Dante. When Dante's parents did come, they were pleased with their son's success, and pleased, too, with the actor chosen to portray him. Sammy and Nick even bore some physical resemblance to each other.

The monologue ends with the boy's father calling him "son" for the first time. Three years after the show opened, Nick Dante realized more about that scene than he had known at the moment. "That was not the first time my father called me his son. My father used to introduce me as his son all the time. I never *heard* it. That was the first time I ever heard it."

Dancers came to see the show about their lives. For some who had participated in the early meetings and workshops, but who did not end up doing the musical, it was their lives in a literal sense. Tony Stevens and Michon Peacock, Chris Chadman and Candy Brown were all working on the new musical *Chicago*. They all wondered if they had made the right decision.

During the out-of-town tryouts of *Chicago*, Michon was on the phone to Nick Dante every night. " 'Well, what happened tonight? Cassie *didn't* get the job tonight? When are they gonna decide?' I knew exactly what was going on. My heart was there the whole time, and here I was working on *Chicago*, this black, dark thing, somewhere else."

When they came back into town, Chris Chadman remembers how *Chorus Line* was on everybody's lips. "All we kept hearing was '*Chorus Line, Chorus Line, Chorus Line.* Everybody's gonna be a star!' I was getting very nervous. Sammy Williams is gonna be a big star? Sammy Williams and I were in the chorus of *Applause* together. I always had this image that I knew how to do it. I felt that I was more conscientious than most of the dancers around me and I would be one of the first to make it, and I'm hearing about all these other people who had these big parts in *Chorus Line* and I'm dying. Sammy Williams! I mean, I used to give him lectures on how to pull his life together, and now he's got a starring role in a show and I'm in the chorus again!

"So we came back into town and we were rehearsing at the Lunt-Fontanne. I remember all the producers of *Chicago* were *very* nervous about this show called *A Chorus Line*. The producers felt competition because it was money, and I remember everyone, *everyone* was talking about it."

As soon as the cast of *Chicago* had a night off, they all ran to see *A Chorus Line*.

For Michon, who with Tony had launched the whole process: "It was wonderful. It exceeded anybody's idea of what it could be or what it should be or how it could be received. Even me. Anybody could relate to that show. That, I had never dreamed would happen. Since that happened I figure I could die now, that I'd accomplished my mission in life. Absolutely. If nothing else ever happens, that's great. To have been able to have been in the right place at the right time to be the instrument for the cause for the whole thing to get moving. What better thing can you ask for?"

Chris and Candy went down to the Public Theater and stood

in line for cancellations. They got two seats in the second row.

Chris was enjoying himself, hearing stories he had told from his own childhood at the original meeting. He remembers thinking, "Oh, I was really blown away. I couldn't believe it. What I said, it's in the show. That's what really shocked me, that it's in the show. Priscilla's story I remember because that became a song. I went, 'Oh, my God! That's the story she told. They put it to music.' "

Candy and Chris were clutching each other. "It was so incredible," Candy recalls. "And then to hear little things that we knew we had said just kinda crop up. Like somebody had my birthday, and somebody else made one of my little wisecracks."

Chris almost jumped out of his seat when a dancer sang about his father taking his mother to Roseland, then coming home with her shoes in her hand. It was something he had said at the meeting.

Chris recalled various of the show's lines and ideas from the tape sessions and from everybody that he knew. But running through his mind throughout the show was another theme: "How come I'm not up there?"

"So the show is over and, oh, I was just hysterical. I couldn't move and I was crying and, oh, it was just awful. I remember Tommy Tune was behind me and there must've been about half a dozen different people who were very, very much connected to the subject matter. Other dancers or choreographers, or people who really had an emotional attachment to the show, were sitting around us and when everybody left the theater we were still sitting there. We just couldn't move. I didn't know what to do. So we went backstage and I managed to put on a phony smile and congratulate everyone. I mean, I did want to congratulate them. Very few times am I totally astounded by anything. And I was really astounded by the show. I really couldn't believe what I had just seen. It was too good."

Others from the original tape session came to see the show.

Andy Bew: "Blew me away. Everything about it. Because it brought back things that were said that night."

Denise Pence Boockvor: "When I saw my husband's character finishing his wife's sentences I went, 'Do we do that?' I had no idea that was what Michael picked up about us."

Jacki Garland, whose sister was in the company: "All of a sudden I lost my identity. It was really a difficult time for me. I never felt in her shadow before—she had felt it."

Tony Stevens: "People ask me about regrets. Even though I was part of the impetus, I was the midwife. *A Chorus Line* is Michael's. His input and his life and his creativity. He took what we were and made something of it, which is what art is. It's just fabulous and he's the only one who could have done it. I couldn't have done that. He was meant to do it."

The Newman is a cozy one-level theater built on an even rake, giving every audience member a clear, close view of the stage. It was where the show had been born. Backstage, the entire company dressed together. There was a strong ensemble feeling among members of the cast, as well as a rare feeling for the small downtown theater, the embryonic place where it all had come together.

The entire cast received rave reviews, but the critics and the media tended to pay more attention to the larger roles. Though Donna had experienced personal success in the past, the others had not. Suddenly an emotionally charged, explosive situation had a catalyst. As excitement over their success began to grow, so did their egos.

Then the question of money arose. The project that everyone had given to so equally looked as if it would move uptown to Broadway, where the gross revenues of the musical would increase dramatically. Would they share in the show's financial bonanza?

Michael and Nick Dante took one half of one percent of the gross weekly box office income, as well as a prorated share of subsidiary rights, all from their own writers' royalties, and assigned it to the dancers in a complicated formula administered by the accounting firm of Lutz & Carr. Three groups were established —A, B, and C—and each dancer was assigned to one depending on the extent of his or her contribution. Dancers who attended the meetings from which the material was drawn were assigned to the A and B groups. Those whose stories became whole songs, monologues, or characters were in the A group, and those with only peripheral contributions were placed in the B group. The A group received two shares for each one the B group was assigned, and consequently received twice the amount of money. These dancers were not necessarily in the original cast. Candy Brown, for example, dropped out after the first workshop and will never do the show because her story was ultimately assigned to a male role, yet she received A-group shares for the "Gimme the Ball" Richie character.

Members of the original cast who did not attend the meetings or provide information that became part of the script received a share—as the C group—only for as long as they performed in the show. When they left they were eliminated from the formula and everyone else's share increased. An example was Ron Dennis, a member of the second workshop and original cast whose personality shaped Richie but whose story was Candy's. He lost the extra income when he left the company. Although he begrudged no one else the money, over the years he has grown frustrated with a formula that has deprived him of royalty checks many of the other dancers continue to receive.

Michon, who as one of the instigators of the original meetings received A-group income, was "knocked out by Michael's gesture of allowing all these people to participate in the show's financial success. He didn't have to do that." Yet, she found, "The surprising thing was the smallness of the inflated egos of the people who were trying to obstruct that and get more out of it."

The show was receiving the highest compliment the theater had to offer. People came out of the woodwork to jump on board. Michael was sued by writer James Lipton and composer Cy Coleman over the original idea for the show. It was their claim that in discussing a possible musical with Michael some years earlier—an idea that revolved around group therapy—they had given him the basis for *A Chorus Line*. That suit was settled out of court. Eight years later, in 1983, another lawsuit was filed against the authors by an actor claiming to have sent Joe Papp material which became the substance of *A Chorus Line*. But the suit never went anywhere. It is quite safe to say that not one note of music, not one lyric or piece of dialogue, not even the basic conceptual approach of *A Chorus Line* came from outside the process or from anyone who had not participated.

With the exception of the title. *A Chorus Line* had been the original working title of *Twigs*, the George Furth play Michael had directed. He asked Furth if he could have the never-used title, and Furth gave it to him, gratis. Years later Furth, John Kander and Fred Ebb, Cy Feuer, Liza Minnelli, and the Shubert Organization were struggling with a new musical called *The Act* (which had evolved out of a one-woman musical Furth and Marvin Hamlisch had discussed with Michael prior to *A Chorus Line*). Michael saw *The Act* in San Francisco and spent some hours in a hotel room sketching out for them his criticisms of the musical and how to approach fixing it. Michael always remembered his contribution as a way of saying "thanks for the title" to Furth. Others who were there remember his delivery as a stream-of-consciousness tirade that came too late.

In the meantime the show was still downtown, playing in a non-profit theater where, because of the disparity between the show's cost and reduced ticket prices, it was losing money each week. A move was inevitable.

It hardly came as a surprise. The manner in which the show was being put together, with a twenty-piece orchestra and a cast of twenty-four, made it clear that Michael, a Broadway Baby if ever there was one, had his eye on a Broadway run. Kelly Bishop felt all along that Michael was calling the shots. "We would talk on the phone and he would tell me things about how much bigger it was going to get and how much more popular it was going to get and what was going to happen, and I'd say, 'Michael, it's big enough already. This is not going to happen.' And sure enough, within a month it had happened. I mean, every single thing along the way."

Many members of the theatrical community were against the move uptown. They felt the show was too special. There was concern that a large theater would overwhelm the dramatic work, and general audiences would not be interested in the subject matter. However, there was no point in continuing to subsidize the musical downtown. There was also the Shubert Organization, in the form of its chief operating officers, Bernard Jacobs and Gerald Schoenfeld. These men loved the theater second only to loving to see their theaters filled. They offered their flagship house, the Shubert Theater, to *A Chorus Line*, and plans were made to move the musical uptown that summer.

The cast was tired from the marathon rehearsals and had been running on reserve energy for months. Before the move uptown, they all got a week off. More even than the opening on Broadway, they needed the holiday, needed to pull themselves together.

In moving the show uptown, Michael had work to do. The sets and lights all had to be brought up and rehung and focused. The orchestra was placed in the traditional pit, but in order to maintain the stark drama of the original, the orchestra pit was covered with black cloth. No one would see them, and no one would hear them unamplified. The sound would be piped through the speakers as before, but this time the electronic sound system would have to project to almost four times as many people in a large, high space, including two balconies.

Over the preceding years the quality of live music on Broadway had altered. More of it was coming to the listeners filtered through microphones and amplifiers, and A Chorus Line represented another big step in that direction.* As audiences have become more and more preconditioned by recordings, film, and television, they have come to expect the kind of sound that is delivered electronically, and Broadway has acquiesced. Although in his book Broadway Musicals, theater critic Martin Gottfried reported that parts of A Chorus Line were prerecorded and the actors lip-synced to the tapes, nothing of the kind took place. Every voice and instrument was live.

The smaller voices of singers like Priscilla Lopez were delivered through a system that compensated for any weakness in an impressive way. Singers like Kay Cole, with strong theater voices, were not hurt by the microphones. An ordinary audience member could detect no distortion. With the engineer taking the sound and redistributing it for correct balance, the orchestra gained the ability to underscore spoken dialogue, play loudly over lyrics, and utilize brassier instrumentation. What they lost was the spontaneity and timbre that is the sound of the concert hall.

Michael based his decision partly on the orchestrations, which sounded better when electronically mixed before reaching the

---

*That practice actually began in earnest with Promises, Promises, because the score, by Burt Bacharach, was not really a theater score but a pop score. Bacharach had worked only in a recording studio, and attempted to duplicate the sound to which he was accustomed when the show moved into the theater.

audience. But Michael was also very anxious to protect the intimacy of the show and to carry through his notion that it was not a traditional musical comedy. He didn't want to remind the audience that there was an orchestra. To that end he also decided against an overture, and even refused to allow the musicians to warm up in the pit. The audience would never hear the familiar scales and tuning up that warn of an impending musical comedy.

He also insisted on complete blackness prior to the opening number. No musician stand lights were visible, because of the black roof on the pit, and even the exit lights in the theater were turned off during the opening sequence. The unusually severe darkness was an effective way to obtain full attention right at the start. And as Michael Bennett would later say, "Out of the darkness comes *A Chorus Line*."

The New York Shakespeare Festival had received only a small royalty from the financial windfall that was *Hair*, and the directors of the non-profit Festival had no intention of letting that happen again. The production was transferred with funds contributed to the Festival by donors ranging from Mrs. LuEsther Mertz, who had always been a staunch financial backer of the Public Theater, to the Shubert Organization, who could always use a good tenant in one of their theaters. This way, all the proceeds that were not paid out in expenses for the show would be returned to the Shakespeare Festival to help fund future projects.

After their week-long break, the company reassembled in the late summer. Twenty-one months had passed since that first midnight dance class on the Lower East Side. These gypsy dancers had covered an enormous distance in their move uptown to Shubert Alley. But in a very real sense, they were home at last.

CHAPTER X
· · · · · · · · · · · · · · · · · ·
Broadway

A *Chorus Line* had its first Broadway performance on July 25, 1975. With unprecedented advance publicity, preview performances sold out. By the early fall, when the Broadway season traditionally gets under way, the musical was already roaring along.

In those days Broadway theatergoers could choose from an array of successful musicals: *Candide* at the Broadway Theatre, *Chicago* at the 46th Street, *Grease* at the Royale, a return engagement of Pearl Bailey's company in *Hello, Dolly!* at the Minskoff, Linda Hopkins singing Bessie Smith at the Edison, *Pippin* at the Imperial, *Raisin* at the Lunt-Fontanne, *Shenandoah* at the Alvin, *The Magic Show* at the Cort, *The Wiz* at the Majestic, and Scott Joplin's ragtime opera *Treemonisha* at the Uris.

By this time the media had already touted the show and the advance sale was mounting. At a top price of $15, tickets were extremely hard to get. House seats, tightly controlled by the producers, were available directly from the Shakespeare Festival. For a tax deductible donation to the Festival of $50—$150 on a Saturday night—the show could be seen without waiting.

After two and a half months of sold-out uptown previews, *A Chorus Line* had its official critics' Broadway opening at the Shubert Theatre on October 19. (The original date had been set for September 28 but, due to a musicians' strike, was postponed for three weeks.) The opening was arranged to coincide with an Actors Fund benefit performance.

The Actors Fund is the oldest theatrical charity in the country, and provides assistance to anyone working in any capacity in the entertainment industry. It raises money through select benefit performances, whose audiences are comprised primarily of theater insiders, those people who can be counted on to applaud wildly if Lauren Bacall reaches for a high note and hits anything at all. Most of the opening night audience had already seen the show downtown and loved it. Michael Bennett and Joseph Papp were really stacking the deck.

Still, it was opening night on Broadway. The ultimate test. The dancers warmed up, dressed, and took their places in the wings. At the call of "Hit it" they swarmed onto the stage in the dark and waited for the familiar piano chords. A blaze of light struck the stage, and they danced.

Those in the audience that night did more than applaud. More even than stand and scream. That evening the theater community took an extraordinary new musical into its heart.

"After we finished each number," Don Percassi remembers, "the warmth, the love, just came over the stage like a wave. You could feel it come and feel it go. It was unbelievable. It was metaphysical almost. You didn't hear the applause—warmth just enveloped. Everybody was sort of connected for an instant. God, it was fantastic."

After they sang "What I Did for Love," each dancer stepped back into the line for the final elimination. As they did, each one received applause.

As they performed their final kick line, the response was deafening.

Twenty-seven gypsies had arrived on Broadway that night. They felt it, and the audience felt it.

Critically, the show was again met with raves. The city reviewers and then the national media, important for the show's future, wrote glowing reviews. Photographs of the show appeared everywhere. Advance ticket sales skyrocketed and now that the show was situated in a large commercial theater, both the Shakespeare Festival and Plum Productions, Michael's own corporate umbrella, started counting the profits. These included a $5.5 million sale of the film rights to MCA-Universal, the largest sale of stage material to date (though, when adjusted for inflation, less than had been paid for *My Fair Lady* in 1956).

Although the response to *A Chorus Line* may seem typical of a Broadway musical hit—at one time an annual event—it was anything but. Fewer than a dozen musicals in the twentieth century have succeeded to the degree that *A Chorus Line* has.

Michael Serrecchia attributed part of the show's success to timing. "Dance was just starting to come to public awareness and it was very timely and it was very catchy and it was very, very flashy without being glitzy and it was true and heartfelt and it was all the things that make theater wonderful."

Original-cast albums are traditionally made and released as soon after a Broadway opening as possible. The *Chorus Line* album was an important one, because there was the opportunity to go beyond the small circle of Broadway show collectors to sell to the general public. Columbia Records' musical theater specialist Goddard Lieberson, who had produced many of the great original cast albums, came out of retirement to produce it.

Half of the show's nearly two hours of music had to be eliminated for the album. Dance music and reprises usually are. "The Montage" alone ran thirty minutes. But there was room enough for the show's ten major songs.

When the company arrived at the recording studio, Hamlisch approached Ron Dennis.

"Ah, I think we're gonna cut 'Gimme the Ball' from the album, because you say 'shit,' " he said.

"Well," Dennis reacted, "he may as well have told me I was Snow White! I got furious. Pam Blair had been sitting there all morning recording 'Tits and Ass' and I can't say 'shit'? I didn't buy that. I went to Michael."

" 'What's this? What is this?' "

" 'Don't worry about it—the song is gonna be there.' "

Ron Dennis speculated that Hamlisch wasn't totally behind the song because Ron believed Michael Bennett had written most of it, not Hamlisch. "I don't know what went down, but I'm glad I stuck up for myself."

The dancers began to get feedback from members of the audience. Not just applause, but outside the stage door, on the street, and in fan mail. The show had touched a chord in many lives, and people took the time to let the cast know it. The dancers were moved by the enormous number of letters they received. People wrote about how they loved the show, but also about how it had opened a window to their own lives. Young homosexual men wrote in, finding their counterparts in the cast the only ones to whom they could confide their secret. Other letters were accounts of those who had faced rejection, who had suffered unhappy childhoods and broken homes.

The cumulative response to their efforts was monumental, yet just when the dancers should have been sitting back and enjoying their success, just when they might have rested on the joy of good work, might have gone to the theater night after night to perform in a musical that is a pure joy to do, everything changed. When the show moved uptown it lost more than the intimacy shared by all the dancers making up in a single dressing room, more than the camaraderie of a community effort. For better or worse (and unfortunately for most of the dancers it was for worse), it lost its innocence.

Don Percassi watched it change. "It became a Broadway show. It became a different show. It became a commercial show. There's one thing Michael taught me. He said, 'It's show *business*, not *show* business.' "

After the show became such a big hit, understudy Brandt Edwards watched everything "get sort of crazy. The success does it, I think. The thing I hated to see was the separate dressing rooms."

Downtown the dancers had all dressed together in two large rooms. At the Shubert, all the understudies were in the basement and everyone else was on one floor or another upstairs.

Scott Allen, an understudy, felt that "there was a haughtiness to what was going on." Consequently the understudies formed their own little clique, calling themselves the "West Side Five." (The fifth was John Mineo, a longtime Broadway dancer, added as an understudy just prior to the move uptown to cover the opening and several roles.) "We started our own little faction downstairs," Scott recalls, "and we had parties every weekend and we continued in the tradition we started downtown. We always invited everybody but soon they stopped coming. One or two people would come in from time to time and have champagne. Everybody sort of got a little colder. I don't know if *colder* is the right word, but when we hit Broadway, things changed."

For Michael Serrechia: "The change was the most disheartening experience of my life. It moved from a creative artistic gem off-Broadway to a multimillion-dollar moneymaking machine on Broadway."

A split opened not only between the understudies in the Shubert basement and the line overhead, but among all the principals, and between cast and management as well.

Money was the beginning of it. Each performer had originally been paid $100 per week under a workshop agreement with Actors' Equity Association. When they began performing, they became "favored nations," under a special contract that guarantees everyone the same salary. Then a story circulated that Donna was being paid more under the table, out of Michael's own pocket. In sight of financial success, salaries became a contentious issue. Rick Mason said, "That was a big problem for Pam and Priscilla. We were downtown at the studio and I think Pam's agent had heard through Donna's agent that she was getting more money than anyone else and Priscilla pursued it. Priscilla was our spokeswoman. [And the company's union deputy.] Somehow Michael heard. We had a big showdown where we were all sent into the anteroom and *told* not to worry about who gets paid what. He said it was not true. I don't think Donna was in the room at that point. It was all very fishy."

In fact, at the time of that meeting Donna was not getting additional money; she was receiving the same as all others under the "favored nations" agreement.

Downtown at dinner one night, Michael had acknowledged Donna's efforts on behalf of the show and told her: "I know it's not fair. I know you should be getting more." He offered to give her a sum of money out of his own pocket if she ever needed it. But Donna wanted to earn the money, not merely borrow it. That night Michael promised her a substantial increase when the show moved uptown.

Now, after three months on Broadway, the increase had not been forthcoming. Donna, run-down from eight shows a week and publicity events, got a cold. It stretched for a week and Avian telephoned her to find out when they could expect her to return. "I don't know," she said, and the conversation turned to how hard she had been expected to work, and that she was unhappy.

Though no amount of money was ever mentioned, Michael increased her salary to $3,000 a week, which she received when she returned. Unavoidably, the other dancers heard about the new arrangement.

"Michael was trying to be covert about this," she explained. "It's not that he didn't think that people would find out eventually, but he was trying to do what was fair. It wasn't fair for me to get the same as everybody else. They forgot that I had done other shows. I had a credibility and a stature."

At that time other stars of Broadway musicals got larger salaries and percentages that amounted to well over $10,000 a week. Although Donna did not complain about the experience and has no bitter feelings, from then on she decided to do business only through her agents.

Another performer in the show went through a similar ordeal, but the promise of more money was never kept. Michael's position was "You should have got it in writing."

Other jealousies stemmed from the fact that after the show had been frozen, some dancers came out with larger roles than others. Michael was creating a show and there could not be seventeen leading characters. The situation reminded Carole Schweid of something she had read in a book on the Mouseketeers. "They were all jealous of Annette, but Annette was jealous of Darlene."

One day a company spokesperson called everyone downstairs to sign a release for the logo. Everyone signed and each was handed a little balloon with the logo on it: seventeen dancers on line. A week later Bloomingdale's put towels and various paraphernalia on sale displaying the logo featuring the seventeen dancers, and it suddenly dawned on them that they had no financial participation. They said, "We're getting a lawyer."

Management said, "Go ahead, get a lawyer."

Some members of the cast were very angry when they realized that money was being made. They knew that Bloomingdale's was getting a cut, the Shakespeare Festival was getting a cut, and they were sure that Michael was getting his cut. They had only wanted to do the show and would have agreed to anything. Now they felt management had taken advantage of them.

If Michael had walked away and let the cast down, he still asked a lot of them. A photo session was planned with Richard

Avedon, one of New York's most famous photographers. The call was announced with less than the twenty-four-hour notice the union requires. As Equity deputy, Priscilla told the company that they didn't have to do it if they didn't want to. Michael came in and pulled Priscilla into another room. When they returned, he lectured the company severely, threatening each of them with the consequences if they didn't appear at the photo shoot.

At another point their permission was requested for the use of a photograph of the line that would appear on the cover of an André Kostelanetz album, one side of which would be *Chicago* and the other *A Chorus Line*. They were being offered $50 apiece. By this time they were anxious to obtain more of what they saw as the riches of the show. They got together and demanded $500 apiece instead. The offer evaporated.

It must have been difficult, given the original community feeling, to read in *Variety* that Michael was earning $75,000 a week once the touring companies opened—a figure that did not include subsidiary rights. Though *Variety* has a reputation for overquoting grosses, it was not hard to figure that Bennett, Avian, Hamlisch, Kleban, Dante, and Kirkwood personally would be millionaires. In fact, Michael quickly became a multimillionaire. The cast's income seemed to them miniscule by comparison.

However, there was nothing unusual in the arrangements made for those contributing the basic material—the dancers' stories. The raw material for a musical, whether from a play, film, novel, or short story, is traditionally worth one half of one percent to two percent of the gross weekly box office receipts and a proportionate share of subsidiary rights. Under normal circumstances those proceeds usually fall to one author, or two at the most. In the case of *A Chorus Line* they were divided into parts to be shared by all the dancers. If some were unhappy with the formula for that division, it was unfortunate. Michael had done his best to work out a complex program of residuals. As for the uptown salaries, they were, at approximately $650 a week, double the union minimum at the time and a good deal more than any of the dancers had ever earned as members of a chorus.

A feeling of betrayal enveloped the company. But this was not merely because of financial circumstances. There was a far larger problem. Many of the cast members were reacting violently to their sudden good fortune.

They were all dealing with instant stardom, with people trying to jump on the bandwagon. They were wined and dined; they were an instant, overnight success. The pressure mounted on the little band of anonymous dancers. Many overreacted, thinking they were going to become stars.

They were the toast of the town and basking in it. Nancy Lane admits, "I blew so much money. I was so crazy. We got such good paychecks. We were like the highest-paid dancers on Broadway and it was wonderful, because I could do everything I ever wanted to do. Go to nightclubs. This little *pisher* going to nightclubs in evening gowns and furs. I bought jewelry. I didn't save *anything*."

Chuck Cissel talks about something else he observed: "People were taking Valium and a couple of people were smoking grass, and I used to say, 'Listen, guys, you better be able to handle pressure a little better than that.' I mean, really, it's not that heavy when you think about it. You're onstage with a group of people. You aren't alone."

Pressure brought out some dancers' nerves. "Pam Blair would be in the wings going, 'Oh, I can't sing,' " Cissel recalls. " 'I won't be able to hit that note. I'm just not going to be able to make it.' And she'd kick and go, 'Oh, my leg. I'm not warmed up.' And they'd say 'Curtain!' and she'd say, 'I'm not ready. I just can't go on.' I'd snatch her and say, 'Do all this shit downstairs. Don't bring that up on this stage, Pam. This is boring.' "

Others in the cast saw Pam's behavior as simple preparation. Donna says, "It was Pam's way of warming up. She needed to lose her anxiety, needed to do that as an actor." Pam's character, the wise-cracking, foul-mouthed, self-centered, ambitious Val—which Michael had drawn from his professional experience with her—required less nervous tension and more self-assurance than the others. But tolerance was in short supply. The understudies in particular were feeling a lot of anger and friction.

Michael had taken each of the dancers by the hand, and led them to that place where they could strip away the artifice and just express themselves. There were no actor's barriers to stand behind. No separate character or facade to shed after the performance. Michael led them there, then walked away. He now had different concerns. And it was an emotional shock to the company, who still looked to Michael as a father figure.

When the show opened, and they were dealing with the complex strain of success, Michael left them on their own. One of the dancers said it was as if Michael had led them to the top of the mountain, then pushed them off and let them fall. While Michael could no longer cope with taking care of all of them, they still needed and expected it.

Chuck Cissel saw Michael "build them all the way up and then, after the show opened, he just like opened it up and everybody fell through. I think he could've been a little more real. It's a gift the man has. You've got to understand that he's a director and he will feed you whatever you need. 'You're going to be brilliant. You're going to be fabulous. This is what I want you to do when you get out on that stage.' I saw him work every one of those people. Oh, he was cool. He was cool."

Carole Schweid says, "With the original group, everybody got so much care and help. Michael really helped people, really let them go through all their bullshit. I mean, Trish couldn't sing. She was running around the room screaming, 'I can't, I can't, I can't, I can't!' And then Michael led her to a place where she could, and she was wonderful. Well, that was his job. He really created this. That was what he was going to do, and he did it brilliantly.

"It was very intense," she recalls. "Sometimes Michael would just treat people so rudely. I remember walking into the theater with Jim Kirkwood and Nick Dante. Michael said, 'Oh, the writers are here. Hello, Nick. Hello, Jim.' I mean, I felt like: 'Mommy! Mommy! Will you look at me, please!' I felt like a little kid trying to prove myself."

Michael had created *A Chorus Line* for his dancers. He wanted to do something for the gypsies he had spent his youth among, and still revered.

Now Michael had a meeting of the entire company. They sat in the house before a performance.

"Don't make light of this," he cautioned them. "This is a once-in-a-lifetime opportunity, a show like this. Don't use it glibly. Don't treat it lightly." He went on to warn them that they were on their own now. "I am not responsible for all of you. I don't want to be the daddy. I can't be connected to every one of you any longer."

Sammy listened to the speech, then stood up and left—crossing upstage of the cast in a direct affront to Michael.

"Sam, where are you going?" Michael said.

But Sammy said he was leaving.

"If you walk, keep right on walking out of this theater!" Michael screamed.

Sammy kept walking.

But at one time Michael did want to be the daddy. He had known it was the way to obtain their trust. It was because of his relationship with each and every cast member that everyone involved was able to contribute so much and to tell the truth and to be so open. Michael made them all feel that they were in a safe place and that they could say what they wanted and do what they wanted and it would all turn out all right. And then he tried to distance himself from it. It had become too much for Michael. He could not be the daddy for three hundred chorus-liners running around the universe performing the show.

Even outsiders could see it. Candy Brown, now ensconced in *Chicago*, was almost glad she hadn't done the show. "All the shit that went on backstage. It's my feeling—I wasn't there, so I don't know—but it's my feeling that if the man at the helm has got it together, that kind of shit doesn't happen. It starts at the top and comes down. He took seventeen chorus kids and made seventeen pseudo-stars out of them. There was a lot of friction, a lot of animosity, a lot of nervous breakdowns backstage, and in a sense I'm really glad I didn't do it. We had such a wonderful camaraderie backstage at *Pippin*, and even though *Chicago* was kind of messed up—Bobby was fighting with Fred Ebb [the show's co-author and lyricist]—backstage we were having a *ball!* I shared in the percentage and I still get royalties from *A Chorus Line*. Once I got the money, I had no regrets. I hate to say that, because those kids went through agony. A lot of them are still going through it."

Within weeks of its arrival on Broadway, the show that had come from such love and community feeling was engulfed in bitterness and strife. The dancers, exhausted from six straight months of rehearsals, now found themselves at the center of a phenomenally successful show. Yet that success, swirling all around them, was personally elusive, and they began to realize that they were not going to be stars overnight. Tempers grew short, and frictions developed into unbridgeable gulfs.

The fact of the matter was that the company had virtually been *encouraged* to act like children during much of the workshop and rehearsal period. They were pushed to work straight from their emotions and *act out* until enough material had been exposed for Michael to fashion a show. They were all treated like stars. As the show took its final form, when it became a commercial success, their situation changed drastically. They now had to perform the same material consistently, had to replace the spontaneity of their performance with professional skills.

So while the show was a tremendous hit, outside of a weekly salary double what they were used to, not much of this success *really* filtered down to them. Other shows were being created without them. Hollywood lavished money and praise on Michael. The authors went off to write other projects. The dancers began to develop a strange feeling of being left behind, left to play out the same story eight times a week, week after week. Nothing in their lives seemed to have *changed*.

The irony of this was that one of Michael's original reasons for doing the show was his genuine love for dancers in general, and these dancers in particular. He wanted to give them a chance to experience the higher plateaus of success. Having arrived there, most of them could not handle it.

For a long time Nick Dante, the ex-gypsy author, didn't go to the theater, because he just could not "absorb all that crap" going on backstage any longer. For one thing, the company tended to feel that they had written the show themselves. For another, they now felt they were doing all the work for the least reward. Nick recalls one dancer saying to him: "You got it easy. We have to come and do the show eight times a week." But that is the performer's responsibility. At that time the company was being described as "seventeen screaming egomaniacs."

It was difficult for Michael to do anything right. He now had larger responsibilities than to parent the original seventeen dancers. Two brand-new companies were being formed. One, called the national company, would go to San Francisco for a sixteen weeks break-in, then to the Los Angeles Shubert Theatre for an open-end engagement. The second, called the international company, would break in for ten weeks in Toronto, then open in London. The American company would play six months on the West End and then continue their tour while English dancers took over for them. The companies would have to be expanded to approximately thirty-three dancers each, for adequate coverage in case of injuries. The companies also needed stage managers, key musicians, traveling crews, sets, costumes, lights, and five enormous trucks each. "*ACL* on Tour," as it came to be known, carried its own stage floor, extra costumes, the computer light board, hairdressers, masseurs, publicity people, and more. Michael orchestrated it all. He had become more than a director-choreographer. He had become an impresario.

At the same time, his contract with MCA-Universal called for a total of three films, including *A Chorus Line*, scheduled for 1980. Since Michael knew anything he did in Los Angeles would be scrutinized by the movie colony, it was important that he be represented by the best. He insisted the entire original company become the national and go to the West Coast, where they had already started advertisements for "The Original Broadway Cast."

But the company was no longer his to dominate. He had abdicated, and some members of the company began to assert their own identities again, separate from Michael Bennett and *A Chorus Line*. Not all were interested in going to L.A. with the show. Rick Mason had already learned that there was little personal glory in his smaller role of Mark.

"Michael kept playing with us. 'You'll be the toast of the town. You'll go to all these parties.' I knew that if I went to those friggin' parties that I would get 'Oh, I saw the show—which one are you?' The hoopla that he was telling me I was going to be getting—if I didn't get it in New York, then I wasn't going to get it out there. All those business people from L.A. came to New York to see the show because it was such a hit. If I wasn't seen by them in New York, I wasn't going to be seen by them in L.A."

Prior to *A Chorus Line*, Kelly had gone on the road with many shows, had left her husband, had moved into a new apartment, and had suffered the anxiety of being out of work. Now, to be settled on Broadway in a hit gave her a great feeling of security. She didn't want to leave town and she was afraid she would be unable to duplicate her subtle performance in the L.A. Shubert, a new theater in Century City, vast, cold, acoustically poor, and inhospitable to drama. Sheila's dialogue includes a lot of asides, a lot of quick cracks that might be lost if she had to shout them. So Kelly decided she'd at least try to negotiate for more money. "I wanted more money, and again I heard one more time that everybody was going to be 'favored nations,' and I thought, 'This has got to end.' With Donna it had, and I think we all knew that but we accepted it. I didn't suddenly want to see it happening again. So I wanted more money. The money wasn't that good. It was good, but it wasn't *that* good.

"He absolutely would not give it to me. And then he said to me: 'If I were you, I wouldn't let anybody else play Sheila in California.' And I said, 'And you shouldn't.' It stopped right there. I saw the shades go down over his eyes and I knew the conversation was over."

Kelly stayed in New York, as did Rick Mason, Thommie Walsh, Wayne Cilento, and Clive Clerk.

Michael was doing his best to keep people under control. He felt betrayed by the defections. The tables had turned. Not long ago members of the cast had felt paranoia when Michael said a distant "Good morning." Now, with the company turning against him, it was Michael who felt a growing paranoia. But Michael had the money and the position to insulate himself. He purchased a white Rolls-Royce.

And he began the most massive auditions for dancers in Broadway history. All during the show's first season on Broadway, and even before, while it was still downtown, Michael and Bob Avian and Baayork Lee auditioned dancers. They traveled to a dozen major cities, held cattle call after cattle call, and built up their files. In one sense, Michael could not allow himself to fail. He could have failed downtown, where the workshop would have been filed away as noble and then forgotten. But now Michael had gone public. His face was on the cover of the Sunday *New York Times Magazine*. He was interviewed by every periodical. The pressure that faced the cast faced him a hundredfold. It was absolutely necessary for him to duplicate that success in Toronto, London, San Francisco, Los Angeles, Chicago, Washington, Boston, Philadelphia.

As the winter progressed, dancers each day reported to theaters around the country for call backs. If they were lucky enough to get through the first audition, they were assigned potential characters and flown to New York for a more extensive audition in smaller groups, all up for the same roles. For three or four hours they would dance the jazz, ballet, and tap routines, sing a popular song, sing from the show, read from the script; be directed and read again, then talk without the script, improvising. Michael was taking no chances. He reserved the right to make up his mind slowly and carefully. An excitement spread over the whole city, or so it seemed to the dance community. Roles in the show seemed to be the chance of a lifetime.

Meanwhile the original understudies sat in the basement waiting to be asked to move up to the line. Each assumed they would be offered one of the roles they understudied. Then it became clear that Michael did not plan to use any of them in the new companies. They felt they had been lied to. "It seems to me I remember some spoken agreements, but that doesn't matter now," recalls Michael Serrecchia. "It's all blood under the bridge. We referred to that as the Blood Bath: the understudy run-through that Michael came to see in which he sat us all down and told us how incredibly inferior we all were and how we were not capable of sustaining those roles. Which is the complete opposite of what we were told during rehearsals and every time we went on. Why wonder why? You'll never know. If you're told, it doesn't necessarily make it the truth. Maybe Michael doesn't know. Frankly I don't think he does. I still spend a lot of time thinking about it myself."

Not one of them got a role in either of the new companies. They all had to go to Michael's new office and sit across the desk from him as he said, "Well, I'm not going to put you into a part because you're really not right for either of the parts, so come to California with us and have a great time."

Michael wanted all eight understudies to stay with the original company as it went to California. All refused, and all echoed the same sentiment: It seemed silly to go sit in the basement of the Shubert Theatre in California. They might as well stay in the basement of the Shubert Theatre in New York.

No one had it in his or her contract. Nobody got moved up. They felt "screwed over." They felt used.

Hard feelings continued to build. The company was approached to perform their finale during a special event at the Hilton for mayor Abraham Beame. The mayor learned "One" and Michael asked the cast to perform it with him. For Michael, it was a prestigious event. For the dancers, it looked like one more favor for which they would see little return. That afternoon at a rehearsal, the dancers talked it over among themselves. After the rehearsal, Michael announced, "Whoever's doing the show tonight, please stay. Everyone else is excused." Slowly, watching one another for who was going and who was staying, people began making exits. Some left very quickly; some hesitated.

Incredibly, most of the understudies did the benefit. From the line, only Ron Kuhlman and one or two others performed. Brandt Edwards, an understudy, explained: "We were the ones who had just been royally fucked over by not getting an advancement to the line. But I thought, 'Well, I want him to know that I care for the show and I care for him and I'm going to do this.' I even went to the big ball afterward and hung out with the mayor's people and Michael. It was a big thing for him. He was calling 'Abe' by his first name.

"I remember getting a beautiful letter from him. That's when I knew how much it meant to him. The letter proved to me how special it was for the people to support him and not slap him in the face. That's what really hurt him, I think, that his friends turned on him."

It was a time in New York when every dancer's eyes were darting around. Everyone wanted to join *A Chorus Line*, everyone auditioned, and everyone waited breathlessly to see who would get the coveted jobs.

After months of auditions, Michael chose his new casts. An entirely new company would go to London. The original .cast would go to L.A., with replacements for the five who refused to go. Those five, staying on at the Shubert on Broadway, would be joined by fourteen new dancers. All these dancers and their understudies would have to be taught the complex show. Michael chose to hold one lengthy rehearsal period, teach and direct everybody at once, so that he could put together the various companies simultaneously. Rehearsals were held in the basement of City Center, one of the few spaces in the city large enough to contain that many dancers. Preparations for touring companies had never before been held on so massive a scale. It seemed that every time Michael turned around, *A Chorus Line* was breaking ground.

The tours had been set and each of the dancers chosen had been asked to sign a special eighteen-month contract, to which Actors' Equity had agreed. Michael retained the prerogative of juggling his legion of dancers from company to company as he saw fit. Even as rehearsals began, many of them did not yet know whether they were going to stay in New York, go to London or L.A., or travel around the country for the next eighteen months.

On the first morning, nearly one hundred dancers assembled at City Center. There was great tension, excitement, and expectation, for by now they had seen the show, perhaps several times, and knew what they were joining.

Joe Papp appeared, and stepped forward to welcome the group.

"Napoleon will be arriving shortly," he announced.

CHAPTER XI

·················

City Center

The musical had never been taught to anyone before. It really had never been rehearsed, only created. Now it had to be duplicated.

Ron Kurowski, a young dancer who saw the show eight times before he auditioned and was cast in the London company to play Bobby, remembers the excitement: "We did the jazz combination the first day fifty, sixty times. That's how much energy we had. We were the people who had to be good actors, good singers, good dancers to get in. Once it became a smash, they could pick anybody they wanted. So we all wanted to show Michael—'Look! We can do everything!' "

First Michael sat the hundred dancers in a circle and congratulated them.

"Look where you've gotten," he said. "We talk about wanting to be successful in show business, but you people got the job that you wanted. Getting that must feel so great." In effect, he gave the Diana "Wow, you dance on Broadway" speech from the show's last sequence. He gave out all his love of the theater and thanked them for getting out of their homes, getting out of their cities, and not giving up.

Then he started asking questions. He would point to different dancers and ask them to talk. To almost everyone he said, "Speak up." He would say, "Are you listening to everybody else?" He gave a basic acting lesson in voice, diction, and projection; unbeknownst to the dancers, he was conducting their first exercise in listening and speaking in a natural manner.

As the rehearsals progressed, Michael's reputation oftentimes proved more a detriment than an asset. Everybody was incredibly nervous around him, wanting to make a good impression. This only managed to frustrate Michael, because every time he entered the room, the dancers would be so anxious that they couldn't relax and be themselves. He had to walk out of a lot of rehearsals. He just couldn't stay in the room.

The role of Cassie was particularly difficult to cast. Michael had never thought of anyone but Donna for the role, and he was never completely happy with the choreography for "The Music and the Mirror." It was the one thing he had thought about fixing when the show moved uptown, but had never gotten to. With Donna, the number was brilliant. Now others, less perfectly suited, even if equally talented, would have to make the number work.

Sandy Roveta had come to the city a generation earlier with strong technique and dark good looks. She met Michael in the chorus of the 1961 musical *Subways Are for Sleeping* and they grew very close. She went with him to visit his family in Buffalo. He was the brother she never had and she was the woman he could almost love.

"It was a strange relationship," she recalls. "The closest thing to—what would I call it?—an incestuous relationship. Michael had a difficult time with people. He's very difficult when someone loves him. He appears to equate love with being responsible. That means to him clutching, choking."

Then Sandy married the dancer turned choreographer turned television director Tony Mordente. They moved to California and she settled down to be his wife, working only occasionally.

Much later, when Sandy's marriage to Mordente was ending, she stopped in New York to see Michael and his new musical. She was getting a divorce, her life was falling apart, and she had no career. When she saw her old friend Donna McKechnie stand center stage and say, "I'm thirty-two, I need a job," it struck too close to home. She ran out of the theater. "I was in that exact position," she recalls. "It was exactly what was happening to me. I couldn't go back and see Donna. I couldn't go back and see anybody. Michael was out at Fire Island that weekend and I went to see him and I said, 'I'm a mess.'"

She needed a job and Michael invited her to audition for the new companies when they came to California. She gave an excellent reading. She was not acting.

Two days prior to the start of City Center rehearsals, he had still not made up his mind. He asked five women to come to rehearsals and learn the role, without knowing whether they would play it in California, London, or New York. Two would be cast and three would understudy. One of those women was Sandy Roveta. Michael called her two days before the start of rehearsals and made the offer. Sandy refused to understudy, and did not want to sign an eighteen-month contract. Still deeply disturbed over her failing marriage, and too old to start again as a chorus girl, she was eager to work but afraid and feeling vulnerable. So Michael said, "Just come to New York and work on the role and you'll know in three weeks. I won't hold you to a contract. You can go home." On those conditions she agreed. After three days of rehearsal he offered her the role of Cassie in the London company.

Once again, Michael looked to the truth of an actor's life and saw what would be useful. They were old friends and he was well aware—probably even before she saw the show and later auditioned—of her personal problems. He must have known Tony Mordente, involved as they both were in the *West Side Story* generation. When she auditioned for Michael, that audition was eerily similar to the Cassie–Zach audition scene. Here she was trying to make a comeback, propelled back to her first love, dancing, by emotional considerations, and facing a director who had known her in her prime.

And just in case she had any difficulty drawing on painful memories, Michael cast Jeannie Fraser—*the woman now in the life of Sandy's ex-husband, Mordente*—and placed her in the London company also, though he had three companies to choose from.

He said to Sandy: "Jeannie's the Maggie in that company."

"Yeah, I know," she replied.

"Do you want me to make a change?" he asked.

"No." Sandy felt it was not fair to ask. Also, she was smart enough as an actress to know that she could use it. She talked to Jeannie and said, "We can handle this between us."

"It became difficult," she recalls, "only because Tony would show up in places. So it made it very hard on me. She was a nice girl. We just kind of kept our distance.

"Michael's very smart. Michael was very clever in his casting and always has been with this show. I was that character, as Donna was. I used it. He knew. All I had to do was walk out onstage. I didn't have to go grabbing for anything."

When Sandy did walk out on the stage of the Drury Lane Theatre in London, she gave a soul-wrenching performance. Her commitment, vulnerability, and reality had a positive effect on the other actors as well.

Bob Avian asked Michael: "Does she realize what she's doing?" And Michael said, "I don't think so."

But Michael realized.

With three companies being prepared at City Center, there was an enormous amount of work to be done. Five Cassies learning the dance, four or five dancers learning every role. Dance captain Baayork Lee enlisted help, and Clive Clerk and Rick Mason came in, and sometimes others from the original company, to teach the routines. Because the show had never been taught before, it had not been codified either. Sometimes only the original dancer knew exactly what he was doing and what his traffic pattern was. It all had to be figured out, and the new dancers were sometimes frustrated waiting for the information. But the spirit was good and rising with the original company as they looked forward to Hollywood and the next step in their careers. Sometimes it even felt like the family it had been almost a year before.

Michael could work for eight hours on the opening alone. Moment to moment to moment, telling everybody what to do. He was always very specific about what he wanted. Yet the sheer volume of bodies, choreography, and music could be overwhelming. Michael and Bob would say things over and over about the show, but the large numbers of dancers, the high level of energy, made concentration difficult.

Michael explained that he had done everything he could to tell the audience that *A Chorus Line* is *not* a musical.

He had hidden the musicians, dispensed with a main curtain flying out, and used a bare stage. He was insistent that actors not be heard or seen in the wings, and staged the opening as if the audition had actually been going on for two hours before the lights came up.

He was most insistent that actors *listen* while onstage, explaining to them again and again that they did not know what was going to happen, did not know everyone around them. Only Zach, for whom they were auditioning, knew what would happen and would tell them what to do. They were expected to ignore the audience entirely, and were never allowed to push for laughs. He worked hard to get each actor to talk and behave naturally, and fought against the kind of musical-comedy performance that all the dancers were accustomed to giving.

He vigilantly policed the actors on line who were not being called on at the moment. He wanted the company to work together, to support and protect one another, and knew that if the other dancers were shuffling or fidgeting with their clothes or hair, audience focus would be misdirected. He had them intensely watching whichever actor was then speaking, thus encouraging the audience to do the same.

The important thing in the show, as always, was that everyone have his or her own personality. Now, however, this sometimes conflicted with the traditional method of passing a show on from the original cast. Michael and his assistants would say, "Okay, you have to be yourself," and when the dancers were themselves, they'd say, "Uh, well the original cast didn't exactly do it that way. That's not the way it's done."

Michael most of all wanted the actors to be simple and direct. He always said to people: "Just tell a story."

Michael also broke a cardinal rule of direction, though it is more observed in the breach than in the practice. He gave line readings. A director who gives a line reading is taking a risk. It's always done as a last resort by a good director. If he is better than the actor, he makes the actor look bad, and loses the actor's trust. If he is worse, *he* looks bad and ineffective. But the play was in a close and real sense Michael's autobiography, and if he wasn't getting what he wanted, he demonstrated.

During one rehearsal Michael got up and played everybody in the show.

Ron Kurowski says, "He does give line readings. I mean, this is a man of line readings and how do you disagree? I love when he directs by doing the role for somebody, and that's giving line readings, but what he's really giving is the compassion and the logic of the role. His eyes water up and you just fall in love with him doing Maggie or Diana. He just somehow draws you in."

As the six weeks progressed, Michael bore down. He never meant to be rude or crass, but he had no time or energy for politeness either. Once he turned a girl who was playing Bebe toward the mirror and said, "Look, you're no Raquel Welch. You can relate to that." It wasn't so much that the girl was bad-looking. She had a handsome, strong face. It was that he had seen into her soul. She *felt* that she was unattractive, had always felt that way, and was very competitive with other women. It was one of her deepest, most sensitive secrets. Many dancers close to her had hardly even seen it. He had seen it the first day. And knew when to use it. She turned back and gave the simplest, rawest, most heartfelt reading of the lyrics she had ever done. Then she ran crying into the dressing room.

A lot of people didn't like Michael. A lot of people thought he was rude. He seldom handed out compliments. He would jump on one person and not another. He stripped people, made them feel naked, and most of the dancers were ill-at-ease around him.

Sandy Roveta, who had danced through several Broadway generations, thinks that "there's a line that goes through almost every choreographer from Jerome Robbins to Michael Kidd to Bob Fosse to Michael Bennett. Sacrifice a person to get a product. To get a result."

Keeping people off balance was one of Michael's ways, never more useful than for *A Chorus Line*. On the first day, he sat the company down and asked them to open their scripts to the first page and write across it: "I – AM – AT – AN – AUDITION!" It was the one atti-tude, the one basic motivation, the overall action to be played for the entire two hours; and to maintain that thought uppermost in the actor's mind throughout the show, he would go to almost any lengths. Michael liked to fire people to keep the show alive. To keep people on their toes. Before the end of the eighteen months a number of the dancers had been fired. He loved it when people were intimidated by him. Michael purposely kept people on edge, tried to maintain his mystique, loved to get across the feeling "I'm the one. Figure me out."

But at City Center, among the dancers there was still a joy in having gotten into the show and an innocence about Michael's power. Those days of rehearsal were chaotic. Not only was there the show to learn, but two thirds of the company were preparing to leave town for a year and a half. The creators worked with one company from ten A.M. to two, with everybody from two to six, then with another company from six to ten P.M.

Those days were hectic with excitement and hard work, with the sweat of a hundred bodies dancing together. That communion— of shared physical exertion and pride in professional technique— drew the family together.

The international company became Michael's favorite. They were younger and less jaded than the original company, and had not become bitterly divided, nor had they turned against him. They were gypsies who wanted nothing more then to dance in the show they had seen and loved, for the man who had created it. Michael was the one they all did it for.

At the end of the Broadway season (which runs from September through May—a tradition established in the pre-air-conditioning days when New York playhouses closed for the summer), the Antoinette Perry, or Tony, Awards are given in eight performing and ten nonperforming categories. The performing awards go four each to straight plays and musicals, divided by male and female, leads and supporting players. The production awards go to best scenery, costumes, and lighting (not separated into plays and musicals); best director of a play; best director of a musical; best choreography for a musical; best book for a musical; best score (once separate awards for music and lyrics, now thought to be inseparable); and the best play and the best musical. Nominations for these awards are made by a committee of twelve critics. The winner is voted by approximately six hundred members of the theater community: the governing boards of Actors' Equity Association, United Scenic Artists, the Society of Stage Directors and Choreographers, and the Dramatists Guild; the membership of the League of New York Theatres and Producers; and the board of directors of the American Theatre Wing.

At the end of the 1975–76 season, *A Chorus Line* was nominated for best lighting and costume design. Donna McKechnie was nominated as a leading actress. Kelly Bishop and Priscilla

Lopez were placed in direct competition with each other in the supporting actress category. Of the men, Sammy Williams and Robert LuPone competed for best supporting actor. A special Theatre World Award had been given to the entire cast, but the Tonys were the more prestigious awards and the Sunday evening they were announced would be for the cast a splendid mix of buoyant excitement and bittersweet sadness.

On Sunday, April 20, 1976, the company literally hosted the awards. The show was televised live from the stage of the Shubert, the theater that had become their home. The cast would perform their opening number as the television show's opening, and they would close the program with their finale. In between, they would be relegated to offstage, sharing their dressing rooms with dozens of luminaries from the theater, film, and television worlds, as well as with other Broadway casts. The live audience included the community's most prestigious members, and aisle seats were assigned to the nominees.

The cast was called to the theater in the late afternoon to rehearse for the camera. Ordinarily the program, devised as it is for the stage, comes off flat and uninspired. But when Michael Bennett arrived that afternoon and his dancers took the stage, he replaced the television director and stepped into the control booth himself. He chose every camera angle for both his numbers, and dictated the cuts from one camera shot to another as the number developed. For the first time, a musical number on the television Tonys appeared as dazzling as it did onstage.

But the real excitement was generated by the anticipation of the awards. Because, by the very nature of the awards structure, the original premise of a true ensemble was under attack, those members of the cast who had been nominated were even more on edge. Although the experience drew Donna, Kelly, and Priscilla closer than ever, other company members reacted bitterly.

Understudy Michael Serrecchia watched the cast turn fiercely competitive. "My eyes were burning and my heart was crumbling and I just couldn't believe it. I remember sneaking out of the theater early during rehearsal because if I didn't, I was going to have a nervous breakdown. I walked into the first movie theater and I stayed until it was time to go back. The joy and the dream of Tony recognition were gone. It turned into ash because it wasn't worth what I saw beforehand. It was awful. It has nothing to do with what I want to do in the theater." That afternoon Michael Serrecchia vowed never to watch the Tony Awards again.

Whatever Michael Serrecchia or anyone else was feeling disappeared at eight o'clock that night, when the company took the stage for the most glorious performance of the opening number they would ever give. The Tonys began with a film, a helicopter shot of Manhattan, Broadway, Shubert Alley, then came in tight to the theater marquee proclaiming in dazzling lights A CHORUS LINE. The company took their places in the dark as a voice-over announced: "Every plane and bus and train that comes to New York brings more people who have fallen in love—stage-struck romantics who have come to try for the chance to do what they live to do . . . go out on that stage and light up the sky." The curtains rose and the Chorus Line company began "The Audition."

There was an energy onstage that every dancer felt. Suddenly everything else disappeared. The heartache, the frustration, the arguments, the unkept faith, the money, the bitterness—it was all gone. They felt exactly as the two dozen dancers had two and a half years before, at midnight in the small studio, sitting in a circle holding hands. Once again it was all focused. What their lives meant, here on this stage, facing the mirrors. The music began and they danced, barely touching the ground.

Then Zach moved downstage to begin the group jazz combination and the company turned as one to face the audience. The community that had taken those dancers to heart exploded. Every one of the dancers recalls that night vividly. Scott Allen says, "Events like that were wonderful because the energy was so good. It was then that it was at its purest."

After the opening they gathered downstairs and in the wings to watch. Allen had a TV set smaller than a pack of cigarettes. There were video monitors all over the theater but Allen's was the only TV with sound, so the understudy dressing room filled with people.

There, between numbers, Carole Schweid held up a cigarette and a man reached to help her. It was Richard Burton. "He lit my cigarette for me! I thought Baayork was going to faint! She was standing right next to me grabbing my arm. He lit a cigarette and then he put it in my mouth!" For cynical dancers who had stood behind many sweating, off-key, mean-spirited stars, there was still some royalty left in the theater.

All through the evening, they were winning. Michael won for direction, Michael and Bob for choreography, then Dante and Kirkwood for book, Hamlisch and Kleban for music and lyrics. Tharon Musser won for lighting design.

Robert LuPone had been "determined to do the best performance that I could do every night since I was nominated. At least for myself I knew that I gave it everything I had. That's all I could walk away with from that experience. I lost control when they said, 'The winner is . . .' because at that moment I thought, '*I want this award!*' And they said, 'The winner is . . . Sammy Williams,' and I went, 'Oh.' "

For Sammy, that moment was the most satisfying and exciting of the entire experience. All day people had been wishing him good luck. He began to develop the feeling that he might win after all. He had tumultuous, mixed feelings. If he won, he knew that it would be the ultimate confirmation of his success, and might lead to stardom. That was a life he had dreamed of, but which also concerned him because of the demands such a life would place on him.

When he accepted his award he thanked all the people who had helped him win. Then he went home and shut the door behind him. The next day he sat there alone with his Tony, not answering the constantly ringing phone, not knowing what to say.

Donna also won, and for her it was a very special night, because too many nights before, when the excitement rose to a fever pitch, she had gone on out of nerves and later had remembered nothing. She made a silent prayer to herself to stay in the moment. "You're going to appreciate this because this may never happen again, this moment in your life. With a show you love so much."

"I didn't trip on the stairs or anything. I just walked straight and I looked around and I thought, 'I am in the moment,' and I'd never been able to do this. I looked at all these people, Michael and Bob, my mother, and I thought, 'This is a wonderful moment. This may never happen again.' "

A Chorus Line won nine Tony Awards that night. The costumes

lost to flashier designs for shows that have long since closed.
Priscilla lost to Kelly, but some years later won the award for
another show.

The Tony Award performance turned out to be the last night
that unique family would ever be together. Pam Blair had been out
of the show in recent weeks, and on the very next Saturday, the
company was split up for the first time. Five principals and all the
understudies stayed in New York, while fourteen principals headed
for California.

A rehearsal was scheduled for ten A.M. the day after the Tony
Awards. It was a thrill for the new companies of dancers to watch
the original company filing in the next morning, triumphant and
glowing.

After he won the Tony Award, Sammy Williams attempted to
renegotiate his salary. Michael flatly refused him.

Sammy told him he wanted to go to London.

"No," Michael said, "and you're going to be fired if you don't
go to Los Angeles." Michael was trying to keep the company
under control.

Unable to call Michael's bluff, Sammy became incensed. He
complained about Michael's treatment of him to the others in the
company. Although he did deserve to be paid more, he was even
angrier because he felt Michael had betrayed him as a friend.

Michael had withdrawn his emotional support, which had
been such a crucial part of the creative process. Now Sammy, who
was making more money than the dancer he had once been, but
less than what he felt a Tony winner deserved, wanted to negotiate for a larger share. Michael not only closed the iron door but
threatened to withdraw the job, a job that Sammy depended on.
He could not afford to lose it. He went to California.

For Michael, it was all business and it was money and it was a
show. But that was just the trouble. For the dancers it had always
been more than that. When rehearsals were over, when the
reviews were in, Michael moved on and away. Without warning
or explanation, his demands changed. The intimacy of rehearsals
was replaced by a need for professional behavior. It was a difficult
and painful transition for all the dancers. They could not reconcile
the vulnerability they felt doing the performances he had drawn

out of them, the drugs he had participated in, or the half-dozen close friendships he had formed, with this new businesslike producer.

The original company members were upset by the cast's splitting up and the new people coming in. They viewed it as an invasion of something very special; they felt their family being torn apart. By then it was a phenomenal, very famous family. Though everyone tried to keep a stiff upper lip, to many it felt like death.

During the final week before hitting the road, Michael brought the original cast into the City Center rehearsals. He lined them all up in their formation. Then he said, "All right, all the people who are going to California, step back, please." And the dancers stepped back, leaving just Kelly Bishop, Thommie Walsh, Wayne Cilento, Rick Mason, and Clive Clerk.

"They seemed so vulnerable," Don Percassi recalls. "I realized how vulnerable we all were."

For those who were staying, it was especially difficult. They were fewer in number and lacked the challenge Hollywood offered. For Kelly Bishop the pain of separation crystallized during a rehearsal with the new company.

"Of course I was very angry. Even though it was my choice. We get to 'Ballet' and I start to sing, and the tears came pouring out of my eyes at such a rate that they were dripping off my nose and my chin and I was standing there gesturing to Michael, saying, 'I can't . . .' and the piano player's playing and I couldn't sing anything. I was crying so hard and it wouldn't stop until the whole song was over."

Inevitably their last night together—Saturday, April 24, 1976—arrived. The company had two shows that day, only six days after the Tony Awards. Crissy Wilzak was on for Pam Blair: "I don't know how Priscilla kept singing 'What I Did for Love' without just breaking down and crying. It was so tearful, it was just incredible. I just sat there bawling. A lot of other kids were too. I don't know how she kept it together. It was real sad. Real sad."

The three companies divided and went their separate ways. It was the end of the original company of *A Chorus Line*. It was the end of an era.

CHAPTER XII

....

On the Road

For Michael Serrecchia, still an understudy, it took a greater effort to stay than to withdraw. "I had made peace with the situation. First comes the shock, then comes the hurt, then comes the humiliation, then comes the decision. Am I going to leave? I decided I would get over it. I remember distinctly when the second company came in how all the understudies would not come out of the basement. I went out and I bought coffee mugs for every one of those new people in the company. It sounds stupid but it was a hard thing for me to do. I wrote each one of them a note saying "Welcome to the Chorus Line experience," and left it in everybody's dressing room. I had to lie down for a week—it exhausted me. I'd felt robbed but those were not the people who robbed me. Those were not the people who betrayed me. I've decided to stay. I'm going to stay and do it right."

In California, Donna McKechnie's emotions were completely tangled in the show. And Michael, too, uncharacteristically lowered the wall he had built around himself during the first season. Michael asked Donna to marry him.

"When Michael and Donna announced that they were getting married," Nancy Lane recounts, "I just about dropped my drawers! Everybody knew that it was just a big bunch of shit. It was a fling for both of them. And poor Donna—it's just so stupid and it's just so typical. Falling in love with the director. In San Francisco. Poor Ken Howard was *in love* with Donna. So in love with her. Then she just threw him over for Michael."

Donna and the tall, blond, TV-star-handsome Ken Howard had first worked together when he had a two-line, one-punch part in *Promises, Promises.* Since then they had both done a number of other things and their stock had risen on Broadway tremendously. "I was living with Ken Howard. It was an important relationship in my life, very passionate. I loved him very much but I just didn't trust it. We had been on and off again in our lives. The practical side of me said it's gonna be a show-business marriage."

Donna's relationship with Michael wasn't a fling at all. If anything, it was motivated less by the flush of success than by the terror of it. Caught up in a whirlwind of notoriety, money, and responsibilities, both Donna and Michael needed a life jacket.

The problems began for Donna nearly right away. "When the show hit and we started doing publicity, other people would say, 'I can't be bothered with this,' but I was doing, on the average, two interviews a day, because I had already had the experience of being close to something and then giving up the business and losing my stride. I've learned that you have to promote. I worked hard. I did all the interviews that nobody else wanted to do. And got all these awards. Awards you never heard of. Nobody's ever heard of. The Hands-Across-the-Library-Table. These people would hold promotional luncheons and take the hit show and that's the person they would give the award to. I started getting really tired, because it was all about promotion for other people and the show didn't need it after a while.

"It was a very difficult and strenuous time. I didn't allow myself that much private time. I felt like my personal life had taken a lot of abuse. And I felt pretty bad about not being successful in my relationships in the past. The success of *A Chorus Line* pointed up to me that I'm not such a success in personal ways."

Donna's father had never approved of her career; then, just when her work had reached a level at which she was receiving accolades from everyone else, her father passed away. In Donna's mind her family relationship would now never be resolved, and the father she had always wanted would never materialize.

And then there was Michael. "I was in a perfect condition for escaping from real life and I glorified Michael. I had already started feeling more than a camaraderie. A sense of something powerful, an intimacy with Michael. Through the work I felt that I really loved him. He had said things to me in a very confidential way about himself that touched me. All through the period of

A Chorus Line I felt like I had to defend Michael to a lot of people. I came on like Mother Mary sometimes. I felt he was misunderstood, that they did not appreciate his talent.

"I felt that he had given me the opportunity of my life. He once said to me: 'I did this for you.' "

On Michael's side, there is no way to underestimate the Pygmalion syndrome. Donna McKechnie as Cassie Ferguson was Michael's supreme creation. Michael became the sculptor who created his finest statue and begged the gods to bring it to life so he could love her.

With the exception of Donna, the entire original company had turned against Michael. He had tried to go back to those days when he was a chorus boy enjoying the friendships of the dressing room, but had succeeded only in going further forward and distancing himself even more from the kids in the line. The gypsies he had so loved, and wanted to work closely with again, turned ungrateful and shut him out.

There was another factor. Michael's career was moving up another step into the world of corporate entertainment. In the board rooms of MCA-Universal there are important men in dark suits, and dark politics. In the power alleys of Hollywood there are couples on gracious estates and tennis courts, making deals at exclusive Sunday brunches. Michael wanted to move up from the small world of the theater—as had Orson Welles, Herbert Ross, Mike Nichols, Bob Fosse before him—into the larger one of film. A wife would be just the thing.

Finally, there was Michael's homosexual background. As personally comfortable as he may have been, he had to know that a less controversial life-style would be viewed more favorably in Hollywood. And Michael had always loved women, skillfully glorifying many of them over the years in his shows. In *Follies*, in *Company*, in *Seesaw*, and in *A Chorus Line*, the standout roles are the women's.

Michael proposed to Donna. "I could've fallen off the chair when he approached me," she says. "It was shocking to me that he asked me, and it was shocking to me that I did it. It was a terrible mistake in one way. I didn't know him—and this is not to come off naïve.

"It seems bizarre to me sometimes. Talk about soul-searching.

· 177

I'm shy to talk about it because I'm kind of damned if I do and damned if I don't when I talk about Michael."

In spite of sincere feelings and good intentions, it was a mistake. "It was very painful and it was right away. One of the things you wake up the next morning and go, 'My God, I wasn't in reality here.' Then you work a whole year to try to *make* it work. To really be responsible and not to just chalk it off."

They had only just begun when the marriage began to crumble. "My naïveté came in the form of: I had never lived with him before. He was going crazy. He was having a breakdown. I was totally confused by his behavior. He would go away for weeks at a time and I would put up this front. I never knew where he was. He was going through something that I couldn't have fathomed even if he had told me. I think the Chorus Line effect on him was stronger than he let people know or let himself know."

By the time *A Chorus Line* hit the road, cocaine had come well out of the show-business closet. Its quick exhilarating effect is ideal for dealing with the physical exertions of rehearsals, performances, and a demanding schedule. One of the drug's more unusual properties is its tendency to invoke paranoia.

Michael felt his dancers had turned on him. The understudies were reacting to what they perceived as his betrayal of them; the line dancers, to having been abandoned. They all were waiting for him to knock on their dressing room doors, but circumstances prohibited his giving them the exclusive attention he had given them in rehearsal.

At the same time, success surrounded him with sycophants and parasites. He and Donna, then living in a penthouse he had purchased on Central Park South, shared a private joke: Michael would always answer the telephone with "How much?" in reaction to the avalanche of requests for money or help that came on the heels of his public success. Though many people he considered genuine friends were still nearby, they found it difficult to tell a hugely successful, driven, opinionated, manipulative, guarded millionaire that he was acting self-destructively. His drug habit became so severe that he was spending thousands of dollars a week on cocaine, an expense he could easily afford.

At the height of his paranoia, Michael actually imagined himself the victim of a gangster's contract that the original company had taken out on his life. He was convinced that he was going to be hit, and he knew the date.

In the meantime, a huge national publicity campaign had launched the touring companies, and not one of them had let their audiences down. The talented dancers—who had not yet become involved in the bitterness that characterized the show's aura backstage—and the show's momentum carried *A Chorus Line* to new heights of achievement. The original company performed brilliantly in San Francisco, where the Curran Theatre and the sophisticated cultural awareness of the city enhanced audience appreciation of the show. Even though the move to Los Angeles weakened the company, because of the size of the theater and the city's shallow cultural sensibility, *A Chorus Line* became the event of the season. It would be "out" to miss it, and few did.

In London the international company was front-page news. In spite of a raked stage that tended to give the performers knee problems, they danced and performed brilliantly and were received by English audiences with enthusiasm. British stars mingled with the U.S. company, and London's private clubs opened their doors in a round of parties. Not since *West Side Story* had an American musical taken London by storm. For six months the giant Drury Lane Theatre rang with enthusiasm.

"It was more exciting in London because you realized how important theater is to them there," Ron Kurowski explains. "It's not like television. Television is everything to American families, and theater is everything to the British. Shakespeare is theirs. They own Shakespeare and they're so proud of him. There's more theater going on than in New York and that's hard for most Americans to believe. There's more shows, more reasonable prices. Our show had a one-pound ticket, which at that time was a dollar fifty. The whole third balcony was a pound. So people would come back and back and back. The last performance of the American company was packed with people who had seen the show many, many times. They gave every person entrance applause when they said their names."

Backstage, the musical was not protected from the turbulence the other companies experienced. "Michael came to London and told us that we destroyed his show," Kurowski goes on to say.

"After putting ourselves in his arms he left us for months in London with stage managers that just didn't know how to tell us what to do, and we didn't know what we were doing. We were just trying to do the show, we were all real young and most of us inexperienced, and he came back and just lit into us. He came to a Wednesday matinee, didn't tell us he was coming."

Michael's problems were escalating in that second year of *A Chorus Line*. Soon after he put together the new companies, the six months Britain had allowed his American dancers to work in England expired. It was time to assemble a fourth company of English dancers who would take over when the Americans left. The English were not used to slick American musicals or American jazz choreography. They tend to be uncomfortable with the total combination of singing, dancing, and acting that is typical of American musicals, and especially of *A Chorus Line*. Then there was the struggle to master American accents.

"Some of them overdo American accents. They sound like they're from Oklahoma, or they sound cockney. It was such a mix of people," Kurowski remembers. "Their Zach was French and badly cast. He had this thick accent: 'You can't go beck to zee choreze, Cazzee.' And he couldn't do any of the dancing. All he did was the tap. He did the tap combination instead of Larry because he was an old hoofer, and he used a hat. It was all embarrassing."

Once again the role of Cassie created problems. Michael had hired Elizabeth Seal to replace Sandy Roveta, and London was thrilled. It was a big comeback for the favorite hometown actress who had starred in *Irma la Douce*, but she was a little old, even for the mature Cassie.

After dance captain Tom Reed had taught the show to the English company, Michael came in, saw what had been accomplished thus far, and fired her.

The next day it made front-page news. In New York, directors often fire people. The show is the thing. If it doesn't fit with the concept, you're out. But the British simply don't fire people. London's numerous tabloids ran headlines: ELIZABETH SEAL SACKED. HER BIG COMEBACK TAKEN AWAY FROM HER. Though Jimmy Carter was being inaugurated, *A Chorus Line* was much bigger American news.

Then Michael came up with a solution. Donna had not yet appeared in London with *A Chorus Line*. She would do the show. She had done *Promises, Promises* and *Company* in London and was well known there. He felt certain the London public would open their arms to his star.

Michael had left Donna behind in New York, but they had parted on one of their better, communicative nights, and she was looking forward to joining him. She flew to London and walked into a hornet's nest. The next day newspaper headlines read DIRECTOR'S WIFE TO REPLACE SACKED ELIZABETH SEAL. British Actors' Equity went up in arms. The following day the newspapers read BRITISH EQUITY COUNCIL OVERTURNS DECISION. DIRECTOR'S WIFE NOT TO STAR IN SHOW. The excitement included death threats, and Michael and Donna had to be guarded while driving between the Savoy Hotel and the Drury Lane Theatre.

Under increasing time pressure and in an attempt to turn sentiment and publicity in their favor, it was next decided that the girl who had been hired to understudy Cassie would take over the role. Donna went to the theater daily to help her prepare. This dancer wasn't English either, but Latvian, and spoke with an accent. She had bright-red hair and was too heavy for the red costume, so they fitted her with a blue one.

Kurowski was appalled. "Cassie in London had a blue costume! She was not an actress. She was not ready. They had pictures of this girl on the second page putting on her makeup, eye liner all over the place. She was *frightened*. She didn't know what she was doing."

It became a political issue, with Vanessa Redgrave (British Equity's local Bolshevik) on the bandwagon rallying against American artists. Rumors abounded of British actors being paid a pound to vote against permission for Donna to appear. Equity meetings were being called for eight o'clock when working members couldn't get there.

Donna came out of the stage door one day to be knocked against a brick wall by twenty photographers and reporters, while Michael White, the British producer, and Michael Bennett hid behind a car. Taking refuge in his hotel room, Michael had a screaming fit, threatening to abandon the production.

"Michael was totally desperate," Donna recalls. "He was very upset and he must have been going through his paranoid thing then, because he was just totally unreachable. He was having fits of rage, screaming, and all of a sudden what seemed to be a situation where we could help each other turned into a nightmare.

"One day I was rehearsing to go on. The next day I wasn't. Then I had to work with the understudy, so I was working all day and not knowing if I was going on that night. It was just chaos. It was seven days but seemed like seven years. I flew back to New York alone and distraught. It was a break in the relationship. It took me months to understand what happened."

Finally the English company took the stage. They did not continue the run of *A Chorus Line* quite as long as was expected. American musicals are still a product of a uniquely American idiom. The English company had as much trouble with the show as most American actors have with Noël Coward.

The marriage had a short run as well. Michael found the situation claustrophobic. In the end, he said to Donna: "I'll never forgive you for loving me."

"What do you mean?" she asked.

"You made me feel, and I'll never forgive you for that," he replied.

CHAPTER XIII

·················

The Circle Is Broken

The first original company member to walk away from *A Chorus Line* was Kelly Bishop.

In New York, surrounded by new faces, she had refused to sign a new, longer contract, or to go to the Coast. She had been making $650 a week and asked for $1,000, expecting to be negotiated down to $800. Kelly had won a Tony Award for her role as Sheila.

Management refused to give her any raise at all. Though she did not speak with Michael directly, no one else had the authority to make that decision.

So with the expiration of her current contract, she left the show. The other cast members watched to see what would happen. Later, when she was in Los Angeles and the bulk of the company was still working there, she attended a party. She recalls how everyone scrutinized her, as if they could learn something, as if they could find out if she—and one day they—would be all right after *A Chorus Line*.

Just what one was going to do after leaving the family was a problem. Many of the cast had gone on the line as chorus girls and boys and had come back stars. No one wanted to go back to the chorus. But the show had been the real star. *It* was the phenomenon and would continue without them. But without it, many of them were still unknown. The five dancers who had not gone to California were now playing on Broadway surrounded by new faces. They stood out, and suddenly that became another problem.

Wayne Cilento had been told that he was the best dancer in the show. Michael had wanted Wayne's character, Mike Costa, to think and dance like the best dancer in the show. "When I danced, it didn't matter if my leg was over my head three times higher than everyone else—he wanted me to dance that way. He wanted me to stick out." But new stage managers and dance captains on Broadway didn't know the intricacies of the text, or the history behind the show.

"They started telling me that my legs were too high, to put my legs down, and I said no. That's when the friction started happening. They were trying to clean the show and they were making everyone a machine, and I said, 'Fuck you. I *am* Mike Costa. This is what I'm about. Call Michael up. I'll tell you right now that I'm not going to dance like that.' At the same time they were telling me to put my legs down they were telling me that I wasn't exciting anymore onstage. I was one of the original people and I had something in me left over from the original cast that the replacements didn't have and I was sticking out. Plus, I was making too much money. They were hiring people for four hundred dollars— why should they have me?"

After two-and-a-half years of *A Chorus Line*, Wayne left. He joined the new musical *The Act*, starring Liza Minnelli, dancing in the chorus of what was not so much a musical as Minnelli's act. Suddenly the specter of going back to the chorus loomed large in front of the dancers. "Thommie and all these people said, 'You're gonna dance *behind* Liza Minnelli? What the hell is that?' And I said, 'Fuck you all. I'm gonna dance behind Liza Minnelli.' " Wayne got more publicity doing that than he had as Mike Costa. Bob Fosse saw him in the show and offered Wayne his next show, *Dancin'*. Wayne had gone back to the chorus. Somehow the others felt he was letting their side down. Yet the Broadway chorus, partly because of *A Chorus Line*, had changed.

Carole Schweid was moved into the role of Diana when the first replacement was fired. It should have been a triumph for the understudies, but it was too late.

"There was a new stage manager who kept giving me these directions and I *was there* when it all took place." She wasn't functioning well under the mounting pressure; she couldn't lose the ten pounds she needed to; she was exhausted and having vocal problems. "I was fired. I can't blame anybody. I just wasn't on top of it. I had been. But I wasn't. I just couldn't rise to it. I really feel like I blew it. But I would not have missed it. I wouldn't have missed the whole thing for anything."

When Chita Rivera saw Michael Serrecchia dance in the show, she called him up and asked him to dance in her act.

"I remember when I left, I felt about twenty years younger. I felt lighter. I couldn't wipe a smile off my face. Life was beautiful. Where did it come from? I had no idea. I finally put two and two together and realized how much I had suppressed trying to make it work, sticking it out for the money, whatever.

"In Chita's act I wasn't anybody's understudy. I wasn't anybody's lackey. I wasn't second-rate and not good enough. Nope, I was the best.

"When we were downtown it was blown up to be an enveloping force. I've learned not to let myself get that wrapped up in a project. A show will never become my life again. We were bled dry. No more all. It doesn't take all."

Ultimately Michael Bennett did turn to two of the original understudies for help.

Brandt Edwards was sent to the international company as Don Kerr when the first actor was fired. He played London and then continued on tour with the company in the States. He soon found that a good deal of the competition, anger, and bitterness was percolating down to this company as well. In Detroit during a company meeting: "It came out that all the bitter, backbiting stuff that was going on backstage had to affect what went across the footlights, because the show was about honesty. It was very hard for me to believe that you could get out there and do what the show demanded and have this bullshit going on backstage. It wasn't healthy for the show or for the company."

Then one girl said, "We're actors. We should be able to go out and act it."

Brandt looked at her and said, "That's the difference. The original company did not get out there and act it. We went out there and *were*."

It was the backstage politics that caused Brandt to view the more than two years he was with the show with despair. "I saw it turn from something beautiful into something commercial into something sick. That was one of the reasons I wanted to leave. I didn't realize what it had done to my head until I left. It took me ten months to get up the will to work again."

But no amount of offstage bitterness could change what happened for the dancers once they took the stage. All the good work that had transpired in the workshop rehearsals and all the love that had grown between the original cast still resonated. Leaving it was ending it. "I think I started crying Thursday night," Brandt recalls, "and by Saturday night it just hurt. I think it sort of freaked out the other kids in the international company."

Scott Allen was sent to San Francisco to understudy Zach, and went on when Michael was there. Michael told Allen: "I'm very proud of you. You've done this."

None of those dancers who had gone to L.A. were able to make a significant impression. They were applauded onstage. Offstage, most went unrecognized. By the end of the L.A. run, those dancers who had expected to be personally embraced by Hollywood were disappointed and those who expected nothing, were not.

When the L.A. run drew to a close, those members of the original company who had not already left, or planned to leave, were encouraged by management to consider it. The show was no longer theirs, and with varying degrees of relief the remaining members of the original cast departed.

Clive Clerk had stayed in New York and taken over as dance captain. He had also become the Zach understudy. The show took up all his time and he had dropped out of his art studies. After a while he ceased being dance captain and took over the role of Zach in New York, Washington, Philadelphia, and Boston. But after almost three years he had gotten a lot out of the show and decided to get on with his life. He went back to college to continue his design studies, having thoroughly, and without turmoil, enjoyed a wonderful interlude. He had happy memories, but leaving was still very sad. "The experience of a graduation," he described it. "So much had happened to you."

After the California run, Sammy Williams left the show. He chose to stay in Los Angeles, where he tried to break into film and television. His first trip to an agent, however, was a crushing disappointment. The agent told him flat-out what a Tony Award meant in Hollywood: nothing.

In a year and a half, his commercial agent was unable to secure a single audition for him as an actor. He did land a small role on an episode of the television series *Kojak*. He convincingly played a sleazy, goatee-sporting drug dealer, and demonstrated that his acting talent went beyond the role of Paul. But fighting Hollywood typecasting is never easy, and it began to look more and more as if the role of Paul was the only one Sammy would ever play.

Between the lack of jobs, and lack of opportunities to realize his full potential, Sammy reevaluated his life and his success in *A Chorus Line*. For three years Sammy didn't go near a theater, didn't go near an audition, didn't go near an agent. Instead, he worked in a store to support himself.

Little by little he came to approach this period in his life in a more positive manner, to deal with what he saw as his failure to fulfill the promise represented by the Tony Award, and to deal with the Chorus Line experience itself. Gradually he began to want to go back on the stage. He grew restless in his regular job. Then a propitious phone call came from Ron Field.

Field was choreographing the television special *Baryshnikov on Braodway*. He invited Sammy to be one of his dancers. Coincidentally, the national company of *A Chorus Line* was performing a number on the program. Michael was there and asked Sammy for a favor. The dancer who played Paul was leaving the national company. Michael invited Sammy to go back into his original role. Sammy agreed and, after a three-year hiatus, went back to the show he had helped create.

After six weeks he broke his foot. He came back to the company too soon, broke it again, then left the show—this time, he thought, for good.

Don Percassi, the most experienced gypsy, returned to the show in New York and was the last to leave. But his performance, which the inventive, uninhibited actor allowed to get bigger, remained fresh to the end.

The original company shared one thing at the end. For each of them it was "Time to go, time to grow."

Over the years the ex-gypsy author Nicholas Dante suffered both writer's block and debilitating anger toward his co-creators and most of the original cast. He felt his contribution to the success of the show went overlooked. Even among cast members, "None of the kids ever really knew what I wrote," he now realizes.

Although in the workshop process the actors made many contributions, it was still true that Dante had worked hard transcribing and refining the stories, creating the characters through which they would be told, and writing many early drafts.

For over a year he wrote and rewrote, responding to Michael's every whim, and even graciously absorbed James Kirkwood's involvement and collaboration halfway through the process. He still describes it as one of the happiest years of his life.

But the cast made it clear shortly after the Broadway opening that they didn't view him as the legitimate author, and begrudged him his income. In addition, Michael, going on to mount other companies and new shows, shut Dante out from the small inner circle of people that surrounded him. This put Dante into a tailspin of anger and frustration from which he only recovered when a curious incident gave him a new perspective.

More than a decade after the show opened, Nicholas Dante played himself—the role of Paul—for the first time. In a production directed by Baayork Lee and starring Donna McKechnie, the show's co-author danced and performed the now-famous monologue based on his own life. For a number of weeks he became just another dancer.

Several weeks into the run, however, the show was being restaged for a theater in the round, and he felt that a line in the show should be altered. He spoke up and was treated really "shabbily" by a couple of members of the cast, as if he were just one of the dancers and had no right to speak up about the dialogue. It became clear to him that the original cast had never accepted him as more than a dancer, nor thought of him as the show's co-author. Terribly hurt, he left the production the next morning.

He later discovered, through casual business with Michael's attorneys, that Michael considered Dante's royalties a gift for his own life story, and not a reflection of his contribution as co-author.

Nick sees show business as an ungenerous and ungraceful business that has gotten worse, and one which reflects the current shallow, materialistic values of the country. Ironically, one of the goals of the show was to re-create the special feeling of the original midnight meeting, in which dancers who competed directly with one another let down their guards and shared the pains, frustrations, and dreams of their lives. "We succeeded with audiences," Dante feels, "but not for ourselves. The walls went right back up." Dante now sees the original cast, and Michael, as "not a very nice group of people, then or now, and extremely self-involved." He has lost affection for the majority of them, but has made peace with his anger and is writing again.

They were the quintessential Broadway gypsies, yet half of them moved to Hollywood to pursue a different kind of career. For Nancy Lane, "It's the glamour. I mean, it really attracted me. I really wanted to be glamorous. Always. I should be Cher. I would wear all this eye makeup. I'd do all this stuff. Anything to take away from my nose. And my teeth were terrible."

Nancy had her teeth straightened and her nose reshaped, though she had already begun getting roles on television. Trish Garland had cosmetic face surgery, had her breasts enlarged, and began wearing a new hairstyle. She became extremely glamorous and in no way resembled the gawky Judy Turner she had created.

Crissy Wilzak landed a regular job on a sitcom, but she, like most of the ex-New Yorkers, had no illusions about what she was doing. "I hate to say it because I do love television. Why do I love it? The pay is so good. The work is so easy. I find I'm almost overqualified.

"The people just don't have a discipline. As a dancer, when they call 'places,' you're ready to work. You're ready to go through it a dozen times if you have to. People here come shlepping up, fifteen minutes late for work, twenty minutes late—nobody says anything.

"Many's the time after we film I come home and feel like I haven't done anything at all. When you do a show on Broadway, you know you've worked. Many a time I come home feeling empty."

Rick Mason danced on a number of TV specials and a series, and says, "The way they treat dancers in TV and movies is pretty ugly. The conditions you work in, for one. The floors are slick as ice. They're hard—they have to be cement to hold the cameras.

Then it's the way you're treated by other people. Even gofers treat you shitty. I was coming from a show that said something about dancers. I was coming from a city that respected dancers."

Ron Dennis misses New York every now and again, "but to go back and live in that rat race, what am I gonna do? Go back and compete with younger dancers? I don't wanna go back there and be in no one's chorus."

There is a consensus that New York is a tough place to live, and L.A. an easy one. Inevitably, after a decade of fighting the city, many people try Hollywood. The work there pays better and can lead to a different kind of success. No one, after all, has become a real Broadway star since the days of Ethel Merman and Mary Martin and Gwen Verdon. But there is also a consensus that New York is the center of the American theater world, and when you're out of New York, you're out of town. Once in their lives, there was nothing more important than to dance on Broadway.

The show, of course, went on. It's run for years on Broadway, and the two touring companies continued to crisscross America, going back again and again to all the major cities. During those years Michael took another small step toward revolutionizing the American theater. Throughout the long runs of previous hit shows, stage managers and dance captains were almost exclusively responsible for keeping cast replacements up to the standards set by the original cast. Many subsequent companies could be compared to the proverbial sock that has been darned so many times, none of the original thread remains. But Michael ran all three companies from his New York offices, keeping close tabs on each. Although the day-to-day teaching and brush-up rehearsals were conducted by the staff, Michael himself looked in on all the companies with regularity, an unheard-of practice for a top director on Broadway. In the final week prior to a company's geographic move, he would often show up in town, see a performance, and rehearse the company in preparation for its next opening. He would not hesitate to fire dancers whose work he was dissatisfied with, or move dancers around from company to company for balance. In addition, he would direct the actors toward a performance that utilized what each had to offer, in the style of his "Be yourself" approach to the material, rather than toward a carbon—and thus pale—copy of the original.

Michael's standards were always exacting and specific, with every move and beat precise. He never allowed any unauthorized deviation from the material, and that included the staging and acting as well as the written word, all of which was codified in an enormous book from which the stage managers and dance captains worked. To any transgressors he would say, "If it ain't on the page, it ain't on the stage." The result was that subsequent Broadway and local audiences saw a show that was closer in quality to the acclaimed original—an unheralded, almost unnoticed, but significant change in the pattern of national theater.

The show was also done in translation in numerous foreign countries. Roy Smith began as Larry with the national company, became dance captain, and eventually staged several companies overseas. His experience indicates just how American the American musical theater is:

"Latin American countries have no idea how to audition for a show. Two people will come in two days later. 'Oh, I hear you're auditioning for a show.' Three people, four people, five people, and you can't ignore them, simply because there's hardly enough talent there to get the show on. You're desperate. You're looking at people in the street. 'Can you sing? Can you dance?' It took me five weeks in Mexico just to find enough people to do the show.

"They don't have the teachers that we have, so their training is way behind ours. We are so precise and we get on ourselves. If we're not doing something correctly we get in the corner, and dammit, we do it until it's right. In the basement of City Center we'd have ten people in a line going over the 'One' combination on their break. They don't do that.

"It is not the same in foreign countries as it is here, being desperate for a job. You say, 'Couldn't you just kill for this job?' And they would go, 'Well, no. I'll just do something else.'

"It's totally American. It's something that we have invented and it is very, very hard to duplicate."

The musical that many theater insiders felt would not work uptown, because it was too oriented toward show biz, appealed to huge Broadway crowds. After that, they felt it would not appeal to the rest of the country—it was too New York. Both touring companies sold out in every major city they played. Then they felt it would not succeed in London—it was too American—and it was received with open arms. They felt it would not translate well in foreign languages and foreign countries, but productions were successful in Australia, Japan, Berlin, Argentina, Mexico, Sweden, Brazil, Vienna, Paris, and more. Though the show is a demanding one and local talent is not always up to the task, something of its power always comes through.

Perhaps the reason for this can be explained by Ron Kurowski's experience with the production in Hawaii.

"Hawaiians are into love. The Hawaiians taught us how to dance the hula and we taught them 'One.' It was incredible. They wear flowers and they speak of love and they profess love. That last night, it was another heavy closing night. When I sang 'What I Did for Love' on my last night in New York, on my last night with the international, and on closing night in London, I could not do anything but cry and weep. That happened all my life. When I thought of love I would cry. That night, however, [in Hawaii] I sang 'What I Did for Love' right at those people who were my friends, who were screaming and cheering, and I didn't cry. I learned there that you can feel an emotion to a tremendous depth and be proud of it."

"If I never saw Michel Stuart again in my whole life," Donna says, "there's a profound feeling of being next to him. Just standing next to him. There's always a bond. I'm using him only as an example. It sounds corny but it's like a family connection. I feel that way about everybody in the show."

It was the show that drew everyone together. In spite of everything. Trish Garland once said, "I'll be the first one to tell you off, but if anyone ever says anything bad about you kids, I'll fight them." That's the way everyone felt after they left.

It was the show that filled everyone with pride. Not the show that Michael Bennett and Bob Avian, Marvin Hamlisch and Ed Kleban, James Kirkwood and Nick Dante had created. It was the show *they* had created.

All of them were approached by audience members. The cast received letters and visits backstage from people who felt the impact of their work. Strangers would simply approach them at the stage door. First, there would be compliments. Then, sometimes gently, sometimes suddenly, sometimes unknowingly, they would try to say that they had grown themselves, changed, learned something, from seeing the show. Young men who were afraid to confront their parents with their sexuality; young dancers who had suppressed their ambitions and not been able to articulate their need to dance; people from other walks of life who had buried their own unhappiness—they could all now confront those realities. One man told them: "You know, you're gonna make it good for me to go back to work." That's what they had done. And they had not done it with anything Michael Bennett had drilled into them. They had done it with their own lives.

CHAPTER XIV

·················

Hollywood

Hollywood had bought a musical in an era when film musicals were passé. They had bought a theater score in an era when popular music had moved away from show tunes to rock and roll. They had bought a script filled with inner monologues, a dramatic technique that had never worked on the screen. They had bought a story that takes place entirely on one closed, bare set, at a time when films had come to depend more than ever on style over content. They had a passel of characters who had to sing and dance, when movies desperately needed bankable name actors. The financial package—rights, royalties, development, production, prints, and advertising—would add up to an unrealistic break-even figure.

On the basis of all that, one might believe that Universal was brave indeed to take on *A Chorus Line* and, flying in the face of Hollywood convention, intended to make a large budget film that depended on nothing but the strength of a great play. Nothing could be further from the truth. Universal bought *A Chorus Line* because it was a tremendous success, and success is what Hollywood lusts after most of all. Studio executives simply assumed that the creative problems would be solved by the creative people. (Or, to quote Saki, they had the "reckless courage of the non-combatant.")

Shortly after the sale of the film rights, Universal Pictures took a full-page advertisement in *Variety* announcing that in 1980, Michael Bennett would produce, direct, and choreograph the film version of *A Chorus Line*. This coincided with a contractual stipulation, made in 1975, that the film not be released for five years, thus guaranteeing a healthy run for the stage show before a film might subtract from its audience.

The film version turned out to be a project full of surprises. Michael never directed the film, and it took *ten* years to make. The unsurprising finale: Hollywood fell far short of realizing the property's potential.

Michael probably had the finest opportunity to make a good picture since Orson Welles went to Hollywood in 1939 with a final-cut contract. The studio offered to pay for a smaller picture with which Michael could learn the technical conditions of film. Then he would create *A Chorus Line*.

But Michael was under the tremendous strain of his overwhelming success, he was increasingly under the influence of drugs, he was wary of devoting another three years of his life to the same project, and—not unlike many New York artists, from Welles to Woody Allen—he hated Lotusland. He gave up his deal and retreated to the world of the theater.

Hollywood breathed a sigh of relief. If there is anything the studios are uncomfortable with it is the Authentic Genius. Now they had the best of all possible worlds: the property they wanted and the right to make it their way.

A series of script development strategies followed. Director Mike Nichols (whose numerous credits include directing the Broadway musical *The Apple Tree* and producing the Broadway musical *Annie*) and screenwriter Bo Goldman (*The Rose, One Flew Over the Cuckoo's Nest*) attempted the task. Then director Sidney Lumet (whose film credits ranged from *The Pawnbroker* to *Murder on the Orient Express* to *The Wiz*) gave it a try. Then Joel Schumacher (screenwriter of *The Wiz* and director of *The Incredible Shrinking Woman*) contracted to write and direct. Allan Carr (producer of *Grease* and *Can't Stop the Music*) was brought in to produce. Carr enlisted John Travolta to play Zach, and for the first time the project began to hit the newspapers. By now it was 1980 and after five years of false starts, Universal was disenchanted. No one had been able to come up with an acceptable screenplay, and no one had been able to construct a budget to match even the most pessimistic expectations.

Universal suddenly sold the rights to Polygram for $7.8 million.

At Polygram, producers Peter Guber (who had offered $400,000 for the rights on opening night) and Jon Peters took on the project, and they put together a star package. Mikhail Baryshnikov would play Zach. Travolta would play a large part created from various stories (including Cassie's). Jim Bridges (*The China Syndrome, Urban Cowboy*) would write and direct. Their production was budgeted at $18 million and Polygram said no. By 1982, Guber-Peters had lost interest, and Polygram's president, Gordon Stulberg, had been left with one of the most expensive stillbirths in Hollywood history. Stulberg couldn't even get a distributor interested, because by now the financial commitment necessary to make the film was completely untenable.

Stulberg approached Joe Papp, who had since got his feet wet producing the movie version of *The Pirates of Penzance*. Papp was interested and was able to convince Polygram and Universal that he had a chance at getting the original contract rewritten to reduce the crippling royalty package of 20 percent of the gross over $30 million. But Bennett and his collaborators refused to cooperate. After all, the longer the movie went unmade, the less competition there would be for the stage production.

Every time the project reached a new producer, phone calls and offers were made to Michael. Though at times he flirted with the idea, he ultimately avoided any involvement with the film version.

By June of 1985 the inexorable attraction of being associated with *A Chorus Line* hit Cy Feuer and Ernest Martin. Feuer and Martin (who had offered $150,000 for the rights prior to opening night) had produced many original stage musicals on Broadway in the 1940s and '50s, including *Guys and Dolls* and *How to Succeed in Business Without Really Trying*, as well as the notable film version of *Cabaret*, probably the only successful film musical released between *The Sound of Music* and *Flashdance*. Given these credentials, they must have seemed like white knights to Stulberg, who by now had an $8.5 million starting place, no money for development, and a nearly hopeless aura surrounding the project.

Feuer and Martin enlisted screenwriter Arnold Schulman (*A Hole in the Head, Love with the Proper Stranger, Goodbye Columbus, Funny Lady*). He returned to the original premise of the play, opting not to "open it up." Instead the film would be entirely set in the theater. This and a no-name package would keep the production price to $11.5 million.

But setting the story entirely on the empty stage of a theater, far from being faithful to the play, demonstrated a failure to understand the material. *A Chorus Line* is not set on the stage of a theater but in a black box, a vacuum. In fact, more than half of the material takes place in the minds of the dancers, stories anchored in the times and places of their past. The principal problem that so many other writers had grappled with—how to present the inner monologues on film—was not solved but ignored.

Schulman's screenplay appealed to Polygram and to Embassy Pictures, who agreed to capitalize the film and distribute it. At last *A Chorus Line: The Movie* would be made.

Then Feuer and Martin took the New York theater's most famous musical, not only a great Broadway musical but a great Broadway musical *about* Broadway musicals, to . . . an English director and a Hollywood choreographer. Two men with no background whatsoever in Broadway musicals.

Just what that meant was immediately clear to Broadway musical-theater cognoscenti, and who better to put it in perspective than Bennett himself, who, in an interview he gave on the subject of Broadway musicals for the book *Sondheim and Company* several years *before A Chorus Line* was even a gleam in his eye, had said, "I get so annoyed when I read that English directors are coming here to direct American musicals. Unless you've grown up in musicals, you can't do them well."

The choice of Sir Richard Attenborough to direct was facilitated by the coincidence that he and Feuer shared the same agent.

Attenborough and Arnold Schulman compounded one of the property's original problems. From the beginning, every screenwriter on the project was convinced that the Zach–Cassie relationship would have to be expanded. Hollywood's belief that a story without a romance is a movie without an audience fed this theory. But by moving the romance to the forefront, they spent a huge portion of the film on the least important theme, a minor subplot that has no real bearing on the substance of the material. *A Chorus Line* is not about Cassie and Zach any more than it is about "casting a forthcoming Broadway musical," as Richard Attenborough described it in a *New York Times* interview prior to release of the film. *A Chorus Line* is about a dancer's life, not his work. About testing oneself against the highest standards. About needs and wants and hopes and dreams. About life as it is for people who opt for an obscure, short-lived, emotionally charged profession.

One "new" scene is particularly revealing. In the film, after the opening number, Cassie falls out of a taxi, bobbles into the theater, and interrupts the audition in an attempt to get Zach's attention. Where have we seen this before? At the stage musical's *first preview*, when Michael attempted to create an entrance for Donna. The results were disastrous. The audience hated her. Anyone who thought the audience would rather look at the struggle of egos between Zach and Cassie, instead of the young gypsies dancing their hearts out, had no understanding of the material.

In emphasizing the Zach–Cassie relationship, and in casting a name actor (Michael Douglas) as Zach, the filmmakers also badly mistook Zach's part in the play. Zach is not so much a character as a device, which allows the material to be presented in its brutal docudrama form. The theater audience is placed between the dancers and Zach and, with the dancers pleading directly to them, are compelled to become emotionally involved. The film inserted Zach between the dancers and the camera/audience, and attempted to make him more of a three-dimensional character.

The theater audience *became* Zach, while the film audience watched him. The opportunity the lens provided to put the audience in Zach's place with point-of-view shots was ignored. The opportunity to keep Zach the omnipotent mystery man he would be to the young dancers by keeping him in the shadows, heard but unseen, was entirely passed over in favor of a futile attempt to deepen the character.

Michael's original instinct to keep Zach from becoming a well-defined character had been entirely correct. The filmmakers failed completely to identify what it was that made *A Chorus Line* so heartfelt, and plunged into exactly those traps that Michael had so skillfully avoided.

Bowled over by the semi-pornographic dances in *Flashdance*, Feuer and Martin enlisted Jeffrey Hornaday for the crucial job of choreographer. Their reasoning—that the material needed a "contemporary image" (Attenborough again)—turned out to be equally misguided. The desire to give the film a contemporary look did make sense. Film musicals were coming back into acceptability, thanks to input derived from the MTV-video form. This look is based on editing and photography, however, not content, and there was no need to change the fundamental choreographic concept from theater dance to television boogaloo. The result, an angry, sexual, and limited vocabulary, was unflattering to the dancers, and dated the film unnecessarily. The only thing that dates *A Chorus Line* is its costumes, and a few references to that generation's heroes. The choreography itself is timeless.

Their misunderstanding was that choreography is an accoutrement, an embellishment, when in fact it is a much more fundamental function of a great musical. Great choreography transcends time, just as great literature does. And for the same reason. Its vocabulary is not hip or chic, but original and, most of all, reflective of precise dramatic content.

The one thing Hollywood had to offer *A Chorus Line*—visual technique—also failed crucially. Many buffs still feel that the very foundation of *A Chorus Line*'s success was its staging. Within that simple black box, a kaleidoscopic pattern of movement carried the audience along. Unfortunately for lovers of dance, the movie failed even to translate this into first-rate photography. From the first solo, when Mike launches into a tap dance and the camera covers him *from the waist up*, to the *Phantom of the Opera* crane shot on "At the Ballet," the coverage was woefully inadequate. The cinematography didn't allow the superb work of the performers to charge the audience, and never conveyed the wonder and beauty of dance.

When *A Chorus Line: The Movie* disappeared nearly as suddenly as the original musical had stunned audiences more than a decade earlier, a great opportunity was lost. *West Side Story*, *My Fair Lady*, *South Pacific*, *Oklahoma!*, and *Camelot* have all been preserved in thrilling movie versions of once-great Broadway musicals. With the very future of the American musical theater in doubt, it will forever be a tragedy that no film exists of one of the greatest of all.

CHAPTER XV

· · · · · · · · · · · · · · · · · · ·

The Life

A ll the dancers from the original Chorus Line company
thought their success would be permanent. In fact, the
cast dropped from sight, at least from the high profile
they'd enjoyed on the heels of the opening. But the members of
the company went on to many varied achievements, even if they
discovered that security and steady employment in the business
were still elusive.

Michael Serrecchia, Tony Stevens, Chris Chadman, and Rick
Mason all danced in Chita Rivera's nightclub act, some for several
years and around the world. All saw it as one of the greatest
opportunities of their dance careers. Their work was pure dance.
Priscilla Lopez, Ron Kuhlman, Crissy Wilzak, Nancy Lane, and
Candy Brown acted in television series of varying longevity, and
Nancy wrote scripts for several television sitcoms. Don Percassi,
Brandt Edwards, Wayne Cilento, Mitzi Hamilton, Scott Allen, Pam
Blair, Priscilla Lopez, Jane Robertson, and Michon Peacock all con-
tinued to dance and act in Broadway musicals. A number of dancers
crossed over the chorus line, into production: Baayork Lee, Tony
Stevens, Andy Bew, Thommie Walsh, Chris Chadman, and Wayne
Cilento choreographed successfully. Michel Stuart produced several
musicals on Broadway. Kelly Bishop appeared in several films and a
television series. Robert LuPone had leads in a number of ill-fated
musicals. Chuck Cissel released two successful record albums. Kay
Cole returned to the show seven years after she first created Maggie,
as Diana. Sammy Williams also returned to the Broadway company,
but has since left show business. Priscilla Lopez eventually won a
Tony for another performance (*A Day in Hollywood, a Night in the
Ukraine*), and Wayne Cilento earned a nomination for *Dancin'*.

Even this list is misleading. It caters to the kind of labeling that continued to follow the Chorus Line dancers wherever they went, as if any achievement had to be a public one. Trish Garland is a Buddhist district leader in Los Angeles, where Nichiren Shoshu of America is headquartered; Michon Peacock works in New York chapter of the same organization; Robert LuPone created and directed several workshop theater pieces of his own. Clive Clerk returned to his real father's name and, as Clive Wilson, became an award-winning interior decorator. Jacki Garland has had two children; Michon Peacock, one; Wayne Cilento, three; and Andy Bew, five. Their achievements continue to grow. And change.

Donna moved to California, where she appeared in television specials, played guest roles in episodic series, and did five plays. She created and produced a successful musical review called *Let Me Sing and I'm Happy* and a nightclub act for herself, and played the lead in the Chicago company of *I'm Getting My Act Together and Taking It on the Road*. She was forced temporarily to give up dancing because of a crippling bout with arthritis, which was at least partially attributable to the strains in her life. Although unable to walk and told she would not recover, she found a more positively oriented doctor and has now regained the trim body and original grace of Broadway's greatest dancer. To help others who suffer from arthritis she publishes a newsletter and is writing a book on the subject. In 1987 she performed *A Chorus Line* in Japan, and reappeared on Broadway in the role she originated, expecting to stay for eight weeks and remaining for seven months. In 1988 she played Cassie for the premiere engagement in Paris.

Michael and Donna loved each other. For a decade their talents flowed together as one. But their triumphs created for them a new universe, one that neither of them traveled in easily, and it took both of them a good deal of time and trouble to get their bearings. By the time they did, they had lost sight of each other and where they had begun. "The greatest sense of loss for me personally," Donna points out, "was not losing a marriage, but losing a friendship."

They were both hurt and rewarded by the driving ambition they grew up with and recognized in each other. Donna says of Michael: "There was a part of him that strove to be happy, and the happiest moments in his life were when he was working. He loved his work. He knew that finally that is not enough and so the search went on. Each in our own way."

There is a line from the original script in which Cassie says, "It's all straightened out in my mind now. You fell in love because we worked so well together. You fell in love with my work and then a little bit with me." Zach starts to interrupt. She cuts him off, and tells him it's all right, that the result of their affair was a couple of show-stopping dance numbers instead of a baby, but there's nothing wrong with that.

That was written about a year before it came true.

Michael pulled away from Hollywood when he pulled away from Donna. He did not like the world to which he had succeeded, and dropped his deal with MCA-Universal. In New York he bought a tall factory building and renovated it, turning it into the finest rehearsal-studio complex in the city. He rented space at reasonable rates to other dance companies, and to designers. In the basement he built a small theater. From there he produced and directed a number of workshops, two of which resulted in Broadway musicals. *Ballroom* was his first, following *A Chorus Line*. Although it contained half a dozen stunning ballroom sequences, it failed, embittering him. But *Dreamgirls* succeeded. After that production he felt he'd regained some of his equilibrium. He began work on a new musical to be called *Scandal*, but canceled it abruptly after several workshops. There were difficulties with the show, and a rising conservatism in the country and the sudden emergence of AIDS made the sexually oriented subject matter seem outdated. He prepared to direct the world premiere of *Chess* in London but, just prior to rehearsals, was forced by ill health to drop out. Subsequently he sold his building—which in less than a decade had become the hub of the Broadway musical and dance world—to his tenants, and disappeared.

Though rumors abounded, little of his current life leaked out. He quietly moved to Tucson, Arizona, where he prepared to live the last year of his life. AIDS had been diagnosed in the forty-four-year-old man-child, and on July 2, 1987, he died. In an interview before his death, he said, "I thought I was ready for success. No one is."

Michael needed to have total control. At his memorial, his attorney wondered how he would carry on without Michael to advise him, and columnist Liz Smith assured those attending that Michael was watching them all, anxious to redirect and restage the event. His mania for control had a dark side. Only on his own terms could he be generous and supportive. He had desperate, unsatisfied needs to be loved and liked, yet he was incapable of asking for help, or love, and mistrusted those who offered it freely. But he was a vulnerable human being who inspired undying loyalty, and many of his close associates protected him fiercely. He lived his whole life with a vision of what the theater could be at its best, and the emotionally costly manipulations of his casts were in the service of the greatest and only gift he could give them: a musical.

Like many artists, Michael suffered from the nightmare "What if I wake up and find out I'm a fraud?" But Michael was one of two men—the first being Jerome Robbins—who truly understood the American musical theater. In a lifetime of extraordinary theater choreography and direction, *A Chorus Line* will stand as his masterpiece for all time.

Drugs have become embedded in Broadway musicals. Over the run of *A Chorus Line*, dancers turned increasingly from Valium, uppers, and marijuana to cocaine and even heroin. In 1975 the majority of the members of the original company had only flirted with drugs, and not generally in rehearsal and performance. Still, at least one member of the company was badly hooked on hard drugs. By 1980, however, all three companies were awash in cocaine. The problem became so severe that more than once a dancer had to be pulled offstage during his performance and replaced with his or her understudy. Several dancers had to leave the show when they became so dependent upon drugs they were unable to perform. At one point Michael paid for Actors' Equity to sponsor a short "lecture" tour on drug abuse, and a member of the staff visited each company. He spoke about the professional actor's responsibilities, warned the dancers about drugs, and offered information on where to get help. However, the counselor was so out of touch with the volatile young dancers, and Michael Bennett's both forgiving and, by example, encouraging them, that the meeting was less than useful.

Sadly, the musical that gave chorus dancers their greatest

recognition also provided hundreds of dancers with pressure, money, and access, the losing combination that seems to increase susceptibility to drugs. And other Broadway musicals were equally affected. Yet use throughout the country indicates that Broadway's problems are by no means unique.

From the dancers willing to speak out on their experience, two unequivocal statements arise: You cannot be creative on drugs. You cannot find happiness with drugs.

They have all passed thirty; they have all entered that stage of life when the body begins to rebel.

Donna: "What do you do when you can't dance anymore? I think it was important to bring that in. We realized when Michael asked that question that nobody had an answer. Nobody was prepared with options. When he asked that question everybody went, 'What?' Gwen Verdon said it in some interview I read: 'A dancer lives two lives. Dies once when they don't dance anymore.' "

Don Percassi notices "a lot of kids coming up. There's a lot of new talent coming up, and the competition is tough. I went to a couple auditions recently. And I realized who the old gypsy is, and it's me."

A Chorus Line has affected the lives of many dancers, but none so much as the original company. Nancy Lane's parents finally understood what she was doing. They understood that this was what she had to do, what she was happiest doing, and that she shouldn't be a teacher, shouldn't be a social director. They used to come in regularly from New Jersey, and the ushers knew them and would let them stand in the back of the theater. "My mother was telling me this morning," Nancy recalls, "that my brother, who's in college, got his first suit since his Bar Mitzvah, and she said, 'Oh, he looks so wonderful, a man. He's a junior in college—he's a man, wonderful.' And she said, 'Your sister, the only time I felt that way was when your sister got married and I saw her in her wedding gown and, oh, I was *kvelling* and, oh, it was wonderful, she was so beautiful.' And I said, 'Well, sorry, Mom, I disappointed you.' And she said, 'Oh, no, no, *A Chorus Line*. *A Chorus Line* will always be the best, the most exciting thing in our lives.' "

How many people can say they did with their lives what they wanted, and they did it for love? For Michael Serrecchia it started "before I got called in for that audition. I had two, three, four Broadway shows. The stuff I didn't like far outweighed the stuff I did like, and so I decided I was going to leave the business. Twenty-four, I'm going to leave the business. So I sold everything I owned and I bought a two-hundred-dollar car and a tent and I took off cross-country, living in every national park we have, looking for a new place to live and a new career. It was the best thing I ever did because it made me realize that the thing I do is theatrical and the place to do it is in New York. That took me four months—it seemed like four years—of the school of hard knocks. Working in cardbord-box factories, as a dishwasher, selling encyclopedias, waiter, busboy, anything to put enough money in my pocket and gas in the car to get me to the next city. Because I didn't like the one I was in. It was the most wonderful thing I've ever done for myself. It made my commitment ironclad, forged in fire. I knew that I had a gift and I was given a great reprieve in life, being able to get up and dance."

Wayne Cilento knows now that "on Broadway you don't realize where you are when you're doing it. I haven't been in a show for a while and I don't feel like I'll ever get back on that stage in New York. When you're there you take everything for granted. I mean, what's walking in a stage door? Well, it's real fucking special."

Crissy Wilzak thinks: "We were lucky to be living in this time, when finally there was a show about chorus kids. Not just dancers either, but kids in the background singing—which is all I really aspired to do when I came to New York. I think it's a once-in-a-lifetime thing. I think we were really lucky to be living in the time when dancers came of age and there was Michael Bennett to put something like that together. It's something that's not likely to happen again."

Carole Schweid: "I loved at the end of the play saying, 'I don't need to get back anything for this. I did it because I chose to do it.' And that's really how I felt."

Kelly Bishop: "It was a wonderful way to say, 'This is what I gave so many years to. This is what it's really like.' "

Robert LuPone: "I know that they wanted to do a reunion, March something. Bernie Gersten called me about a reunion and would I be interested. I said no. Do I regret it? It's a useless question. I lived it."

Scott Allen: "It's a good feeling. It's a wonderful feeling. They're warm memories."

Nancy Lane: "It's all right. Enough with *A Chorus Line*. Good-bye, good luck, only live and be well, never knock on my door again, thank you very much."

Not one of them regrets either the Chorus Line experience or his life as a dancer.

Don Percassi: "People used to ask me, they'd say, 'If I study this summer, and I go to school this summer, could I do the show? Could I be on Broadway?' I say, 'Van Cliburn, Horowitz, did they study for a summer?' There's no instant anything. Kids don't realize that today. It takes years. I looked around me and all those kids, there were so many years of dancing. My mother could've sent me to Yale and Oxford University, God knows, for the amount of money and time and effort put into it."

Wayne Cilento: "Study. There's a lot of dancers that don't study now. Everyone thinks that they can go to a discotheque and shake their ass and then come to Broadway and be dancers. I think it's real sad that producers and directors and choreographers take a lot of these people because they have blond hair or blue eyes or they have a big ass or they're ethnic or they're skinny or they're tall. They don't go for talent and they're really blowing the whole professionalism of Broadway. They think they can get away with it by singing maybe one audition song, taking one jazz class a week, not taking ballet classes at all. It's real sad."

Kelly Bishop: "Learn your art. Learn your trade. That's it. It's not an easy life. It's not one I'd really encourage anybody in. Some people have a love for it and they'll do it, and they're going to do it anyway whether you discourage them or not. Those are the people who should do it."

Nancy Lane: "Don't be afraid to be individual. I think that's real important to remember. Just be yourself. Don't try to be anybody else. Just try and make it on what you have, and if you have it, you'll make it. Be sure of yourself. Keep smiling and keep walking. And don't look back."

Mitzi Hamilton: "Do it because you have to do it. When you have to dance, there's no other way, but know that it's not going to last forever. I see young dancers and I remember the trip that I went through when I was that age. We can't tell them any different. It's like a fix—you need it. You gotta dance and there's no two ways about it. I came to New York and did what I wanted to do. I danced on Broadway. But I never realized that when I actually did it, what was I gonna do next? Now that that time has come I'm still at a loss, because I'm not prepared."

Rick Mason: "Pursue your career but also have something to fall back on. Don't forsake schooling. Your dreams are important because they propel you, but be realistic in life. You're one of *thousands* that are striving and having those same dreams. It's hard, because at that point your dreams are all the realism you need. We meet kids now that want to become dancers and they say, 'I heard you were in *A Chorus Line*. I want to go to New York too.' I want so badly to say, 'Don't.' "

Tony Stevens: "You have to just love it more than anything. You're gong to find yourself unhappy if you don't really love it so much. I mean, it's just gotta be the most fulfilling thing."

Chris Chadman: "My advice is to know what you want, because if your desires are true, then you can put up with anything. I think it's about desire. It's the desire that keeps you going, because everything else is transient and superficial."

Barry Bostwick: "If you want to dance, dance. It's stupid and simple, but if you want to dance, don't smoke. If you want to dance, don't drink. If you want to dance, don't act. If you want to dance, don't sing. *Dance.* If you want to dance, don't get married at the age of seventeen, because it's going to hold you back from a certain flexibility in your life, where you have to be on the road. In any discipline there's a trade-off. I think as a dancer you trade off more than most other art forms do."

Donna McKechnie: "This is something I would pass on to other people: The struggle and the proving and the auditioning will always be there."

Michael Serrecchia: "Never stop moving and always be true to yourself."

CHAPTER XVI

·················

Glittering Finale

Flashback: Broadway. September 12, 1866. Niblo's Gardens. A handsome, three-thousand seat theater at the corner of Broadway and Prince Street in Manhattan.

A melodrama is about to open, and it's going to be a stiff. A good deal of money has been spent on sets and costumes, but the plot, a loose adaptation of the Faust legend, is tedious and dull.

At the last minute the manager, William Wheatley, has an idea. Some days before, the Academy of Music on Fourteenth Street burned down, stranding a French ballet company in New York City. Wheatley quickly makes an arrangement with them, and when *The Black Crook* opens, they are a part of it.

It goes splendidly. Whenever the plot bogs down, one hundred dancers speed on stage in low-cut diaphanous costumes, through which can be seen shapely legs in cloth tights. (These alone are cause for a libidinous revelation, and the church tries, and fails, to prohibit their display.) The dancers perform their routines delightfully, and irrespective of the plot. The melodrama is a smash. *The Black Crook* is the first American musical comedy.

Dancers have been the backbone of the American musical ever since, but they remained anonymous for over a hundred years. Then, in 1975, they were brought out of obscurity for a long-deserved, revolutionary bow. This bow was a musical by, about, and starring the latest generation of gypsies.

On September 29, 1983, the current Broadway company of *A Chorus Line*, still at the Shubert Theatre on West Forty-fourth Street, played its 3,389th performance and became the longest-running show—play or musical—in the history of Broadway.

. . . .

On that night Michael Bennett, exceeding even his own leaps of entrepreneurial imagination, arranged a performance that many theater lovers speak of as one of the most extraordinary events of their theatergoing lives.

Michael and the New York Shakespeare Festival arranged for 330 dancers who had appeared in the show since it first opened off-Broadway to come from all over the country and participate in the performance. The majority of the original company appeared (Nancy Lane and Pam Blair could not get out of television commitments, and Robert LuPone declined), and the week was a grand reunion for dancers who had worked together over the years.

Backstage the week of preparations was an emotional event. Members of the original company, and dozens of dancers who had been fired on Michael's semiannual visits to inspect his companies, still harbored resentment toward him. Donna hadn't seen Michael since the divorce six years earlier. Yet somehow the event allowed past history to take its proper place. Donna and everyone involved put the grand musical, which meant so much to them, at the fore, and left the backstage turmoil unexpressed.

On Sunday night, before the week began, everyone was invited to a party at Michael's rehearsal studios. This broke the ice and became the time for reunion. The next morning, work could begin in earnest.

On Monday morning of the three-day rehearsal period, three hundred dancers gathered in the Shubert Theatre. When Michael appeared he received a spontaneous round of applause from the dancers. As the different groups were sorted out, the original company members found themselves standing on the line in their original places. The rest of the crowd, milling around the house awaiting their turn and chatting to renew old gypsy acquaintances, suddenly felt a chill, and one by one heads began to turn to the stage. It grew quiet. And there they were, the original dancers, as if the clock had gone back to 1975. They received an ovation from the others. That was for themselves alone, a show of sheer respect.

As rehearsals progressed, all the dancers who had performed in the show felt once more the power of a *A Chorus Line* and enjoyed the clarity of Michael's direction. It became apparent, too, that

Michael was staging a very special performance of the show, although, put together in pieces as it was, none of the dancers was aware of the overall design.

The stage floor had been reinforced to hold the weight of three hundred dancers. Tharon Musser had added lights to illuminate the aisles for the finale. Preparations had cost close to half a million dollars.

On Thursday, an afternoon dress rehearsal before an invited theater-wise audience was videotaped for the archives at Lincoln Center. Afterward, the dancers had dinner as guests of a dozen theater restaurants. Then, in front of a celebrity-studded, black-tie audience, the 3,389th performance—held at 10:30 P.M. to accommodate the dancers who were currently in other musicals—took place. It was preceded and followed by a gala party in Shubert Alley.

The current New York company danced the opening, but in the dark just prior to the first lineup they changed places with the original group. When the lights came on, a sign lit up over their heads announcing THE ORIGINAL COMPANY. Each of them looked as if no time had passed, and each performed his or her portion of the show with tremendous passion, energy, and skill.

The audience went crazy. The ovation was simply enormous.

Throughout the evening one company replaced another. Three girls sang "Dance: Ten; Looks: Three" together as if they were the Andrews Sisters; "Nothing" was sung in Japanese; seven Cassies backed up Donna McKechnie in her solo dance; seven Pauls ghosted behind Sammy Williams; the last scene featured the foreign companies speaking their own languages; rows of dancers stood in each place for "What I Did for Love." Michael had created one of the most sensational events in theater history, topping himself again and again.

In the finale, a quadruple line of dancers entered until the stage was filled, then more chorus lines flooded the entire house until the aisles to the top balcony were bursting with dancers. The spectacle and size of it were awesome. A thunderous response rocked the house. The audience rose to their feet spontaneously, drowning out the last chorus of "One" in a wave of cheering.

When it was over, Michael walked onto the stage and thanked the audience. Then, doing what he did best, he directed them.

He instructed an entire row of patrons in the orchestra to "get up and go stand in the back, to make room for a mobile camera." Laughing, two dozen bejeweled and tuxedoed audience members trooped up the aisle as they were directed by the little maestro, and the finale was repeated for the television news cameras from one more angle.

Then Bennett took the stage again and introduced the authors and designers connected with the making of the show. Behind him, 330 dancers stood in their diamond-studded beige costumes.

Following the performance Shubert Alley rang with excitement. The audience was drained by the experience, but their faces continued to glow. Alexander Cohen, one of Broadway's oldest showmen, who has seen and heard it all, said, "Don't do it again. My heart couldn't take it!"

Donna McKechnie: "I know certain things about life because of dreams that were attained and shattered with this experience. In many ways it was the most painful experience I've *ever* endured. I felt it in my bones even then. I also felt how profound it was and how much it was giving me. It's too quick and too easy to say, 'Oh, I wouldn't have wanted to do that.' The reward of having a theatrical experience like that comes once in a lifetime."

A Chorus Line is a show about dignity. Michel described it just that way shortly after it opened. He pointed to the American tendency to look to material success as a measure of achievement. The Chorus Line audience begins by willingly judging the dancers along with the director. As the musical progresses, and the dancers become real individuals, the audiences divorces itself from the director's viewpoint. They don't want to see the dancers judged, and they come to view the whole process as inhuman, if unavoidable. The dance audition becomes a metaphor, and in life, each member of the audience undergoes it. The nobility with which the dancers stand upon the line, waiting for a disembodied voice to decide their fate, is the climax—not the ultimate decision, which finds half of them losers and half winners. In *A Chorus Line*, audiences *feel* what it means to do something for love.

The extreme likability of each of the musical's characters was in large part responsible for the show's phenomenal commercial success, because it brought people back to the theater again and again. Thus *A Chorus Line's* success can be traced directly to the original dancers, because they provided from their own lives, from their own joy and ebullience in dancing, the sources of the play's characters. Through the long, emotionally and physically exhausting workshop process, and from their voluntary submission to the manipulations of their director, the musical was fashioned. *A Chorus Line* was created from the souls of the original cast.

Their time in the sun would end. Another show like it would not come again in their generation. Other shows would hardly furnish them the glory they had once known, even if they were still young enough, strong enough, driven enough.

And how far, really, had they come? Hardly anyone can now name the twenty-seven dancers who blazed across the Broadway stage in 1975.

The business will take away their fame. They will lose their strength, their looks, their magnificent grace. Yet what they once had, which few others ever have in a lifetime, can never be taken away. For one incandescent moment, they were one singular sensation.

DENNY MARTIN FLINN played Greg and Zach in the international touring company of *A Chorus Line* from April 1980 to October 1982.